The
Philosophy
Of
Spinoza

Special Edition

By
Baruch Spinoza

Edited
by
Joseph Ratner
Shawn Conners

El Paso Norte Press
Special Edition Books

The Philosophy of Spinoza – Special Edition
by Baruch Spinoza

Edited by Joseph Ratner, Shawn Conners

First Edition – February 2010

Published by
EL Paso Norte Press
El Paso, Texas

ISBN 1-934255-28-9
ISBN13: 978-1-934255-28-5

Printed in the United States of America

The Philosophy of Spinoza

PREFACE

Selections usually need no justifications. Some justification, however, of the treatment accorded Spinoza's *Ethics* may be necessary in this place. The object in taking the *Ethics* as much as possible out of the geometrical form, was not to improve upon the author's text; it was to give the lay reader a text of Spinoza he would find pleasanter to read and easier to understand. To the practice of popularization, Spinoza, one may confidently feel, would not be averse. He himself gave a short popular statement of his philosophy in the *Political Treatise*.

The lay reader of philosophy is chiefly, if not wholly, interested in grasping a philosophic point of view. He is not interested in highly meticulous details, and still less is he interested in checking up the author's statements to see if the author is consistent with himself. He takes such consistency, even if unwarrantedly, for granted. A continuous reading of the original *Ethics*, even on a single topic, is impossible. The subject-matter is coherent, but the propositions do not hang together. By omitting the formal statement of the propositions; by omitting many of the demonstrations and almost all cross-references; by grouping related sections of the *Ethics* (with selections from the *Letters* and the *Improvement of the Understanding*) under sectional headings, the text has been made more continuous. It is the only time, probably, dismembering a treatise actually made it more unified.

In an Appendix, the sources of the selections from the *Ethics* are summarily indicated. It would be a meaningless burden on the text to make full acknowledgments in footnotes. For the same reason, there has been almost no attempt made to show, by means of the conventional devices, the re-arrangements and abridgements that have been made. Every care has been taken not to distort in any way the meaning of the text. And that is all that is important in a volume of this kind.

Wherever possible Spinoza's own chapter headings have been retained; and some of the sectional headings have either been taken from, or have been based upon expressions in the text. It would have been more in keeping with contemporary form to use the title *On Historical Method* or *The New History* instead of *Of the Interpretation of Scripture*; a chapter on *Race Superiority* would sound more important than one on *The Vocation of the He-*

i

brews; but such modernizing changes were not made because the aim has been to give the reader a text as faithful to the original as the character of this volume would allow.

The selections have been taken from Elwes' translation of the *Tractatus Theologico-Politicus*, *A Political Treatise* and the *Improvement of the Understanding*; and from White's translation of the *Ethics*. These translations are no longer in copyright and hence it was not necessary to secure permission from the publishers to use them. Nonetheless, grateful acknowledgment is their just due.

White, in his translation, uses, not altogether without reason, the stilted term "affect" instead of the natural English term "emotion." "Affect" is closer to the Latin and it more clearly indicates the metaphysical status of the emotions as "modes" or "affectiones" of Substance. Still, practically no one has followed White in his usage. The reasons are not difficult to discover. Besides being a stilted term, having no legitimate English status, "affect" very often makes the text extremely obscure, even unintelligible to one who has no antecedent knowledge of it, because besides having also its ordinary English meaning, "affect" is used by White to mean "mode" or "modification" ("affection") as well. In the circumstances, therefore, I thought it advisable to change "affect" to "emotion" and "affection" to "modification" or "mode." I also corrected White's translation of the Definition of Attribute by deleting the word "if." In spite of the need for these changes, it was desirable to use White's translation because it is the most accurate and elegant extant.

I am indebted to Mr. Houston Peterson, of Columbia University, for suggesting to me the idea of arranging a volume of selections from Spinoza. I am alone responsible, however, for the actual selections and arrangements, and for the idea of taking the *Ethics* out of its geometrical form. Professor Morris R. Cohen, of the College of the City of New York, read this volume in manuscript; I am indebted to him for some valuable suggestions. I am also indebted very greatly to a friend (who prefers not to be acknowledged) for invaluable help in getting the manuscript into shape.

JOSEPH RATNER.

October, 1926.

CONTENTS

PAGE

PREFACE   i

THE LIFE OF SPINOZA   1

INTRODUCTION TO THE PHILOSOPHY OF SPINOZA   11

FIRST PART

ON GOD

CHAPTER

    I. OF SUPERSTITION   38

    II. OF THE INTERPRETATION OF SCRIPTURE   39

    III. OF PROPHETS AND PROPHECY   59

    IV. OF THE VOCATION OF THE HEBREWS   76

    V. OF THE DIVINE LAW   81

    VI. OF THE CEREMONIAL LAW   91

    VII. OF MIRACLES   100

    VIII. OF THE DIVINE NATURE   112

SECOND PART

ON MAN

    IX. THE NATURE AND ORIGIN OF THE HUMAN MIND   132

    X. THE NATURE AND EXTENT OF HUMAN KNOWLEDGE   144

    XI. DETERMINISM AND MORALS   155

    XII. THE ORIGIN AND NATURE OF THE EMOTIONS   168

    XIII. THE PSYCHOLOGY OF THE EMOTIONS   185

THIRD PART

ON MAN'S WELL-BEING

XIV. OF HUMAN BONDAGE   195

XV. THE FOUNDATIONS OF THE MORAL LIFE   205

XVI. OF THE FOUNDATIONS OF A STATE   226

XVII. OF SUPREME AUTHORITIES   237

XVIII. FREEDOM OF THOUGHT AND SPEECH   249

XIX. OF HUMAN FREEDOM   257

XX. OF HUMAN BLESSEDNESS AND THE ETERNITY OF THE MIND 268

APPENDIX   278

The Life of Spinoza

Baruch de Spinoza was born into the Jewish community of Amsterdam on November 24, 1632. His parents were Jews who had fled, along with many others, from the vicious intolerance of the Inquisition to the limited and hesitant freedom of Holland. At the time Spinoza was born, the Jewish refugees had already established themselves to a certain extent in their new home. They had won, for example, the important right to build a synagogue. Still, they did not enjoy the complete freedom and peace of mind of an independent and securely protected people. Although one could be a Jew in Amsterdam, one had to be a Jew with considerable circumspection. Whatever might prove in any way offensive to the political authority had to be scrupulously eschewed. For, as is always the case, minority groups which are simply tolerated have to suffer for the offenses of any of their members. The Jews of Amsterdam thoroughly understood this. They knew that any significant default on the part of one member of their community would not, in all likelihood, be considered by the authorities to be a default of that one person alone—a failing quite in the order of human nature; they knew it would be considered a manifestation of an essential vice characteristic of the whole community. And the whole community would have to suffer, in consequence, an exaggerated punishment which the individual delinquent himself may well not merit.

It was inevitable that the intellectual life of the Jews of Amsterdam should bear the marks of their inner and outer social constraints. Their intellectual life was cramped and ineffectual. Indiscriminate erudition, not independent thought, was all the Jewish leaders, connected in one way or another with the Synagogue, were able to achieve. It was far safer to cling to the innocuous past than it was to strike out boldly into the future. Any independence of thought that was likely to prove socially dangerous as well as schismatic was promptly suppressed. The humiliation and excommunication (circa 1640) of the indecisive martyr Uriel da Costa when he ventured to entertain doctrines that were not orthodox, were prompted as much by political as by religious considerations. It is true, many of the faithful were attracted by Cabbalistic wonders and the strange hope of being saved from a bitter exile by a Messianic Sabbatai Zevi. But these wayward deviations, in reality not so very far removed from orthodox tradition, exhibited only the more clearly the fearsome inner insecurity which a strained formalism in thought and habit bravely attempted to cover.

The Philosophy of Spinoza

In such social and intellectual atmosphere Spinoza grew up. Of his early life, practically nothing is known. His parents, we know, were at least fairly well-to-do, for Spinoza received a good education. And we know that he was, when about fifteen years of age, one of the most brilliant and promising of Rabbi Saul Levi Morteira's pupils. Everyone who then knew Spinoza expected great things of him. He proved himself to be a very acute rabbinical student; at that early age already somewhat too critical, if anything, to suit the orthodox. But all felt reasonably confident he would become a distinguished Rabbi, and perhaps a great commentator of the Bible. Of course, of the orthodox sort.

But the Rabbis were early disillusioned. Spinoza soon found the learning of the Synagogue insufficient and unsatisfactory. He sought the wisdom of secular philosophy and science. But in order to satisfy his intellectual desires it was necessary to study Latin. And Latin was not taught in the Synagogue.

An anonymous German taught Spinoza the rudiments of the language that was to enable him to enter into the important current of modern ideas especially embodied in the philosophy of Descartes. Francis Van den Ende gave him a thorough technical, not literary, mastery of it. And Van den Ende taught Spinoza much more besides. He acquainted him with the literature of antiquity; he gave him a sound knowledge of the contemporary fundamentals of physiology and physics; and it was he possibly, who introduced him to the philosophy of Descartes and the lyrical philosophic speculation of Bruno. He did much also (we may easily infer) to encourage the independence of mind and the freedom in thinking Spinoza had already manifested in no inconsiderable degree. For although this Van den Ende was a Catholic physician and Latin master by profession, he was a free thinker in spirit and reputation. And if we are to believe the horrified public suspicion, he taught a select few of his Latin pupils the grounds of his heterodox belief. As one can easily understand, to study Latin with Van den Ende was not the most innocent thing one could do. Certainly, to become a favorite pupil and assistant teacher of Van den Ende's was, socially, decidedly bad. But Spinoza was not deterred by the possible social consequences of his search for knowledge and truth. He took full advantage of his opportunities and did not hesitate to follow wherever his master might lead.

Van den Ende was also something of a political adventurer; he finally paid the unsuccessful conspirator's price on the gallows in Paris. It is not at all unlikely that Spinoza's hard-headed political and ethical realism was, in significant measure, due to his early intimacy with his variously gifted and interesting Latin master. We know that Spinoza was at least strongly attracted, in later life, by the Italian political insurgent Masaniello, for Spinoza drew a portrait of himself in the Italian's costume. Machiavelli's influence, too, upon Spinoza was very great—an influence that would but be a continuation of Van den Ende's.

Spinoza may have been indebted to Van den Ende for one other thing: his only recorded romance. There is some question about this indebtedness because tradition does not speak very confidently, in some essentials, about Van den Ende's daughter Clara Maria. Clara, tradition is agreed, was intellectually and artistically well endowed, although she was not very good looking. In her father's absence on political affairs she took his place in the school, teaching music as well as Latin. But tradition is somewhat disconcerting when it comes to Clara's age when Spinoza knew her. According to some chronological researches, the fair object of Spinoza's supposed devotion, was only twelve years old. Hardly of an age to warrant Spinoza's love, unless he loved her as Dante loved Beatrice. A somewhat improbable possibility. The tradition that is less sparing of Clara's age is, however, even more sparing of her character: the success of Spinoza's supposed rival—a fellow-student by name, Kerkrinck—is attributed to the seductive powers of a pearl necklace. In spite of the fact that tradition reckons this gift to have been of decisive importance, one does not like to believe that a girl of high intellectual and artistic ability could be so easily and fatefully overcome by a mere trinket. Still less does one like to believe that Spinoza fell in love with a girl whose mind was so far removed from the joys that are eternal and spiritual. But, of course, it is conceivable that the girl took the trinket symbolically; or else that Spinoza, who had given all his time to rabbinical and philosophical studies was, in the circumstances, quite justifiably deceived.

Spinoza had not yet been graduated from his student days when the Synagogue thought him a fit object for official censure and threat. It seems Spinoza was betrayed into overt indiscretion by two fellow-students from the Synagogue, who asked for his opinion regarding the existence of angels, the corporeality of God and the immortality of the soul. Spinoza's answers were not complete, but incomplete as they were, they yet revealed a mind that was, to the faithful, shockingly astray from the orthodox path. Spinoza was to have elaborated upon his answers at a later date but the students had heard, apparently, quite enough. Instead of returning to Spinoza they went to the authorities of the Synagogue. The authorities were quite disposed by Spinoza's association with Van den Ende and his perceptible neglect of ceremonial observances, to believe him capable of any intellectual villainy. They promptly set about to reclaim the erring soul. Report has it they sought two means: they offered Spinoza an annuity of 1,000 florins if he would, in all overt ways, speech and action, conform to the established opinions and customs of the Synagogue; or, if he did not see the wisdom and profit of compliance, they threatened to isolate him by excommunication. Again social politics as much as established religion demanded the action the Synagogue took. Their experience with Uriel da Costa was still very fresh in their minds and they must have felt fairly confident that Spinoza would be warned by the fate of his heretical predecessor if not counseled by the wisdom of the Fathers. But Spinoza was of a firmness they did not reckon on. He did not hearken to their censure nor cower at their threat. The thirty days or so in which he was given to reform passed without discovering in him any change. Excommunication had to be pronounced. When barely twenty-four years old, Spinoza found himself cut off from the race of Israel with all the prescribed curses of excommunication upon his head.

Spinoza was not present when excommunication was pronounced upon him. He had left Amsterdam to stay with some Collegiant friends on the Ouwerkerk road, for, so one tradition relates, an attempt had been made by one of the over-righteous upon Spinoza's life soon after he became an object of official displeasure. Although Spinoza was, throughout his life, ready to suffer the consequences of his opinions and actions, he at no time had the least aspiration to become a martyr. When Spinoza heard of his excommunication he sent a spirited and unyielding reply. The spirit if not the words of that reply (not yet discovered) eventually made its way into the *Tractatus Theologico-Politicus*. For the rest of his life, whenever he had occasion to refer to the Jews, Spinoza referred to them as he did to the Gentiles—a race to which he did not belong. And immediately, with the perfect grace and humor of a cultured mind, he changed his name from Baruch to Benedict, quite confident one can be as blessed in Latin as in Hebrew.

The subsequent course of Spinoza's life was almost completely untroubled, though it was unmitigatingly austere. He took up the trade of polishing lenses as a means of earning his simple bread. He was somewhat influenced in his decision by the advice in the *Ethics of the Fathers* that everyone should do some manual work. But it was also quite the fashion at that period for learned men, interested in science, to polish lenses, as a hobby of course, not as a means of support. Spinoza's choice was not altogether wise in spite of its learned associations and the fact that he soon gained an enviable reputation as a young scientist. The early recognition Spinoza received from men like Henry Oldenburg, the first secretary of the Royal Society, from Robert Boyle and Huyghens, was hardly adequate recompense for the fine dust he ground which aggravated his inherited tuberculosis and undoubtedly considerably hastened his death. Spinoza's accomplishment in his chosen trade was not merely practical. Many looked forward, with warranted confidence, to the time when Spinoza would make a distinguished contribution to the science of optics. But the only strictly scientific work Spinoza left behind (long considered to have been lost) was a short treatise on the rainbow.

All Spinoza's intellectual energy went into service of his philosophy. His earliest philosophical work (rediscovered (1862) in translated Dutch manuscript) was a *Short Treatise on God, Man and His Well-Being*. It is a fragmentary, uneven work, chiefly valuable for the insight it gives into the workings and development of Spinoza's mind. The *Ethics*, in the completed form in which we have it (no manuscript of it is extant) has the incredible appearance of a system of philosophy sprung full-grown from an unhesitating mind. Even a most cursory reading of the *Short Treatise* completely dispels this preposterous illusion. The *Ethics* was the product of prolonged and critical toil.

But just how prolonged it is difficult to say. For already as early as 1665 almost four-fifths of the *Ethics* seems to have been written. We learn as much from a letter Spinoza wrote to one of his friends promising to send him the "third part" of his philosophy up to the eightieth proposition. From the letter it is fairly clear that at that time the *Ethics* was divided into three, not five, parts. Also, in letters written that same year to William Blyenbergh one finds expressed some of the chief conclusions published five years later in the *Tractatus Theologico-Politicus*. And Spinoza wrote, at this early period, not conjecturally or speculatively, but as one writes who knows the firm and tested grounds of his belief. Why the *Ethics, in final form, began to circulate privately only two or three years before Spinoza's death*, and why his work on *The Improvement of the Understanding* and his *Political Treatise* were left unfinished, must remain something of an insoluble philosophico-literary mystery.

The only book Spinoza published in his own lifetime above his own name was his *Principles of Descartes' Philosophy Geometrically Demonstrated* with an appendix of *Cogitata Metaphysica* which he had dictated to a youth (one "Cæsarius") "to whom (he) did not wish to teach (his) own opinions openly." Discretion, as he had already learned and later formally stated and proved, was not inconsonant with rational valor. The only other book Spinoza published in his lifetime—the *Tractatus Theologico-Politicus*—bore on its title page Spinoza's initials only, and the name of a fictitious Hamburg publisher. When Spinoza heard, sometime later, that a Dutch translation of this work was being prepared, he earnestly beseeched his friends to forestall its publication (which they did) because only its Latin dress saved it from being officially proscribed. It was then an open secret who the author was. Spinoza's personal rule to incur as little official displeasure as possible made him abandon his final literary project entertained in 1675. When he began negotiations for the publication of the *Ethics* a rumor spread that he had in press a book proving that God does not exist. Complaint was lodged with the prince and magistrates. "The stupid Cartesians," Spinoza wrote Oldenburg "being suspected of favoring me, endeavored to remove the aspersion by abusing every where my opinions and writings, a course which they still pursue." In the circumstances, Spinoza thought it wisest to delay publication till matters would change. But, apparently, they did not change, or change sufficiently. The *Ethics* was first published about a year after Spinoza's death.

In spite of the consensus of adverse, and somewhat vicious opinion, the author of the *Tractatus* did find favor in the eyes of some. The Elector Palatine, Karl Ludwig, through his secretary Fabritius, offered Spinoza the chair of philosophy at Heidelberg (1673). But Spinoza graciously declined it. Although a more welcome or more honorable opportunity to teach could not be conceived, it had never been his ambition to leave his secluded station in life for one involving public obligations. Even in his secluded corner, he found he had aroused more public attention and sentiment than was altogether consonant with the peace and retirement he sought. Besides, he did not know how well he could fulfill the desires of the Elector by teaching nothing that would tend to discomfit established religion.

Spinoza had, in his young days, learned what extreme dangers one must expect to encounter in a righteous community become inimical. In his last years, he experienced a stern and tragic reminder. Two of Spinoza's best friends, Cornelius and Jan de Witt, who had by a change in political fortune become enemies of the people, were brutally murdered (1672). Spinoza for once, when this occurred, lost his habitual philosophic calm. He could restrain neither his tears nor his anger. He had to be forcibly prevented from leaving his house to post a bill, at the scene of the murder, denouncing the criminal mob. A somewhat similar crisis recurred shortly afterwards when Spinoza returned from a visit to the hostile French camp. The object of his mission is not unequivocally known. Some think it was to meet the Prince of Condé solely in his private capacity of philosopher. It is certain Spinoza was advised the French King would acknowledge a dedicated book by means of a pension—an advice Spinoza did not act upon. Others think his mission was political. His reputation as a distinguished man would have made him a very likely ambassador. This conjecture would seem more probable, however, if the de Witts, his intimate friends, had been still in political power, instead of in their graves. But whatever Spinoza's mission was, when he returned to the Hague, the populace branded him a French spy. Spinoza's landlord feared his house would be wrecked, by an infuriated mob. This time Spinoza exerted the calming influence. He assured Van der Spijck that if any attempt were made on the house he would leave it and face the mob, even if they should deal with him as they did with the unfortunate de Witts. He was a good republican as all knew. And those in high political authority knew the purpose of his journey. Fortunately, popular suspicion and anger dissipated this time without a sacrifice. Still, the incident showed quite clearly that though Spinoza did not desire to be a martyr, he was no more afraid to die than he was to live for the principles he had at heart.

Spinoza's character, manifested in his life, has won the high admiration of everyone not bitterly hostile to him. And even his enemies maintained and justified their hatred only by inventing calumnious falsehoods about him. Unfounded rumors of an evil nature began to circulate during his lifetime, and naturally increased in virulence and volume after his death. At that period in human history, it was popularly recognized that nothing good could be true, and nothing vile could be false of an atheist—which was what Spinoza, of course, was reputed to be. Oldenburg even, for years unflaggingly profuse in expressions of devoted friendship and humble discipleship, an eager and fearless advocate (supposedly) of the truth, a friend who lamented the fact that the world was being denied the invaluable products of Spinoza's unsurpassed intellect, and who, therefore, constantly urged Spinoza, by all the advice of friendship, to publish his work without delay, irrespective of popular prejudice— even Oldenburg began to conceive a far from complimentary opinion of Spinoza after the publication of the *Tractatus Theologico-Politicus*! So prevalent were the groundless rumors that the Lutheran pastor, Colerus—the source of most of our information—felt obliged in his very quaint summary biography to defend the life and character of Spinoza. To his everlasting credit, Colerus did this although he himself heartily detested Spinoza's philosophy which he understood to be abhorrently blasphemous and atheistic. Colerus' sources of information were the best: he spoke to all who knew Spinoza at the Hague; and he himself was intimate with the Van der Spijcks with whom Spinoza had lived the last five years of his life, and with whom Colerus was now living—in Spinoza's very room.

Spinoza's courage and strength of mind are as impressively manifested in the constant daily life he lived as in the few severe crises he resolutely faced. For the twenty years of his excommunication he lived in comparative retirement, if not isolation. The frugality of his life bordered on asceticism. All his free time and energy Spinoza dedicated with unusual single-hearted devotion to the disinterested development of a philosophy he knew would not be very acceptable to the general or even special philosophic reader. His mode of life is all the more remarkable because it was not determined by embittered misanthropy or passionate abhorrence of the goods of the world. It was dictated solely by what he understood to be, in his circumstances, the reasonable life for him. Although he was an eager correspondent, and had many friends whom he valued above all things that are external to one's own soul, his interest in his own work kept him from carrying on, for any length of time, an active social life. He believed, too, that it is part of the wisdom of life to refresh oneself with pleasant food and drink, with delicate perfumes and the soft beauty of growing things, with music and the theater, literature and painting. But his own income was too slender to allow him much of these temperate riches of a rational life. And always, rather than exert himself to increase his income, he would decrease his expenditure. Still, he no doubt enjoyed the little he had. He found very palatable, most likely, the simple food he himself prepared in later life; and he must have gained additional satisfaction from the thought that he was, because of his own cooking, living more safely within his means. The pipe he smoked occasionally (let us hope) was fragrant; the pint of wine a month very delectable. For mental recreation he read fairly widely in literature, observed the habits of insects, with the microscope as well as the naked eye. He also sometimes drew ink or charcoal sketches of his visitors and himself. A fairly plausible rumor has it that Rembrandt was his teacher. Unfortunately, all of Spinoza's sketches were destroyed.

Although Spinoza wanted to be independent and self-supporting he was not irrationally zealous about it. He did not accept all the financial help his friends were eager to give him, but he did accept some. One of his young friends, Simon de Vries, before his early death occurred, wanted to bequeath all of his estate to Spinoza. But Spinoza persuaded him not to deprive his own brother of his natural inheritance. Even the annual 500 florins de Vries finally left him, Spinoza would not altogether accept, offering the plea that so much wealth would surely take his mind away from his philosophy. But he would accept 300 florins, a sum he felt would not be burdensome or dangerous to his soul. This annuity he regularly received until his death. His friends the de Witts, pensioned him too; the heirs to the estate contested Spinoza's claim, whereupon Spinoza promptly withdrew it. This high-minded action corrected their covetousness, and from the de Witts, too, he received financial help until his death.

Spinoza's relations with the humble folk he stayed with exhibited the modesty and grace of character that endeared him to his intimate friends. When he was

8

tired working in his own room, he would frequently come down to smoke a pipe and chat with his landlady and landlord about the simple affairs that filled their lives. His speech was "sweet and easy;" his manner of a gentle, noble, beauty. Except for the occasion when the de Witts were murdered, Spinoza never showed himself either unduly merry or unduly sad. If ever he found that his emotions were likely to escape his wise control, he would withdraw until such danger had passed. We find the same characteristics exhibited in Spinoza's correspondence. Although he found some of his correspondents sometimes very trying, he never failed to be as courteous and considerate as the circumstances would permit. Even when one Lambert de Velthuysen provoked his righteous indignation, Spinoza tempered his caustic reply before sending it off.

Spinoza lived the ethics he wrote. As is the *Ethics*, so is his life pervaded by a simple grandeur. And as he lived, so did he die. He had not been feeling very well, and had sent for his friend and physician Dr. Ludwig Meyer. A chicken broth was ordered for Spinoza of which he partook quite healthily. No one suspected that he was this time fatally ill. He came down in the morning, and spoke for some time with his hosts. But when they returned from a visit that same afternoon (Sunday, Feb. 21, 1677) they learned the sad, surprising news that Spinoza had gently passed away, the only one by his bedside, his doctor and friend.

Spinoza sought in his lifetime neither riches, nor sensual pleasure, nor fame. He wrote and published his books when he could and thought advisable because part of his joy consisted in extending, as he said, a helping hand to others, in bringing them to see and understand things as he did. If they did not see, or obdurately refused to understand, he did not consider it part of his task to overcome them. He was animated by no missionary zeal. He was content to search for the truth and to explain what he found as best he could. The truth, he devoutly believed, would make us free. But it was truth that we understood, not truth that was forced upon us. He was quite satisfied to leave in his desk the manuscript of his *Ethics*. People in his lifetime did not want to listen to him. If ever they did after his death, they were cordially welcome to. In death as in life they would find him faithful to his ideal.

Spinoza has often been likened to the old Hebrew prophets. He does not, it is true, exhort the people to follow in the path of righteousness; it is the philosopher's task simply to show the way. But the morality Spinoza stands for is the old prophetic morality purified and made consistent with itself. And Spinoza was, in his own time, as the prophets were in theirs, a heretic and a rebel, a voice calling in the wilderness—a wilderness that was later to become the very citadel of civilization. Excommunicated by the Jews and vilified by the Gentiles during his lifetime, Spinoza has, since his death, been canonized by both alike as the most saintly and exalted of philosophers. Like his forerunners of old, Spinoza was a prophet *in* Israel, *for* Mankind.

INTRODUCTION TO THE PHILOSOPHY OF SPINOZA

I

Spinoza's philosophy has suffered not a little from the highly abstruse and technical form in which the *Ethics* is written. Some, who are not inured to the hardships of philosophy, quite naturally jump to the conclusion that its formidable geometry contains only the most inscrutable of philosophic mysteries; and a wise humility persuades them to forego the unexampled enlightenment a mastery of the difficulties would yield. Others, who are devoutly wedded to what they consider the unreservedly empirical character of modern (that is, true) philosophy, avoid the *Ethics* because they are convinced, on general principles, that only a mind hopelessly lost in the dark night of medieval speculation could conceive of philosophy in such ultra-deductive fashion. Reason was for so long servile to idle theology, it is not at all surprising that a work exemplifying reason to such high degree as does the *Ethics*, should receive scant respect from intrepid empiricists. It is so easy to confuse the rationalizations of reason with the nature of reason itself.

Spinoza did not, however, choose the geometrical order because he thought his philosophy too profound for ordinary exposition; nor did he choose it because he was enmeshed in medieval philosophic speculation. He chose it because his fundamental philosophic aim was to establish ethics on a thoroughly tested, scientific foundation; and geometry, an exemplar of all mathematical science, most completely embodied, at that time, the highest scientific ideal. Man, Spinoza held, is a part of Nature, and Nature is governed by eternal and immutable laws. It must be just as possible, therefore, to apply the mathematical method to man, as it is to apply it to matter. It must be possible to determine, with the certitude obtainable in the exact sciences, what things are good for man and what means he has for attaining them.

Spinoza's belief in the self-sufficing, lawful order of Nature, and the adequacy of the natural powers of our mind to understand the mysteries (popularly so appraised) of heaven and earth, the singular expository style of the *Ethics* emphasizes in unmistakable fashion. Even for our understanding of God's own nature, Divine Revelation, as commonly interpreted in Spinoza's day and our own, is wholly unnecessary. We need only the revelation afforded by the natural powers of reason operative in us. In geometry, we do not blindly accept conclusions on faith, nor do we reject them by authority. We are guided in our discovery of the true and the false, solely by the light of our natural understanding. And the truths we discover are not temporary fabrications of the human mind, but eternal truths about the nature of things. Perhaps no other single aspect of Spinoza's philosophy distinguishes Spinoza from the medievalists as thoroughly as does his use of the geometrical order of exposition; and no other single aspect, perhaps, justifies as thoroughly Spinoza's claim to rank with the moderns if not even the contemporaries.

The geometer's method of starting with definitions and axioms and proceeding from proposition to proposition especially appealed to Spinoza, apart from the fact that geometry was an ideal science, because, for Spinoza, the essence of logical method consists in starting out with ideas that are of utter simplicity. Then, if the ideas are understood at all, they can only be clearly and distinctly understood. The absolutely simple we can either know or not know. We cannot be confused about it. And ideas which are clearly and distinctly understood are, according to Spinoza, necessarily true. Such unambiguously simple and therefore necessarily true ideas Spinoza believed his definitions and axioms expressed. Furthermore, if we gradually build up the body of our science by means of our initial simple ideas, justifying ourselves at every step by adequate proof, our final result will necessarily be as firmly established and as certainly true as the elementary ideas we started with. The reliability of this whole procedure more than compensates for its tediousness—a defect Spinoza expressly recognizes.

Unfortunately, however, there are other defects in the geometrical method when it is applied to philosophy, far more serious than its tediousness,—defects, moreover, Spinoza apparently did not recognize. Even though the geometrical method is pre-eminently scientific, it is hardly a form suitable for philosophy. The Euclidean geometer can take it for granted that the reader understands what a line or plane, a solid or an angle is. For formality, a curt definition is sufficient. But the philosopher's fundamental terms and ideas are precisely those in need of most careful and elaborate elucidation—something which cannot be given in a formal definition or axiom. Also, in the geometrical form, the burden of the author's attention is shifted from the clarification of the propositions to the accurate demonstration of them. Which, in a philosophical treatise, is most unfortunate. For though it is undoubtedly highly desirable that the philosopher should observe the same care and precision as the scientist, admitting nothing he cannot prove, it is nevertheless just as well for the philosopher to take reasonable care that what he is conscientiously proving is understood. That Spinoza did not always take such care but considerably overestimated the self-evidence of his definitions and axioms and the simplicity of many of his important propositions, is an unhappy fact conclusively established by the increasing volume of Spinozistic literature.

II

However, in spite of the difficult, and to the literary repellent form of the *Ethics*, the catholicity of Spinoza's influence has been extremely remarkable. In time, his influence bids fair to equal in range, if not in gross extent, the as yet unparalleled influence of the artist-philosopher Plato. It took about a hundred years for Spinoza to come into something of his own. For the *Ethics* was condemned with the *Tractatus Theologico-Politicus* as an atheistic and immoral work. Only when the romantic philosophers of Germany, following the lead of Lessing and Jacobi, found in Spinoza a man who was, as they thought, after their own heart, did Spinoza's mundane fortune change. As a result of their efforts, Spinoza ceased to be a philosopher to be execrated in public (though furtively read in private), and became a philosopher to be eulogized on all occasions in most rhapsodic, if bewildering, terms. Many others too, besides professional philosophers, began to read Spinoza with much sympathy and unbounded admiration. Goethe, Matthew Arnold, Heine, George Eliot, Flaubert, Coleridge, and Shelley—to mention only a few distinguished lay names—found in Spinoza a powerful, stimulating and, in varying degrees, congenial thinker. To-day, after having been one of the liberating thinkers of mankind who was read but not honored, Spinoza is fast becoming one of the canonized of mankind who are honored but not read.

The reason for Spinoza's magnificent influence is not difficult to discover: his philosophy deals in a grand, illuminating way with all that is of profoundest importance in human life. There is no material the universe offers for man's life but Spinoza seeks to understand and explain its rational function and utility. For Spinoza set before himself the hard task of laying down the principles whereby men may guide themselves aright in all the affairs of life—the lowest as well as the highest. His philosophy, as a result, is at once the most exalted and the most matter of fact. There is no high sentiment or glorious ideal to which Spinoza does not give proper attention and a proper place. And yet he propounds nothing in his ethical theory that cannot be clearly seen by reason and that cannot be fully substantiated by the history of man. Spinoza's ethics is perfectly balanced, eminently sane. And there is, pervading it all, a stately sustained resolution of mind, a royal, often religious spirit and calm.

And Spinoza's thought, if not all of his terminology, is refreshingly modern and contemporary. We find in him, as in contemporaries, an utter reliance upon the powers of the human mind. All dogmatism, in the pristine connotation of unexamined adherence to the doctrines of tradition, is absent from his thought. Spinoza is thoroughly critical, for only modern philosophic arrogance, in first full bloom in Kant, can justly monopolize the term "critical" for itself. Naturally, though, Spinoza is unfamiliar with the whole apparatus and style of philosophic thinking which the last two centuries of excessively disputatious and remarkably inconclusive philosophy have created. Spinoza has his own technical philosophic style, inherited to some extent, but to a much larger extent transformed by him for original use. But technical as his style may be, it is simplicity itself when compared with the horrific styles which were, until the last few decades, alone thought adequate to express the profound and esoteric mysteries of modern philosophy. The philosophic jargon of the 18th and 19th centuries is now almost universally discarded, and with it preternaturally recondite and ineffectual modes of thought. Those who have achieved at least some of the new simplicity in thought and expression are better able than any others to enter into the heart of Spinoza's philosophy, into the open secret of his thought. For apart from the mere stylistic difficulties of the *Ethics* and some detail of his metaphysical doctrine, the few great and simple ideas which dominate his philosophy are quite easy to understand—especially if one uses the *Tractatus Theologico-Politicus* as an introduction to them. It was an unexpressed maxim with Spinoza that even at the risk of keeping our heads empty it is necessary we keep our minds simple and pure.

III

The central controlling idea of Spinoza's philosophy is that all things are necessarily determined in Nature, which he conceives to be an absolutely infinite unified and uniform order. Instead of maintaining that God is like man magnified to infinity, who has absolute, irresponsible control of a universe which is external to him—the rather rude anthropomorphic account of the ultimate nature of the universe contained in the Bible—Spinoza maintains that God is identical with the universe and must be and act according to eternal and necessary laws. God is Nature, if we understand by Nature not merely infinite matter and infinite thought,—the two attributes of Nature specifically known to us—but infinite other attributes the precise character of which we can never, because of our finitude, comprehend. Within this Being—God, Nature or Substance (the more technical, philosophic term)—there is no dichotomy; and there is outside of it no regulative or coercive intelligence such as the Biblical God is conceived to be. Whatever is, is one. And it is, in the special Spinozistic sense, supremely perfect because absolutely real. There is, considered in its totality, no lack or defect in Nature. There can be, therefore, no cosmic purposes, for such purposes would imply that Nature is yet unfinished, or unperfected, that is, not completely real. Something that cannot possibly be true of an absolutely infinite Being.

Spinoza's conception of an absolutely infinite universe is a vast improvement upon the pent-in, finite medieval universe inherited from Aristotle. It exceeds by infinity, in breadth of vision, even our contemporary notion of an infinite physical cosmos. And his conception of universal necessity is as great an advance upon the view that transformed natural occurrences into miraculous events. Miracles, according to the Bible, most clearly exemplify God's omnipotence; for omnipotence in the popular mind consists in nothing so much as in the ability to satisfy any purpose or whim no matter how transitory it is, or how incompatible with what has been antecedently desired or done. Miracles may be extraordinary occurrences with reference to the order of Nature, but they are, with reference to God, commonplace exhibitions of His Almighty power. For Spinoza, however, miracles, did they actually occur, would exhibit not God's power, but His impotence. The omnipotence of the one absolutely infinite Being is not shown by temperamental interruptions of the course of events; it is manifested in the immutable and necessary laws by which all things come to pass.

Spinoza's conception of the universe, flawlessly operating under necessary laws, effectively disposes of miracles. And to dispose of miracles is one of Spinoza's primary concerns. For as long as miracles happen, organized knowledge and rational control—the bases of a rational life—are both impossible for man.

If events were not absolutely conditioned by the determinate nature of things, instead of science, we should have superstition, and magic instead of scientific control. When a god governs the universe according to his transitory and altogether personal whims, or when chance, without a god, reigns, man is hopelessly at the mercy of the flux of events. In the conduct of his affairs memory is of no use to him, and forethought is impossible. In such cases man, as we read in his history, and could easily conclude from his nature, piteously grasps for salvation at whatever happens his way. All things are then loaded with ominous powers the strength of which is directly proportionate to the hope or fear that enthralls him. If the universe were lawless, the irony of man's fate would forever be what it was when he lived in abysmal ignorance: when in bitterest need of sane guidance, he would be most prone to trust to the feeblest and most irrational of aids. On the other hand, if things are determined by necessity, nothing happening either miraculously or by chance, science and a commensurate power of scientific control is possible for man. No more important argument could Spinoza conceive in favor of his doctrine.

IV

But the very doctrine which Spinoza placed at the heart of his philosophy because of the inestimable advantages man could derive from it, people loudly objected to on the ground that it robbed man's life of all moral and religious value. Determinism, they exclaimed, reduces man to the rank of inanimate Nature; without "free-will" man is no better than a slave, his life doomed by an inexorable fate. True enough, nothing is more abhorrent or more deadly to the striving soul of man than to be bound in a fatalistic doctrine. But the anti-determinists wildly confuse a perverted determinism of ends with a scientific determinism of means. And only the former determinism is truly fatalistic. This confusion is to be found equally central in Henry Oldenburg's inconsequential letters to Spinoza and in Bernard Shaw's shamelessly silly Preface to *Back to Methuselah*. Fundamental confusions remain astonishingly stable throughout the centuries.

Spinoza, when he maintained that all things are necessarily determined by the laws of their own being, certainly did not mean to say that, for example, the toothbrush I shall buy to-morrow will be determined by the stellar dust of æons ago. He did not wish to maintain that the infinite occurrences of the past were slowly but persistently moving to that far from divine or distant event. No aboriginal astronomer royal could have predicted the pending purchase merely by exhaustively analyzing the then stellar dust. For toothbrushes and their purchase are determined by the nature of human beings, not by the nature of embryonic stars. And Spinoza's doctrine of necessity maintains that all events are determined by their proper causes, not that everything is immediately caused by some antediluvian event. And this is true even though we can start from any event in the present, no matter how trivial, and go back to an event causally antecedent, and from that to another, even until we recede into the stellar dust itself. But this only amounts to saying, what is undoubtedly true, that neither I nor the toothbrush could now exist if the stellar dust, and the whole series of intervening events, had not existed. But this is totally different from saying that the stellar dust existed that I might exist to-day and buy a toothbrush to-morrow, or, what equals the same, that I and the toothbrush exist so that the stellar dust and the exceedingly long consequence of natural events should have a final purpose, an ultimate end—even if not an ideal fulfillment. Now only when causality, as in the latter case, is perversely teleological is determinism fatalistic. Fatalism is the result only when the ends of activity are necessarily but arbitrarily determined. But when causality is not arbitrarily teleological, or when only the natures of things, the instruments or means of activity are necessarily determined, then determinism involves no fatalism at all.

The only truly fatalistic systems which have had an important influence in the history of mankind, have been certain religious systems—the Christian religion among them. The energies of western men were, for over fourteen centuries, robbed of all vitality and meaning because Christian theology irrevocably fixed the end of life, and man could do nothing to alter it significantly in any respect. Arbitrary teleological determinism is, in the Christian religion, the philosophic root of other worldliness. And it was no alleviation of the state of affairs that miracles could happen in the realm of Nature, that is, that Nature was not determined, but was undetermined, accidental, or "free." On the contrary, it was a decided aggravation that there existed side by side with a perverse teleological determinism for the other world, an instrumental indeterminism for this world. For the latter served as effectively to put the means of man's life, as the former did to put his end, out of his present reach and control.

Contrast the modern and contemporary Christian period with the medieval and pre-medieval Christian period. What a vast difference there is! With the introduction of the modern period man's energies were almost instantaneously liberated. And why? Because of Chancellor Bacon's discovery of the value of empirical investigation? Hardly. For this discovery had been made long before Bacon. But it was only after Bacon that the discovery had a great effect because an enormous intellectual transformation had already partly taken place in the time between the first medieval discovery of the empirical method and Bacon's proclamation of it. The enormous change was that determinism had been transferred from ends to means; and indeterminism from means to ends. Mathematical physics had, as a system for explaining Nature, supplanted theology.

With scientific determinism firmly established in the realm of Nature and arbitrary determinism thoroughly disestablished in the realm of ends, the two-fold fatality that crushed man with its oppressive power, automatically disappeared. On the one hand, the world ceased to be haunted by demonic powers; it was no longer a miraculous world subject constantly to capricious perturbations. It was no longer a world alien to man's nature and it therefore ceased to be sheerly brutal to him. For the world is brutal only as long as we do not understand it. As soon as we do, it ceases to be brutal, and becomes quite human, if not humane. Knowledge transmutes a brute existent into a rational instrumentality. And, on the other hand, man could now espouse any end consonant with his nature. He was no longer bound and dwarfed by an alien, superimposed end which is just as sheerly brutal to man's soul as an alien world is sheerly brutal to man's body.

Of course, the ends that are consonant with man's nature are determined by his nature, so that it may seem we have not really escaped the fatality of "determinism." This is, however, only seemingly so. Because, according to the teleological determinism of Christian theology the ends were fixed independently of the natures that were to fulfill them; just as, according to instrumental indeterminism events were caused independently of the natures of the things that caused them. Otherwise there would be nothing miraculous about miracles and nothing virtuous about Calvinism. But if the ends are the ends of our natures,—that is, if teleological determinism is not perverse and arbitrary but rational and scientific—we are, as Spinoza constantly points out, free. Only when we are subject to alien ends or the ends of alien natures are we enslaved. For freedom is not opposed to necessity or determinism; it is only opposed to an alien necessity or alien determinism. Freedom consists not in absolute indetermination, but in absolute self-determination. And self-determination is the very last thing that can be called fatalistic.

Because Spinoza knew that freedom consists in self-determination he was saved from falling into the absurdities of Rousseau's "Back to Nature" doctrine even though Nature is, for Spinoza, the origin of everything and its laws, the only laws that are divine. Still, the purpose and conduct of man's life, if they are to be rational, must be defined by man's nature not by any other nature; if man is to be free, he must be guided by the particular laws of his own being, not by the laws of any other being least of all by the general laws of so totally dissimilar a being as absolutely infinite Nature. There is as much sense and rationality in exhorting us to go back to the Realm of Nature, as there is in exhorting us to go on to the City of God.

There is, in Spinoza's system, no teleological determinism (in the perverted theological usage explained above); but neither is there, in Spinoza's system, any "free-will" for man. And the hue and cry that is always raised when "free-will" is denied, was raised against Spinoza. The clamorous moralists protest that "free-will" is the necessary (*sic!*) foundation of all morality, and hence of religion. This is the starting point of Bernard Shaw's no less than of Henry Oldenburg's infuriated argument. And, unfortunately, no less a thinker than William James starts from the same misguided assumption. And yet nothing can be more certainly clear than that if man as a matter of fact has no "free-will" it is the very height of absurdity to maintain that man's morality necessarily depends upon his having "free-will." Something man does not possess cannot be made any condition, let alone *the* indispensable condition of his being able to live a moral life. Man's morality must be based upon his nature; and what his nature is cannot be antecedently determined in accordance with the demands of any special moral theory. Moral theory must be based upon man's nature; not man's nature upon moral theory.

Far from "free-will" being a necessary foundation of morality "free-will" would make all morality, of the kind we know and the "free-will"-ists want, absolutely impossible. The central condition of moral life is responsibility. So central is it, that it is now acknowledged as such in all the penal codes of civilized countries. But if man has, instead of a determinate nature, "free-will", responsibility can in no way be fixed. Education, too, is necessarily impossible. Hence all punishment would have to be retributive. Moral strife, as well as legal penalties, would bear all the stigmata of unmitigated, imbecilic cruelty. This is not the case however if man has an absolutely determinate nature. Education is possible. And therefore although crime loses none of its evil character, punishment can lose all of its inhuman sting. The necessary condition of human morality is responsibility not irresponsibility; reliability not unreliability; certainty not uncertainty; a firm will, not a "free" will.

"Free-will" is necessary only in theological apologetics. According to Christian theology, if man did not have "free-will" it would follow that God is the Author of all the evil of the world. Something which is not quite in keeping with His perfect goodness. By a queer twist of mind, theologians therefore gave man, and not God (as they should have done) "free-will." But they gave man "free-will" not to enable him to live virtuously, but to enable him to sin. If man were able to live virtuously as well as sinfully of his own "free-will" he would then be altogether independent of God, which can in no way be admitted or allowed. Hence the bitter and heart-rending cries of orthodox, especially evangelical ministers that if left to themselves they can only sin! They can live virtuously only when they are absolutely coerced so to live by God! Their radical inability to understand or believe the self-reliant moral person grows from the very heart of their theology. For "free-will"—the only freedom they know—is the necessary condition, not of man's morality, but of God's!

There is no fatalism in Spinoza's system. Fatalism is the moral value of a theory of the universe. That theory is fatalistic, which makes the activities man cherishes either futile or impossible. Any system that puts man at the mercy of the flux of events does precisely this. This is necessarily done by a system according to which the universe does not faithfully observe an immutable order, does not obey certain fixed and eternal laws. Nothing is as fatal as an accident; no universe as fatalistic as an accidental universe.

There is no fatalism in Spinoza's system because there are no accidents in Spinoza's universe. All things are necessarily determined by immutable laws, and man, who is an integral part of the universe, is necessarily without "free-will." In Spinoza's system, ends, being undetermined (as contrasted with their being determined in the theological sense explained above) they can exercise no fatalistic power; and means, although determined (in the strict scientific sense) are similarly impotent because they are, in the life of man, subordinate to ends. Consequently, Spinoza was able to write upon Human Freedom with a truth and clarity and force excelling by far all theological, teleological, "free-will," idealistic philosophers from Plato to Josiah Royce. Spinoza was able to write thus because, not in spite of the fact that he placed at the heart of his philosophy the doctrine of necessity; because, not in spite of the fact that he developed the only complete system of philosophy strictly consistent with the principles of natural science or mathematical physics. Spinoza is, perhaps, the only thoroughly emancipated, the only thoroughly modern and scientific philosopher that ever lived. And he is, much more certainly, the only thoroughly emancipated, the only thoroughly modern and scientific ethicist that ever lived.

To-day, in view of the extensive dominion and authority of science, the objections against Spinoza's doctrine of necessity can hardly be as self-righteous and as loud as they were two centuries ago. The principle of the uniformity of Nature has become the established foundation of natural science. And it is also acknowledged, except in the recent ranks of superstition, that man is a part of Nature, not independent of it.

Man's connection with Nature is, in Spinoza's system, at least as intimate as it is in the latest system of natural science. The original doctrine of the origin of species, Spinoza would have found entirely in harmony with his general philosophy, although what he would have thought of subsequent evolutionary extravaganzas, it is impossible to say. Darwinian biology made man consubstantial with the animal kingdom; Spinoza's metaphysics makes man's body consubstantial with the infinite attribute of extension or matter, and his mind consubstantial with the infinite attribute of thought which is the mind of Nature or God. Man, as a "mode" of extension and thought, is necessarily subject to the laws of these two attributes of which he is compounded. The fundamental relation of man to the universe, set forth in the Bible, is radically transformed. Man is no longer an only child of God, enjoying his privileges and protection (occasionally tempered by inexperienced punishments); he is a mode of two attributes of substance inexorably determined by their universal, immutable laws.

V

Of all the laws of the universe, it was Spinoza's chief object to discover the mental laws. That there were such laws his metaphysics assured him; and the existence to-day of a science of psychology substantiates his belief. The most popular of recent psychologies—Freudianism—is based upon the principle that nothing whatever happens in the mental life of man, waking or asleep, that is not specifically determined by ascertainable causes. Psychoanalytic therapy would be impossible otherwise. Psychiatry, too, has conclusively demonstrated that only metaphorically is the subject matter it deals with in the region of the "abnormal." Actually, the insane are subject to laws of behavior which can be scientifically studied no less than the sane. They are no more possessed of an evil, designing spirit, as our witch-burning ancestors consistently believed, than the ordinary human being is possessed of "free-will."

Spinoza's psychology is dialectical. But it is no indictment of his psychology to point out that it is. It is true, his formal definition of sorrow, for instance, fails supremely to touch the strings of a sympathetic heart. But the philosophical psychologist is not a novelist. The recent claim that "literary psychology" is the only valid psychology, is as well founded as the claim would be that only a "literary physics" is valid. Mathematical physics gives us no more a picture of the actual physical universe than Spinoza's psychology gives us a picture of the mental and emotional life of an actual human being. But the failure of these sciences to give us a picture of the living world in no way invalidates their truth, or deprives them of their utility.

Consider, as an example, Spinoza's psychological law freely expressed in the dictum that Paul's idea of Peter tells us more about Paul than about Peter. This conclusion follows strictly from fundamental principles of Spinoza's abstract, dialectical psychology; but its truth or its practical applicability is because of that not in the least impaired. Indeed, because of its dialectical form its range of meaning is greatly increased. Spinoza's dictum applies to what William James called the "psychologist's fallacy." It also applies to what John Ruskin called the "pathetic fallacy." Again, it applies to the fallacy Franz Boas exposed and which he may justly have called the "anthropologist's fallacy." And it applies also to what one may, with a great deal of benefit, dub the "ethicist's fallacy." For the very same constitutional weakness of man to identify confusedly his own nature with that of the object he is contemplating or studying, is most flagrantly and painfully evident in the fields of theoretical and practical ethics. The "ethicist's fallacy" is the source of all absolutism in theory, and all intolerance in practice.

All four fallacies just enumerated come under Spinoza's dictum as special cases come under a general law. And these four are by no means the only instances of the common habit of mind. From no field of human endeavor is the mischief-working fallacy ever absent. We find it lodged in the judge's decision, the propagandist's program, the historian's record, the philosopher's system. In the field of metaphysical poetry it has recently been identified by Santayana as "normal madness." In its milder forms, the fallacy is now known by everyone as the "personal equation"; in its pronounced, abnormal manifestations it is known by the psychoanalysts as "transference." It is a Protean fallacy woven into the emotional texture of the human mind. Nothing, for it, is sacred enough to be inviolate. For Spinoza discovered it sanctimoniously enshrined even in the Sacred Scriptures. As he brilliantly shows us in the *Tractatus Theologico-Politicus*, the prophets' ideas about God tell us more about the prophets than about God.

The far-reaching significance of Spinoza's propositions is one of their most remarkable characteristics. This is due to the fact, contemporary philological philosophers notwithstanding, that Spinoza defined the essence, the generating principle, not the accidental qualities, of the human mind.

Another example may not be out of place. Spinoza's proposition that anything may be accidentally (in the philosophic sense of "accident") a cause of pleasure, pain, or desire seems to explain the essence of all the particular variations of the psychological phenomena known now by all who have been aroused to the significance of their vagrant cryptic slumbers, as the phenomena of symbolism, sublimation, and fetich worship. Spinoza's proposition explains all the phenomena adequately because among the fundamental human emotions, Spinoza like Freud—if we discount the recent attempt to go beyond the pleasure-principle—reckons only three: desire, pleasure and pain. And with Spinoza, as with the Freudians, it sometimes seems that desire is more fundamental than the other two, for desire expresses, in Spinoza's terminology, the essence of man. Desire however may be stimulated by almost anything. It requires the least sanity of mind, therefore, to prevent one from scandalously over-emphasizing one particular class of objects—of desire.

The striking similarity, if not identity, between Spinoza's psychological doctrines and those of contemporaries, serves to give conclusive lie to the crass contemporary contention that Truth instinctively shuns the philosophical study, and that she only favors the laboratory or clinic where she freely comes and frankly discloses herself to the cold, impersonal embrace of mechanical instruments.

It is not altogether fortuitously that Spinoza's psychology embraces so readily contemporary psychological conceptions. Spinoza made a psychological, if not psychoanalytical, analysis of some portions of Scripture. And Scripture is a very rich human material. Besides having to explain the diverse and conflicting accounts the different Scriptural authors gave of the nature of God, Spinoza had to account for the superstitious beliefs commonly held by men that are incorporated in the Bible—the beliefs in omens, devils, angels, miracles, magical rites. Spinoza had to account for all these by means of his analysis of human nature since he would not grant the existence of supernatural beings and powers. Spinoza's psychology adequately performs the task. His psychology demonstrates with unsurpassed thoroughness and clarity how human emotions, when uncontrolled in any way by intelligence, naturally attach themselves to all sorts of bizarrely irrelevant and absurd things, and stimulate the imagination to endow these things with all the qualities and powers the disturbed hearts of ignorant men desire. Ignorant and frustrated man, Spinoza showed, frantically dreams with his eyes open.

VI

Spinoza's method in psychology is dialectical, but his interest is practical. His psychology one might almost say is a moral psychology. Spinoza wants to explain mental phenomena through their primary causes because a knowledge of man's nature is the radical cure for his ills. The greatest obstacle man has to contend against is his emotional nature. Not that it is inherently degraded or sinful—the grotesque superstition some religious moralists have maintained; but man's emotional nature masters, more often than not, man's rational nature, and leads man astray. When the emotions are unrestrained and undirected by knowledge and intelligence, they violently attach themselves to anything that chances to excite them. Their stark immediacy vitiates man's judgment. He is unable, while under their sway, to select and follow the course that is best, because his mind is engulfed in the evanescent present. In his hectic desire to gain the passing pleasure, man loses his ultimate good.

But man's salvation, just as much as his damnation, is within his own control. Salvation or blessedness is something man can achieve by his own efforts; it is not something he can achieve only by Divine Grace. For it is no innate perver-

Concepts

sion of soul, no inherent wickedness of man, no malicious "free-will" that causes him to follow the lure of the Devil rather than the light of God. The very elements in man's nature which cause him to fall are the means by which he can make himself rise. He can pit one emotion against another and the stronger will not merely win, but will win over, the weaker. And it is in the nature of the emotions not to have only one satisfying object, but to be able to derive satisfaction from almost any object whatsoever. The most spiritual forms of human love have the same emotional foundations as the most bestial forms of human lust.

To learn how to become master of one's emotions, to learn how to free oneself from their bondage, is, therefore, the primary condition of sustained and rational happiness. The key to virtue, Spinoza independently agreed with Socrates, is knowledge of oneself. Only when we understand ourselves can we control our emotions. And only when we have our emotions under control are we able consistently to direct our activity towards a definite, rational goal. Our activity then follows from our own nature, and not from the nature of external things which arouse our emotions and determine their strength. And, as already noticed, to be the necessary cause of our own activity is, according to Spinoza, to be free.

It is impossible, of course, for man ever to be the sole cause of his activity. To be such, he would have to be an entirely independent being—an absolute power—something he can never be. No matter how eloquently misguided enthusiasts extol the powerful merits of man's "free-will" it will always be true that man's emotions, sensations and ideas change very significantly with the organic changes that occur in his body. The emotions, sensations and ideas of a child differ from those of a man, and those of a man in maturity differ from those of a man decrepit with old age. And these and similar changes are quite beyond the control of man.

However, without denying man's intimate dependence upon Nature, it is still possible to distinguish between those activities which follow, in an important degree, from a man's individual nature—whatever it may happen to be at the time—and those activities which follow only from his own nature in conjunction with the nature of other things. The movement of my pen on paper would be impossible without the general order of Nature which allows such phenomena as motion, pen and paper, to exist. Nevertheless, I can profitably distinguish between the movement of my pen on paper and the movement of my body through stellar space. The former movement follows, in an important sense, from my own peculiar constitution; the latter, from the constitution of the stellar system. Likewise, but more significantly for human welfare, one can distinguish broadly between the activities and the passivities of the mind; between man as an agent, a doer—man's intellect; and man as a patient, a sufferer—man's passions. In this creative age such distinction should be singularly easy to draw. In moral terminology one can distinguish between man as free and man as enslaved.

Since man can never be the sole cause of his activity, he can never be wholly free. The range of human power is extremely limited, and Spinoza is ever careful to point that out. Spinoza is no incurable optimist, no Leibnizian Pangloss who believes this is, for man, the best of all possible worlds. To be humanly idealistic it is by no means necessary to be super-humanly utopian. But neither is Spinoza a shallow Schopenhauerian pessimist. Spinoza's realistic appraisal of man's worldly estate is entirely free from all romantic despair. This world is no more the worst than it is the best of all possible worlds for man. Although man cannot completely alter his evil estate, he can better it. And the wisdom of philosophy consists in recognizing this fact and discovering what ways and means there are for bringing such betterment about.

This Spinoza has in mind throughout the devious courses of his philosophy. It is present to him when he delineates the character of Nature or God, when he outlines the nature of the mind and its emotions, no less than when he specifically addresses himself to the task of describing the way to the highest blessedness of man. Indeed, so intent is Spinoza upon reaching his ethical goal, and making all his doctrines contributory to it, he purposely omits to treat of many philosophical problems because they are, though interesting in themselves, of too little value for the conduct of man's life. His philosophical system, as a result, is in many respects merely sketched in massive outline.

VII

The dominant ethics of Christian civilization has made a special point of disregarding the intimate connection that exists between human nature and rational conduct. Morality has been identified, not with living a life according to a rational plan and an adequate conception of an ideal form of human existence, but with a strained attempt to live in accordance with an inherited system of coercive social habits. Of this morality, the Puritan is the popular type. Only in quite recent years has some advance been made back to the sane naturalistic conception of morals which is found in the Greeks and also in Spinoza.

The Philosophy of Spinoza

It is a fundamental point with Spinoza that the ceremonial law, as he puts it in the *Tractatus Theologico-Politicus*, can at best secure man wealth and social position. Man's highest blessedness can be secured by the divine law of Nature alone. Here Spinoza and Rousseau are at one. It was relevant to Spinoza's purpose to treat only of religious ceremonial law; but his conclusions apply with equal force and relevancy to social and political ceremonial law as well. Spinoza's distinction between ceremonial and divine law is peculiarly significant and illuminating when applied to marriage. For to-day in marriage, if anywhere, is it glaringly evident that the legal or religious or social ceremonial law can at best secure man or woman wealth and social position. Happiness or blessedness lie altogether beyond its powerful reach. Marriage is sanctified and made blessed not by the ceremonial law of priest or city clerk but by the divine law of love. Natural love, or love free from all ceremonial coercions, is not merely not a questionable source of marital happiness: it is the only source. The ceremonial law, the legal or religious marriage custom, has nothing whatsoever to do with human happiness. If by "free" love is meant love free from all legal, social and religious ceremonial restraints, then free love is, according to Spinoza, the only basis of rational marriage.

No man ever treasured the joys of the spirit more than did Spinoza; but he did not because of that nourish a savage antagonism against the body. The very bases of his philosophy of the mind saved him from any such disastrous folly. What Havelock Ellis says "We know at last" Spinoza knew all the time—"that it must be among our chief ethical rules to see that we build the lofty structure of human society on the sure and simple foundations of man's organism." It is because Spinoza knew this so thoroughly and remembered it so well that he devotes so much of his attention to the nature of the human mind and the human emotions in a treatise on ethics.

Mind and body are not intrinsically alien or inimical to one another. They are co-operative expressions of the one reality. The mind is the idea of the body and "in proportion as one body is better adapted than another to do or suffer many things, in the same proportion will the mind, at the same time, be better adapted to perceive many things." Purely psychologically, all that we can ever discover about the regulating influence glands have upon personality can only go to corroborate, not to improve this general position. And morally, the implications are equally far-reaching and profound.

The virtue of the mind is not to despise or reject but to understand and transform. And it clearly must be more excellent for the mind to know both itself and the body than it is for the mind to know itself alone. For natural science is the result when the mind organizes into a system what are, in their own nature, simply apprehensions of bodily existences; and art is the result when the mind transfuses with an ideal quality of its own what are, in their own nature, simply apprehensions of bodily excellences of form or motion, color or sound. Matter is, in its nature, no more hostile to spirit than body is alien to mind. Paradise is not a non-or super-physical realm; it is a physical realm made harmonious with the ideality of the soul. Spirit is an appreciation, a transmutation of matter. For the lover, the physical embrace is a spiritual revelation.

The fundamental metaphysical law from which Spinoza's ethical system flows is that everything endeavors to persist in its own being. This law is the metaphysical equivalent of the first law of motion in physics which is itself the equivalent of the law of identity in logic. By his law Spinoza does not mean anything which anticipates the nineteenth-century doctrine of the competitive struggle for existence. On the contrary, nothing is so clear to Spinoza as the fact that the most efficient way of preserving one's own being is not by competitive but by co-operative activity. Especially is this true of human beings. By his own efforts a solitary man cannot, even after he has been nursed to maturity, maintain himself in a decent manner. Certainly he is unable successfully to resist his foes. But with the aid of his fellows man can develop a highly complex and tolerably stable civilization, all the excellences of which he can enjoy at the comparatively small risk of becoming a victim of its dangers. Social organization is the natural expression of man's fundamental endeavor to preserve himself. A perfect social organization naturally expresses the highest form of human existence—individualism without anarchy and communism without oppression.

Consistent with his primary law of being, Spinoza defines virtue not in terms of negations, inhibitions, deficiencies or restraints; virtue he defines in terms of positive human qualities compendiously called human power. Virtue is power, however, not in the sense of the Renaissance ideal of "manliness" as we glimpse it, for instance, in Benvenuto Cellini; nor is it power in the vulgar sense of dominion which seems to be the confused ideal of some ultra-contemporaries; virtue is power in the sense of the Greek ideal that virtue is human excellence. It was therefore very natural for Nietzsche who consciously went back to the Greeks to hail Spinoza as his only philosophical forerunner, the only philosopher who dwelt with him on the highest mountain-tops, perilous only for those who are born for the base valleys of life. And it was equally natural for Nietzsche to fail to see the important differences between his own violent and turbid thinking and the sure and disciplined thinking of Spinoza—on those very points upon which Nietzsche thought they agreed.

Perfection and imperfection are, in Spinoza's thought, identical with the real and the unreal. The perfect is the completed, the perfected; the imperfect, the uncompleted, the unperfected. These terms have, in their first intention, no specifically ethical significance. Nature is perfect, that is, absolutely real or completed; but in no intelligible sense is Nature ethically good. However, it is possible to convert non-ethical into ethical terms. We can do this by designating, for example, a certain type of character as the "perfect" type. If we reach that type we are perfect or supremely "good"; insofar as we fall short of it, we are imperfect, or "bad."

Just what constitutes human excellence is determined in each case by the specific nature and relations of the individual involved. The excellence of a child is not that of a man; and the excellence of a free man differs from that of a slave. For the parent, the perfect child is docile, beautiful and full of promise; for the ruler, the perfect man is industrious, respectful of law and order, eager to pay taxes and go to war; for the free man, the perfect man is a rational being, living a harmonious life in knowledge and love of himself, his neighbor and God. Moreover, within any one class the excellences vary in harmony with the variations in the individuals. There is no excellence in general.

But because ethical standards are quite human and vary, they do not lack, therefore, all validity. They are within their range of applicability, absolute, even though they are, in a more comprehensive universe, relative. A just appreciation of the relative nature, but absolute value of specific ethical judgments, is above all things vitally necessary in ethics. Such appreciation saves the ethicist from the pernicious fallacy of erecting personal preferences into universal laws; and it also saves him from falling into the ethical abyss where all things are of equal value because all things are equally vain.

Ethical tolerance is different from ethical sentimentality. Everyone has the sovereign natural right to cherish the excellence in harmony with his character. But the equality extends no further. A comprehensive estimate of the powers of the mind can be made and they can be arranged in a series of increasing value. No arrangement can ever be absolutely final and authoritative, for what one free man considers the highest perfection of human life, another will consider to be only of secondary importance. Still, all free men will agree that certain powers of the mind are superior to others. But superiority is not rationally endowed with legislative power over others. The free man is superior to the slave, but he has, because of that, no rational right to dominate him; neither is it his office to revile or despise him; the slave was given his nature, he did not ask for it.

But if it is not the office of the free man to dominate or revile the slave still less is it the divinely appointed office of the slave to rule and revile the free man—universal democratic prejudices notwithstanding. And in support of the independent, and in case of contest, superior right of the free man we have the very highest authority for those who do not trust themselves to be guided by reason. God Himself has pronounced upon this tremendous issue. And not in mere words, but by unmistakable deeds. When Lucifer, the first absolute democrat or equalitarian, the first one to maintain that no one was better than he was, raised his impious standard, God assembled all His faithful hosts together and hurled Lucifer out of Heaven into Hell. And justly so. For Lucifer had, by his foul, sacrilegious doctrine and action, revealed himself to be the Prince of Darkness not the Prince of Light. To our untold and everlasting misery the Prince of Darkness who failed to ensnare the majority of angels did succeed in ensnaring the majority of mankind. So irredeemably so, even the sweetly and tenderly lyrical Prince of Peace had to be sent to us bearing a ghastly sword.

Reason is not, according to Spinoza, a constitutive power in man's life; it is a regulative principle. Spinoza is, in the traditional usage of the term, anything but a rationalist in his ethics. Only if rationalism consists in being unflaggingly reasonable is Spinoza an avowed and thorough-going rationalist. Reason has, for Spinoza, no transcendental status or power, and it plays no dictatorial rôle. Reason, for him, is essentially an organizing not a legislative power in man's life. To take a phrase from Professor Dewey, reason, for Spinoza, is reconstructive not constitutive. The power of the intellect is not some underived, original, independent power which can impose or, better, superimpose its categorical imperatives upon human conduct. The power of the intellect is wholly derivative, dependent upon the nature of the things that it understands.

Reason gives man the power and insight to organize his life on the basis of his knowledge, to chose an end harmonious with his nature, what is for his best advantage—the basis of all virtue—and to select and control the means by which it can be attained. For the happy governance of our lives the object we must chiefly understand is ourselves. Because—in Matthew Arnold's line— "the aids to noble life are all within." When we become creatures conscious of our natural endowment we cease to be blind instruments of our natures and become rational, intelligent agents. For intelligence, in the fundamental sense of the word, consists in knowing what we are and understanding what we can do.

A man who governs his life according to the dictates of reason tries, insofar as possible, to harmonize his conflicting interests. He balances, impartially, future with present goods, and he bases his decision upon the broad foundation of all his needs. He does not madly satisfy or repress one passion at the expense of the rest of his nature. He satisfies a maximum rather than a minimum of his desires, evaluating them not merely by numerical strength but by quality and duration. It is only stupid and pernicious confusion that makes man's moral problem consist in his discovering instead of a good "relative" to his nature, an "absolute" good, good for no nature at all. Man's real moral problem is to secure a permanent good instead of a transitory good; a more inclusive good instead of a more restricted good; a higher good instead of a lower good. Morally, it matters nothing whether an intellectual good is "absolute" or whether it is only "relative" to man's mind and his power of comprehension. But it matters everything, morally, whether an intellectual good is more or less permanent, more or less inclusive, more or less valuable than a sensory good. This is the real moral problem man is faced with. And this is the moral problem Spinoza considers and solves.

Everybody knows what is Spinoza's solution. One permanent intellectual good is, according to him, of more importance and value in the life of man than countless transitory sensory pleasures. The object most permanent in character and greatest in value is Nature or God. The highest virtue of the mind, therefore, the highest blessedness of man, consists in the intellectual love of Nature or God. Thus Spinoza passes from ethics to religion, which in his thought almost imperceptibly blend together.

VIII

The beginning and the end, as familiar wisdom has long since propounded, are the same. The ultimate origin of man is God, and the final end, the blessed crown of life, is to return to God in fullest knowledge and love. The philosopher who was during his lifetime and for over a century after his death constantly execrated for being an atheist (he occasionally still is by some hardy fools) made God a more integral part of his system than did anyone else in the whole history of philosophy. Spinoza did not do occasional reverence to God; he did not, in lightly passing, perfunctorily bow to Him; God is the veritable beginning and end of all his thought.

The intellectual love of God does not demand as basis a knowledge of the cosmic concatenation of things. Omniscience alone could satisfy such a demand. The intellectual love of Nature or God depends solely upon a knowledge of the order of Nature, upon a knowledge of the infinite and eternal essence of God. And such knowledge is within the limits of our reach.

30

We can apprehend the eternal essence of God because the temporality of our thought is accidental to its meaning. It is the nature of reason to see things under the form of eternity. And we can apprehend the infinite essence of God or Nature because every particular finite thing is a determinate expression of the infinite. The law of causality requires that there be an essential identity of nature between cause and effect; otherwise it would follow that something can be produced from nothing. Since cause and effect belong to the same realm of existence, to the same attribute of Nature, whenever we apprehend the essence of a particular thing, we necessarily apprehend the infinite essence of that attribute of Nature. For the infinite, with Spinoza, is not so much an extent as a quality of being. Thus from the comprehension of any particular thing, we can pass to a comprehension of the infinite and eternal.

This is most commonly understood, curiously enough, not in religion, but in art. The ecstatic power of beauty makes the soul lose all sense of time and location. And in the specific object the soul sees an infinite meaning. Indeed, one can almost say that the more specific or limited the artistic object, the more clearly is the absolute or infinite meaning portrayed and discerned. A sonnet is oftener than not more expressive than a long poem; the *Red Badge of Courage* reveals more impressively than does the *Dynasts* the absolute essential horror of war. There are present, apparently, in the more pronounced mystical visions, characteristics similar to those of significant esthetic apprehensions. These visions are extremely rare and fleeting. But then we can be at the highest peaks only seldom and for a short while. But in a moment we see eternity, and in the finite, the infinite. It is for this reason Spinoza says the more we understand particular things the more do we understand God.

The great religious significance of Spinoza's doctrine of the intellectual love of God is that it establishes religion upon knowledge and not upon ignorance. The virtue of the mind is clearly and distinctly to understand, not ignorantly to believe. There is no conflict between science and religion; religion is based upon science. There is a conflict only between science and superstition. Mysteries, unknown and unknowable powers, miracles, magical rites and prayerful incantations are instruments not of religion but of superstition which has its origin in ignorant and ignominious fear.

The free man does not fear and he is not consumed by fear's boundless conceit. He has no apprehensive conscience which unceasingly interprets all unusual or untoward events as being deliberate signs of a god's impending wrath. The free man knows that man is, cosmically considered, impressively insignificant. Human loves and hatreds, human joys and sorrows are, in the face of the eternal and infinite, the littlest of little things. Human nature is only an infinitely small part of absolutely infinite Nature; human life only a very tiny expression of infinite life. Inordinate conceit alone could conceive Nature to have been made designedly either for our pleasure or our discomfort. The stars were not hung in the heavens so that we may steer our petty courses across the seas; nor were the sun and moon put in their places so that we may have the day in which to waste ourselves in futile labors and the night to spend in ignorant sleep. Even if there were a cosmic drama—which there is not—man is too trivial to play in it a leading rôle. The free man knows all this; but his heart is tempered and strong. He can contemplate his place in the universe without bitterness and without fear. For the free man's love, as his worship, flows from his knowledge of God.

IX

Spinoza is unsparing in his criticisms of the superstitions which are in, and which have grown up around, the Bible. All Spinoza's major conclusions have been embodied directly or indirectly in what is now known as "the higher criticism" of the Bible, which is the basis of the Modernist movement. It was Spinoza who established the fact that the Pentateuch is not, as it is reputed to be, the work of Moses. It was Spinoza, also, who first convincingly showed that other of the Scriptural documents were compiled by various unacknowledged scribes; not by the authors canonized by orthodoxy, Jewish or Gentile. The wealth of philological and historical material at the disposal of the contemporary Biblical investigator is incomparably richer than it was at Spinoza's time. But modern scholarship has only added more material—only extended in breadth Spinoza's modest researches. In depth, nothing new has been achieved. The principles of investigation and interpretation, and the general results Spinoza arrived at have not been improved upon in the least, nor is it at all likely that they ever will. Spinoza founded himself upon bed-rock.

Spinoza's aim in revealing the defectiveness of the Bible was not theological but philosophical. Orthodox Biblical conceptions had in his day, as they still have to a certain extent in ours, a peculiarly sanctified power, because they were institutionalized and made the basis of an authoritative system of conduct. The misbegotten doctrines therefore could not be questioned with impunity, for a criticism of the doctrines on intellectual grounds was invariably construed as an attack upon the vested customs. The misfortunes of history made dissent from palpable absurdities capital heresy. Social and religious bigotry burned scientific men with political ardor.

However, although Spinoza suffered in his own person from religious persecution, he never for one moment held as did, for example, Voltaire, that the Church is the wily and unregenerate instrument of vicious priests. On the contrary, Spinoza was quite sure that many of the clergy were among the noblest of men, and that the Church was in large measure a very salutary institution for the masses who cannot learn to govern themselves by force of mind. But Spinoza was unalterably opposed to any encroachment of Church authority upon the just liberties of men. Especially did he object to the Church extending its prohibitive power over men's thinking. It is the business of the Church to inculcate "obedience" in the masses; not to dictate to philosophers what is the truth. The fundamental purpose of Spinoza's attack upon the Bible is to free philosophy from theology; not to destroy the Church but to disestablish it.

Many readers of Spinoza conclude that because Spinoza tolerated Church authority in matters of public morality he therefore either did not in his own thought thoroughly adhere to his principles or else he was excessively cautious, even timid, and did not fully or consistently express his mind. No one would deny that there is some accommodation in Spinoza's language. He certainly followed the practical wisdom of the thinkers of his day. Even so, however, Spinoza was by no means as cautious as was Descartes. Anyway, accommodation does not fully account for Spinoza's attitude on this question; in fact, it does not account for any significant feature of it.

Spinoza never believed a sound metaphysics was, for the masses, the indispensable basis of a good moral life. The multitude, he was firmly convinced, are controlled by their passions and desires, not by knowledge and reason. The coercive law of the State and Nature, not philosophy, keep them living within the bounds necessary for social order and human well-being. Far from it being necessary to tell the masses only the truth Spinoza believed, as did Plato before him, that it may even be necessary in order to rule the masses successfully in the ways of wisdom and virtue to deceive them to a greater or lesser extent. Such deception is, as a political expediency, morally justified, for the rulers would be lying in the interests of virtue and truth.

Spinoza did not suffer from the fond contemporary delusion that the salvation of mankind will come about when philosophers become like all other people. He knew, as Plato did, that the day of ultimate, universal happiness will dawn rather when all other people become like philosophers. In the meantime, it is the height of moral and political folly to act as if that day had arrived or else could be ushered in by morning. Spinoza had nothing but contempt for facile-tongued, feather-brained Utopians. He loved humanity too sincerely to mislead humanity or himself that way. And so we find in Spinoza's *Ethics* as in his *Tractatus* two systems of morals—one for the many who are called, and one for the few who are chosen. In the *Tractatus*, the religion of the many is summarily called "obedience"; in the *Ethics* it is more fully shown to consist of utilitarianism in the conduct of our affairs, high-mindedness towards our fellows, and piety towards Nature or God. To this is added, as the rare religion of the few, what is designated in both treatises alike as the intellectual love of Nature or God.

X

Spinoza's religion is as naturalistic as his ethics. By making God and Nature equivalent terms Spinoza was not merely resorting to equivocation to escape the penalty of his views. The identification of God and Nature fully embodies Spinoza's doctrine that there is no supernatural realm; and therefore if man is to have a God at all, Nature must be that God. To contend, as so many do, that "true religion" must be based upon the existence of a supernatural realm, no matter whether or not such a realm exists, is as absurd as to contend that "true morality" must be based upon man's "free-will" no matter whether or not man has "free-will." Spinoza's system has been called pantheistic. But it is pantheistic only in the sense that whatever man considers Godlike must be found in Nature, for no other realm exists, and there are no gods.

But the question is always raised, how is it possible to love a Being indifferent to our human miseries and blind to our hopes? How is even an intellectual love of such a Being possible? Man, as his religions show, wants God to be a father, a protector, One who cherishes man's desires and cares for his wants. The least anthropomorphic of religions wants God to be the depository of abstract human ideals. But Spinoza's God is not even as human as this. Nature does not constitute the ideal type for man.

Religion is, it is true, man's search for comfort and security in an alien and hostile world. The simple demand of the human heart is to be recognized and to be loved. Love is the magic touch that transforms all that is barren and cold into all that is rich and warm and fruitful. But man is neither loved nor recognized by the immensities of the universe. And in face of the illimitable stretches of time and space even the stoutest heart involuntarily quakes. We cannot consider the vast power of the universe without feeling crushed and becoming despondent. And ignorant man cannot see in the finite things about him the full expression of the infinite beyond. He cannot derive any moral strength or comfort from the world about him because he conceives that world to be an implacable instrument of a god's uncertain, inexplicable will. He therefore cosmically projects, in a frenzy of despair, his crying human demand. And out of the wastes of space there arises for him a personal God.

Anthropomorphic religions reveal man at his weakest, not at his best. Man's true grandeur is shown when he transcends by his own power of mind his insistent human desires. He can then stand free before the Almighty. He may tremble, but he is not afraid. For his strength of soul is grounded not in the external world but in his own ideal. If we are born under a lucky star, and are fortunate and happy lovers of the ideal, the ecstasy of the mystic's beatific vision is ours. But even if we are born under an unlucky star, and are misfortunate and unhappy lovers of the ideal, we still have the ideal to which we can hold fast and save ourselves from being shattered in our despairs, from dying in spirit, which is far more terrible than any death in the body could possibly be. We have the ideal to give us the strength, if we are lovers of God, to go to the cross with Jesus; or, if we are lovers of Virtue, to drink the hemlock with Socrates.

The intellectual love of God is a devotion purged of all fear, of all vain regrets and even vainer hopes. The wild and angry emotions of sorrow and pain leave the strong and noble heart of man like the tidal waves leave the scattered rocks of the shore. As the rocks, when the waves return to their depths, smile securely in the glistening sun in the sky, so does the brave, free heart of man, when the passionate deluge is spent, smile serenely in the face of God. The free man is born neither to weep nor to laugh but to view with calm and steadfast mind the eternal nature of things.

To know the eternal is the immortality we enjoy. But to know the eternal we must forget about ourselves. We must cease to be consumed by a cancerous anxiety to endure in time and be permanent in space. In the order of Nature our own particular lives are of no especial importance. And unless we recognize this, we are necessarily doomed to a miserable fate. We must recognize that our mere selves can never give us ultimate fulfillment or blessedness of soul. Only by losing ourselves in Nature or God can we escape the wretchedness of finitude and find the final completion and salvation of our lives. This, the free man understands. He knows how insignificant he is in the order of Nature. But he also knows that if only he can lose himself in Nature or God then, in his own insignificant particularity, the eternal and infinite order of Nature can be displayed. For in the finite is the infinite expressed, and in the temporal, the eternal.

It is this knowledge that makes man free, that breaks the finite fetters from his soul enabling him to embrace the infinite and to possess eternity. Once man is reconciled to the petty worth of his own person, he assumes some of the majestic worth of the universe. And the austere sublimity of soul that inscribes on the grave of the beloved *God is Love*, inscribes, when it is chastened and purified by understanding, on the grave of all that is merely human *Nature is Great*. Religion is the joy and peace and strength that is all understanding.

JOSEPH RATNER.

FIRST PART

ON GOD

The multitude, ever prone to superstition, and caring more for the shreds of antiquity than for eternal truths, pays homage to the Books of the Bible, rather than to the Word of God.

SPINOZA

The Philosophy of Spinoza

CHAPTER I

OF SUPERSTITION[1]

Men would never be superstitious, if they could govern all their circumstances by set rules, or if they were always favored by fortune: but being frequently driven into straits where rules are useless, and being often kept fluctuating pitiably between hope and fear by the uncertainty of fortune's greedily coveted favors, they are consequently, for the most part, very prone to credulity. The human mind is readily swayed this way or that in times of doubt, especially when hope and fear are struggling for the mastery, though usually it is boastful, over-confident, and vain.

This as a general fact I suppose everyone knows, though few, I believe, know their own nature; no one can have lived in the world without observing that most people, when in prosperity, are so over-brimming with wisdom (however inexperienced they may be), that they take every offer of advice as a personal insult, whereas in adversity they know not where to turn, but beg and pray for counsel from every passer-by. No plan is then too futile, too absurd, or too fatuous for their adoption; the most frivolous causes will raise them to hope, or plunge them into despair—if anything happens during their fright which reminds them of some past good or ill, they think it portends a happy or unhappy issue, and therefore (though it may have proved abortive a hundred times before) style it a lucky or unlucky omen. Anything which excites their astonishment they believe to be a portent signifying the anger of the gods or of the Supreme Being, and, mistaking superstition for religion, account it impious not to avert the evil with prayer and sacrifice. Signs and wonders of this sort they conjure up perpetually, till one might think Nature as mad as themselves, they interpret her so fantastically.

Thus it is brought prominently before us, that superstition's chief victims are those persons who greedily covet temporal advantages; they it is, who (especially when they are in danger, and cannot help themselves) are wont with prayers and womanish tears to implore help from God: upbraiding reason as blind, because she cannot show a sure path to the shadows they pursue, and rejecting human wisdom as vain; but believing the phantoms of imagination, dreams, and other childish absurdities, to be the very oracles of Heaven. As though God has turned away from the wise, and written His decrees, not in the mind of man but in the entrails of beasts, or left them to be proclaimed by the

38

inspiration and instinct of fools, madmen, and birds. Such is the unreason to which terror can drive mankind!

Superstition, then, is engendered, preserved, and fostered by fear. If any one desire an example, let him take Alexander, who only began superstitiously to seek guidance from seers, when he first learned to fear fortune in the passes of Sysis (Curtius v. 4); whereas after he had conquered Darius he consulted prophets no more, till a second time frightened by reverses. When the Scythians were provoking a battle, the Bactrians had deserted, and he himself was lying sick of his wounds, "he once more turned to superstition, the mockery of human wisdom, and bade Aristander, to whom he confided his credulity, inquire the issue of affairs with sacrificed victims." Very numerous examples of a like nature might be cited, clearly showing the fact, that only while under the dominion of fear do men fall a prey to superstition; that all the portents ever invested with the reverence of misguided religion are mere phantoms of dejected and fearful minds; and lastly that prophets have most power among the people, and are most formidable to rulers, precisely at those times when the state is in most peril. I think this is sufficiently plain to all, and will therefore say no more on the subject.

The origin of superstition above given affords us a clear reason for the fact, that it comes to all men naturally, though some refer its rise to a dim notion of God, universal to mankind, and also tends to show, that it is no less inconsistent and variable than other mental hallucinations and emotional impulses, and further that it can only be maintained by hope, hatred, anger, and deceit; since it springs, not from reason, but solely from the more powerful phases of emotion. Furthermore, we may readily understand how difficult it is to maintain in the same course men prone to every form of credulity. For, as the mass of mankind remains always at about the same pitch of misery, it never assents long to any one remedy, but is always best pleased by a novelty which has yet proved illusive.

This element of inconsistency has been the cause of many terrible wars and revolutions; for, as Curtius well says (lib. iv. chap. 10): "The mob has no ruler more potent than superstition," and is easily led, on the plea of religion, at one moment to adore its kings as gods, and anon to execrate and abjure them as humanity's common bane. Immense pains have therefore been taken to counteract this evil by investing religion, whether true or false, with such pomp and ceremony, that it may rise superior to every shock, and be always observed with studious reverence by the whole people—a system which has been brought to great perfection by the Turks, for they consider even controversy impious, and so clog men's minds with dogmatic formulas, that they leave no room for sound reason, not even enough to doubt with.

But if, in despotic statecraft, the supreme and essential mystery be to hoodwink the subjects, and to mask the fear, which keeps them down, with the specious garb of religion, so that men may fight as bravely for slavery as for safety, and count it not shame but highest honor to risk their blood and their lives for the vainglory of a tyrant; yet in a free state no more mischievous expedient could be planned or attempted. Wholly repugnant to the general freedom are such devices as enthralling men's minds with prejudices, forcing their judgment, or employing any of the weapons of quasi-religious sedition; indeed, such seditions only spring up, when law enters the domain of speculative thought, and opinions are put on trial and condemned on the same footing as crimes, while those who defend and follow them are sacrificed, not to public safety, but to their opponents' hatred and cruelty. If deeds only could be made the grounds of criminal charges, and words were always allowed to pass free, such seditions would be divested of every semblance of justification, and would be separated from mere controversies by a hard and fast line.

Now seeing that we have the rare happiness of living in a republic, where everyone's judgment is free and unshackled, where each may worship God as his conscience dictates, and where freedom is esteemed before all things dear and precious, I have believed that I should be undertaking no ungrateful or unprofitable task, in demonstrating that not only can such freedom be granted without prejudice to the public peace, but also, that without such freedom, piety cannot flourish nor the public peace be secure....

I have often wondered that persons who make a boast of professing the Christian religion, namely, love, joy, peace, temperance, and charity to all men, should quarrel with such rancorous animosity, and display daily towards one another such bitter hatred, that this, rather than the virtues they claim, is the readiest criterion of their faith. Matters have long since come to such a pass that one can only pronounce a man Christian, Turk, Jew, or Heathen, by his general appearance and attire, by his frequenting this or that place of worship, or employing the phraseology of a particular sect—as for manner of life, it is in all cases the same. Inquiry into the cause of this anomaly leads me unhesitatingly to ascribe it to the fact, that the ministries of the Church are regarded by the masses merely as dignities, her offices as posts of emolument—in short, popular religion may be summed up as a respect for ecclesiastics. The spread of this misconception inflamed every worthless fellow with an intense desire to enter holy orders, and thus the love of diffusing God's religion degenerated into sordid avarice and ambition. Every church became a theater, where orators, instead of church teachers harangued, caring not to instruct the people, but striving to attract admiration, to bring opponents to public scorn, and to preach only novelties and paradoxes, such as would tickle the ears of their congregation. This state of things necessarily stirred up an amount of controversy, envy, and hatred, which no lapse of time could appease; so that we can scarcely wonder that of the old religion nothing survives but its outward forms (even these, in the mouth of the multitude, seem rather adulation than adoration of the Deity), and that faith has become a mere compound of credulity and prejudices—aye, prejudices too, which degrade man from rational being to beast, which completely stifle the power of judgment between true and false, which seem, in fact, carefully fostered for the purpose of extinguishing the last spark of reason! Piety, great God! and religion are become a tissue of ridiculous mysteries; men, who flatly despise reason, who reject and turn away from understanding as naturally corrupt, these, I say, these of all men, are thought, Oh lie most horrible! to possess light from on High. Verily, if they had but one spark of light from on High, they would not insolently rave, but would learn to worship God more wisely, and would be as marked among their fellows for mercy as they now are for malice; if they were concerned for their opponents' souls, instead of for their own reputations, they would no longer fiercely persecute, but rather be filled with pity and compassion.

Furthermore, if any Divine light were in them, it would appear from their doctrine. I grant that they are never tired of professing their wonder at the profound mysteries of Holy Writ; still I cannot discover that they teach anything but speculation of Platonists and Aristotelians, to which (in order to save their credit of Christianity) they have made Holy Writ conform; not content to rave with the Greeks themselves, they want to make the prophets rave also; showing conclusively, that never even in sleep have they caught a glimpse of Scripture's Divine nature. The very vehemence of their admiration for the mysteries plainly attests, that their belief in the Bible is a formal assent rather than a living faith: and the fact is made still more apparent by their laying down beforehand, as a foundation for the study and true interpretation of Scripture, the principle that it is in every passage true and divine. Such a doctrine should be reached only after strict scrutiny and thorough comprehension of the Sacred Books (which would teach it much better, for they stand in need of no human fictions), and not be set up on the threshold, as it were, of inquiry.

As I pondered over the facts that the light of reason is not only despised, but by many even execrated as a source of impiety, that human commentaries are accepted as divine records, and that credulity is extolled as faith; as I marked the fierce controversies of philosophers raging in Church and State, the source of bitter hatred and dissension, the ready instruments of sedition and other ills innumerable, I determined to examine the Bible afresh in a careful, impartial, and unfettered spirit, making no assumptions concerning it, and attributing to it no doctrines, which I do not find clearly therein set down....

FOOTNOTES:

[1] From the Preface to the *Tractatus Theologico-Politicus*.

CHAPTER II

OF THE INTERPRETATION OF SCRIPTURE[2]

When people declare, as all are ready to do, that the Bible is the Word of God teaching men true blessedness and the way of salvation, they evidently do not mean what they say; for the masses take no pains at all to live according to Scripture, and we see most people endeavoring to hawk about their own commentaries as the word of God, and giving their best efforts, under the guise of religion, to compelling others to think as they do: we generally see, I say, theologians anxious to learn how to wring their inventions and sayings out of the sacred text, and to fortify them with Divine authority. Such persons never display less scruple and more zeal than when they are interpreting Scripture or the mind of the Holy Ghost; if we ever see them perturbed, it is not that they fear to attribute some error to the Holy Spirit, and to stray from the right path, but that they are afraid to be convicted of error by others, and thus to overthrow and bring into contempt their own authority. But if men really believe what they verbally testify of Scripture, they would adopt quite a different plan of life: their minds would not be agitated by so many contentions, nor so many hatreds, and they would cease to be excited by such a blind and rash passion for interpreting the sacred writings, and excogitating novelties in religion. On the contrary, they would not dare to adopt, as the teaching of Scripture, anything which they could not plainly deduce therefrom: lastly, these sacrilegious persons who have dared, in several passages, to interpolate the Bible, would have shrunk from so great a crime, and would have stayed their sacrilegious hands.

Ambition and unscrupulousness have waxed so powerful, that religion is thought to consist, not so much in respecting the writings of the Holy Ghost, as in defending human commentaries, so that religion is no longer identified with charity, but with spreading discord and propagating insensate hatred disguised under the name of zeal for the Lord, and eager ardor.

To these evils we must add superstition, which teaches men to despise reason and Nature, and only to admire and venerate that which is repugnant to both: whence it is not wonderful that for the sake of increasing the admiration and veneration felt for Scripture, men strive to explain it so as to make it appear to contradict, as far as possible, both one and the other: thus they dream that most profound mysteries lie hid in the Bible, and weary themselves out in the investigation of these absurdities, to the neglect of what is useful. Every result of their diseased imagination they attribute to the Holy Ghost, and strive to defend with the utmost zeal and passion; for it is an observed fact that men employ their reason to defend conclusions arrived at by reason, but conclusions arrived at by the passions are defended by the passions.

If we would separate ourselves from the crowd andescape from theological prejudices, instead of rashly accepting human commentaries for Divine documents, we must consider the true method of interpreting Scripture and dwell upon it at some length: for if we remain in ignorance of this we cannot know, certainly, what the Bible and the Holy Spirit wish to teach.

I may sum up the matter by saying that the method of interpreting Scripture does not widely differ from the method of interpreting Nature—in fact, it is almost the same. For as the interpretation of Nature consists in the examination of the history of Nature, and therefrom deducing definitions of natural phenomena on certain fixed axioms, so Scriptural interpretation proceeds by the examination of Scripture, and inferring the intention of its authors as a legitimate conclusion from its fundamental principles. By working in this manner everyone will always advance without danger of error—that is, if they admit no principles for interpreting Scripture, and discussing its contents save such as they find in Scripture itself—and will be able with equal security to discuss what surpasses our understanding, and what is known by the natural light of reason.

In order to make clear that such a method is not only correct, but is also the only one advisable, and that it agrees with that employed in interpreting Nature, I must remark that Scripture very often treats of matters which cannot be deduced from principles known to reason: for it is chiefly made up of narratives and revelation: the narratives generally contain miracles—that is, [as we shall show in a later chapter], relations of extraordinary natural occurrences adapted to the opinions and judgment of the historians who recorded them: the revelations also were adapted to the opinions of the prophets and in themselves surpassed human comprehension. Therefore the knowledge of all these—that is, of nearly the whole contents of Scripture, must be sought from Scripture alone, even as the knowledge of nature is sought from nature. As for the moral doctrines which are also contained in the Bible, they may be demonstrated from received axioms, but we cannot prove in the same manner that Scripture intended to teach them, this can only be learned from Scripture itself.

If we would bear unprejudiced witness to the Divine origin of Scripture, we must prove solely on its own authority that it teaches true moral doctrines, for by such means alone can its Divine origin be demonstrated: we have shown that the certitude of the prophets depended chiefly on their having minds turned towards what is just and good, therefore we ought to have proof of their possessing this quality before we repose faith in them. From miracles God's divinity cannot be proved [as I shall show], for miracles could be wrought by false prophets. Wherefore the Divine origin of Scripture must consist solely in its teaching true virtue. But we must come to our conclusion simply on Scriptural grounds, for if we were unable to do so we could not, unless strongly prejudiced, accept the Bible and bear witness to its Divine origin.

Our knowledge of Scripture must then be looked for in Scripture only.

Lastly, Scripture does not give us definitions of things any more than nature does: therefore, such definitions must be sought in the latter case from the diverse workings of nature; in the former case, from the various narratives about the given subject which occur in the Bible.

The universal rule, then, in interpreting Scripture is to accept nothing as an authoritative Scriptural statement which we do not perceive very clearly when we examine it in the light of its history. What I mean by its history, and what should be the chief points elucidated, I will now explain.

The history of a Scriptural statement comprises—

I. The nature and properties of the language in which the books of the Bible were written, and in which their authors were accustomed to speak. We shall thus be able to investigate every expression by comparison with common conversational usages.

Now all the writers both of the Old Testament and the New were Hebrews: therefore, a knowledge of the Hebrew language is before all things necessary, not only for the comprehension of the Old Testament, which was written in that tongue, but also of the New: for although the latter was published in other languages, yet its characteristics are Hebrew.

II. An analysis of each book and arrangement of its contents under heads; so that we may have at hand the various texts which treat of a given subject. Lastly, a note of all the passages which are ambiguous or obscure, or which seem mutually contradictory.

I call passages clear or obscure according as their meaning is inferred easily or with difficulty in relation to the context, not according as their truth is perceived easily or the reverse by reason. We are at work not on the truth of passages, but solely on their meaning. We must take especial care, when we are in search of the meaning of a text, not to be led away by our reason in so far as it is founded on principles of natural knowledge (to say nothing of prejudices): in order not to confound the meaning of a passage with its truth, we must examine it solely by means of the signification of the words, or by a reason acknowledging no foundation but Scripture.

I will illustrate my meaning by an example. The words of Moses, "God is a fire" and "God is jealous," are perfectly clear so long as we regard merely the signification of the words, and I therefore reckon them among the clear passages, though in relation to reason and truth they are most obscure: still, although the literal meaning is repugnant to the natural light of reason, nevertheless, if it cannot be clearly overruled on grounds and principles derived from its Scriptural "history," it, that is, the literal meaning, must be the one retained: and contrariwise if these passages literally interpreted are found to clash with principles derived from Scripture, though such literal interpretation were in absolute harmony with reason, they must be interpreted in a different manner, *i.e.*, metaphorically.

If we would know whether Moses believed God to be a fire or not, we must on no account decide the question on grounds of the reasonableness or the reverse of such an opinion, but must judge solely by the other opinions of Moses which are on record.

In the present instance, as Moses says in several other passages that God has no likeness to any visible thing, whether in heaven or in earth, or in the water, either all such passages must be taken metaphorically, or else the one before us must be so explained. However, as we should depart as little as possible from the literal sense, we must first ask whether this text, God is a fire, admits of any but the literal meaning—that is, whether the word fire ever means anything besides ordinary natural fire. If no such second meaning can be found, the text must be taken literally, however repugnant to reason it may be: and all the other passages, though in complete accordance with reason, must be brought into harmony with it. If the verbal expressions would not admit of being thus harmonized, we should have to set them down as irreconcilable, and suspend our judgment concerning them. However, as we find the name fire applied to anger and jealousy (see Job xxxi. 12) we can thus easily reconcile the words of Moses, and legitimately conclude that the two propositions God is a fire, and God is jealous, are in meaning identical.

Further, as Moses clearly teaches that God is jealous, and nowhere states that God is without passions or emotions, we must evidently infer that Moses held this doctrine himself, or at any rate, that he wished to teach it, nor must we refrain because such a belief seems contrary to reason: for as we have shown, we cannot wrest the meaning of texts to suit the dictates of our reason, or our preconceived opinions. The whole knowledge of the Bible must be sought solely from itself.

III. Lastly, such a history should relate the environment of all the prophetic books extant; that is, the life, the conduct, and the studies of the author of each book, who he was, what was the occasion, and the epoch of his writing, whom did he write for, and in what language. Further, it should inquire into the fate of each book: how it was first received, into whose hands it fell, how many different versions there were of it, by whose advice was it received into the Bible, and, lastly, how all the books now universally accepted as sacred, were united into a single whole.

All such information should, as I have said, be contained in the "history" of Scripture. For, in order to know what statements are set forth as laws, and what as moral precepts, it is important to be acquainted with the life, the conduct, and the pursuits of their author: moreover, it becomes easier to explain a man's writings in proportion as we have more intimate knowledge of his genius and temperament.

Further, that we may not confound precepts which are eternal with those which served only a temporary purpose, or were only meant for a few, we should know what was the occasion, the time, the age, in which each book was written, and to what nation it was addressed.

Lastly, we should have knowledge on the other points I have mentioned, in order to be sure, in addition to the authenticity of the work, that it has not been tampered with by sacrilegious hands, or whether errors can have crept in, and, if so, whether they have been corrected by men sufficiently skilled and worthy of credence. All these things should be known, that we may not be led away by blind impulse to accept whatever is thrust on our notice, instead of only that which is sure and indisputable.

Now, when we are in possession of this history of Scripture, and have finally decided that we assert nothing as prophetic doctrine which does not directly follow from such history, or which is not clearly deducible from it, then, I say, it will be time to gird ourselves for the task of investigating the mind of the prophets and of the Holy Spirit. But in this further arguing, also, we shall require a method very like that employed in interpreting Nature from her history. As in the examination of natural phenomena we try first to investigate what is most universal and common to all Nature—such, for instance, as motion and rest, and their laws and rules, which Nature always observes, and through which she continually works—and then we proceed to what is less universal; so, too, in the history of Scripture, we seek first for that which is most universal, and serves for the basis and foundation of all Scripture, a doctrine, in fact, that is commended by all the prophets as eternal and most profitable to all men. For example, that God is one, and that He is omnipotent, and He alone should be worshiped, that He has a care for all men, and that He especially loves those who adore Him and love their neighbor as themselves, etc. These and similar doctrines, I repeat, Scripture everywhere so clearly and expressly teaches, that no one was ever in doubt of its meaning concerning them.

The nature of God, His manner of regarding and providing for things, and similar doctrines, Scripture nowhere teaches professedly, and as eternal doctrine; on the contrary, we have shown that the prophets themselves did not agree on the subject; therefore, we must not lay down any doctrine as Scriptural on such subjects, though it may appear perfectly clear on rational grounds.

From a proper knowledge of this universal doctrine of Scripture, we must then proceed to other doctrines less universal, but which, nevertheless, have regard to the general conduct of life, and flow from the universal doctrine like rivulets from a source: such are all particular external manifestations of true virtue, which need a given occasion for their exercise; whatever is obscure or ambiguous on such points in Scripture must be explained and defined by its universal doctrine; with regard to contradictory instances, we must observe the occasion and the time in which they were written. For instance, when Christ says, "Blessed are they that mourn, for they shall be comforted," we do not know, from the actual passage, what sort of mourners are meant; as, however, Christ afterwards teaches that we should have care for nothing, save only for the kingdom of God and His righteousness, which is commended as the highest good (see Matt. vi. 33), it follows that by mourners He only meant those who mourn for the kingdom of God and righteousness neglected by man: for this would be the only cause of mourning to those who love nothing but the Divine kingdom and justice, and who evidently despise the gifts of fortune. So, too, when Christ says: "But if a man strike you on the right cheek, turn to him the left also," and the words which follow.

If He had given such a command, as a lawgiver, to judges, He would thereby have abrogated the law of Moses, but this He expressly says He did not do (Matt. v. 17). Wherefore we must consider who was the speaker, what was the occasion, and to whom were the words addressed. Now Christ said that He did not ordain laws as a legislator, but inculcated precepts as a teacher: inasmuch as He did not aim at correcting outward actions so much as the frame of mind. Further, these words were spoken to men who were oppressed, who lived in a corrupt commonwealth on the brink of ruin, where justice was utterly neglected. The very doctrine inculcated here by Christ just before the destruction of the city was also taught by Jeremiah before the first destruction of Jerusalem, that is, in similar circumstances, as we see from Lamentations iii. 25-30.

Now as such teaching was only set forth by the prophets in times of oppression, and was even then never laid down as a law; and as, on the other hand, Moses (who did not write in times of oppression, but—mark this—strove to found a well-ordered commonwealth), while condemning envy and hatred of one's neighbor, yet ordained that an eye should be given for an eye, it follows most clearly from these purely Scriptural grounds that this precept of Christ and Jeremiah concerning submission to injuries was only valid in places where justice is neglected, and in a time of oppression, but does not hold good in a well-ordered state.

In a well-ordered state where justice is administered everyone is bound, if he would be accounted just, to demand penalties before the judge (see Lev. v. 1), not for the sake of vengeance (Lev. xix. 17, 18), but in order to defend justice and his country's laws, and to prevent the wicked rejoicing in their wickedness. All this is plainly in accordance with reason. I might cite many other examples in the same manner, but I think the foregoing are sufficient to explain my meaning and the utility of this method, and this is all my present purpose. Hitherto we have only shown how to investigate those passages of Scripture which treat of practical conduct, and which, therefore, are more easily examined, for on such subjects there was never really any controversy among the writers of the Bible.

The purely speculative passages cannot be so easily traced to their real meaning: the way becomes narrower, for as the prophets differed in matters speculative among themselves, and the narratives are in great measure adapted to the prejudices of each age, we must not, on any account, infer the intention of one prophet from clearer passages in the writings of another; nor must we so explain his meaning, unless it is perfectly plain that the two prophets were at one in the matter.

How we are to arrive at the intention of the prophets in such cases I will briefly explain. Here, too, we must begin from the most universal proposition, inquiring first from the most clear Scriptural statements what is the nature of prophecy or revelation, and wherein does it consist; then we must proceed to miracles, and so on to whatever is most general till we come to the opinions of a particular prophet, and, at last, to the meaning of a particular revelation, prophecy, history, or miracle. We have already pointed out that great caution is necessary not to confound the mind of a prophet or historian with the mind of the Holy Spirit and the truth of the matter; therefore I need not dwell further on the subject. I would, however, here remark concerning the meaning of revelation, that the present method only teaches us what the prophets really saw or heard, not what they desired to signify or represent by symbols. The latter may be guessed at but cannot be inferred with certainty from Scriptural premises.

We have thus shown the plan for interpreting Scripture, and have, at the same time, demonstrated that it is the one and surest way of investigating its true meaning. I am willing indeed to admit that those persons (if any such there be) would be more absolutely certainly right, who have received either a trustworthy tradition or an assurance from the prophets themselves, such as is claimed by the Pharisees; or who have a pontiff gifted with infallibility in the interpretation of Scripture, such as the Roman Catholics boast. But as we can never be perfectly sure, either of such a tradition or of the authority of the pontiff, we cannot found any certain conclusion on either: the one is denied by the oldest sect of Christians, the other by the oldest sect of Jews. Indeed, if we consider the series of years (to mention no other point) accepted by the Pharisees from their Rabbis, during which time they say they have handed down the tradition from Moses, we shall find that it is not correct, as I show elsewhere. Therefore such a tradition should be received with extreme suspicion; and although, according to our method, we are bound to consider as uncorrupted the tradition of the Jews, namely, the meaning of the Hebrew words which we received from them, we may accept the latter while retaining our doubts about the former.

No one has ever been able to change the meaning of a word in ordinary use, though many have changed the meaning of a particular sentence. Such a proceeding would be most difficult; for whoever attempted to change the meaning of a word, would be compelled, at the same time, to explain all the authors who employed it, each according to his temperament and intention, or else, with consummate cunning, to falsify them.

Further, the masses and the learned alike preserve language, but it is only the learned who preserve the meaning of particular sentences and books: thus, we may easily imagine that the learned having a very rare book in their power, might change or corrupt the meaning of a sentence in it, but they could not alter the signification of the words; moreover, if anyone wanted to change the meaning of a common word he would not be able to keep up the change among posterity, or in common parlance or writing.

For these and such-like reasons we may readily conclude that it would never enter into the mind of anyone to corrupt a language, though the intention of a writer may often have been falsified by changing his phrases or interpreting them amiss. As then our method (based on the principle that the knowledge of Scripture must be sought from itself alone) is the sole true one, we must evidently renounce any knowledge which it cannot furnish for the complete understanding of Scripture....

If we read a book which contains incredible or impossible narratives, or is written in a very obscure style, and if we know nothing of its author, nor of the time or occasion of its being written, we shall vainly endeavor to gain any certain knowledge of its true meaning. For being in ignorance on these points we cannot possibly know the aim or intended aim of the author; if we are fully informed, we so order our thoughts as not to be in any way prejudiced either in ascribing to the author or him for whom the author wrote either more or less than his meaning, and we only take into consideration what the author may have had in his mind, or what the time and occasion demanded. I think this must be tolerably evident to all.

It often happens that in different books we read histories in themselves similar, but which we judge very differently, according to the opinions we have formed of the authors. I remember once to have read in some book that a man named Orlando Furioso used to drive a kind of winged monster through the air, fly over any countries he liked, kill unaided vast numbers of men and giants, and such like fancies, which from the point of view of reason are obviously absurd. A very similar story I read in Ovid of Perseus, and also in the books of Judges and Kings of Samson, who alone and unarmed killed thousands of men, and of Elijah, who flew through the air, and at last went up to heaven in a chariot of fire, with horses of fire. All these stories are obviously alike, but we judge them very differently. The first only sought to amuse, the second had a political object, the third a religious object. We gather this simply from the opinions we had previously formed of the authors. Thus it is evidently necessary to know something of the authors of writings which are obscure or unintelligible, if we would interpret their meaning; and for the same reason, in order to choose the proper reading from among a great variety, we ought to have information as to the versions in which the differences are found, and as to the possibility of other readings having been discovered by persons of greater authority....

... The difficulties in this method of interpreting Scripture from its own history, I conceive to be so great that I do not hesitate to say that the true meaning of Scripture is in many places inexplicable, or at best mere subject for guess work; but I must again point out, on the other hand, that such difficulties only arise when we endeavor to follow the meaning of a prophet in matters which cannot be perceived, but only imagined, not in things, whereof the understanding can give a clear and distinct idea, and which are conceivable through themselves: matters which by their nature are easily perceived cannot be expressed so obscurely as to be unintelligible; as the proverb says, "a word is enough to the wise." Euclid, who only wrote of matters very simple and easily understood, can easily be comprehended by any one in any language; we can follow his intention perfectly, and be certain of his true meaning, without having a thorough knowledge of the language in which he wrote; in fact, a quite rudimentary acquaintance is sufficient. We need make no researches concerning the life, the pursuits, or the habits of the author; nor need we inquire in what language, nor when he wrote, nor the vicissitudes of his book, nor its various readings, nor how, nor by whose advice it has been received.

What we here say of Euclid might equally be said of any book which treats of things by their nature perceptible: thus we conclude that we can easily follow the intention of Scripture in moral questions, from the history we possess of it, and we can be sure of its true meaning.

The precepts of true piety are expressed in very ordinary language, and are equally simple and easily understood. Further, as true salvation and blessedness consist in a true assent of the soul—and we truly assent only to what we clearly understand—it is most plain that we can follow with certainty the intention of Scripture in matters relating to salvation and necessary to blessedness; therefore, we need not be much troubled about what remains: such matters, inasmuch as we generally cannot grasp them with our reason and understanding, are more curious than profitable.

I think I have now set forth the true method of Scriptural interpretation, and have sufficiently explained my own opinion thereon. Besides, I do not doubt that everyone will see that such a method only requires the aid of natural reason. The nature and efficacy of the natural reason consists in deducing and proving the unknown from the known, or in carrying premises to their legitimate conclusions; and these are the very processes which our method desiderates. Though we must admit that it does not suffice to explain everything in the Bible, such imperfection does not spring from its own nature, but from the fact that the path which it teaches us, as the true one, has never been tended or trodden by men, and has thus, by the lapse of time, become very difficult, and almost impassable, as, indeed, I have shown in the difficulties I draw attention to.

There only remains to examine the opinions of those who differ from me.

The first which comes under our notice is, that the light of nature has no power to interpret Scripture, but that a supernatural faculty is required for the task. What is meant by this supernatural faculty I will leave to its propounders to explain. Personally, I can only suppose that they have adopted a very obscure way of stating their complete uncertainty about the true meaning of Scripture. If we look at their interpretations, they contain nothing supernatural, at least nothing but the merest conjectures.

Let them be placed side by side with the interpretations of those who frankly confess that they have no faculty beyond their natural ones; we shall see that the two are just alike—both human, both long pondered over, both laboriously invented. To say that the natural reason is insufficient for such results is plainly untrue, firstly, for the reasons above stated, namely, that the difficulty of interpreting Scripture arises from no defect in human reason, but simply from the carelessness (not to say malice) of men who neglected the history of the Bible while there were still materials for inquiry; secondly, from the fact (admitted, I think, by all) that the supernatural faculty is a Divine gift granted only to the faithful. But the prophets and apostles did not preach to the faithful only, but chiefly to the unfaithful and wicked. Such persons, therefore, were able to understand the intention of the prophets and apostles, otherwise the prophets and apostles would have seemed to be preaching to little boys and infants, not to men endowed with reason. Moses, too, would have given his laws in vain, if they could only be comprehended by the faithful, who need no law. Indeed, those who demand supernatural faculties for comprehending the meaning of the prophets and apostles seem truly lacking in natural faculties, so that we should hardly suppose such persons the possessors of a Divine supernatural gift.

The opinion of Maimonides was widely different. He asserted that each passage in Scripture admits of various, nay, contrary meanings; but that we could never be certain of any particular one till we knew that the passage, as we interpreted it, contained nothing contrary or repugnant to reason. If the literal meaning clashes with reason, though the passage seems in itself perfectly clear, it must be interpreted in some metaphorical sense. This doctrine he lays down very plainly in Chap. xxv. part ii. of his book *More Nebuchim* for he says: "Know that we shrink not from affirming that the world hath existed from eternity, because of what Scripture saith concerning the world's creation. For the texts which teach that the world was created are not more in number than those which teach that God hath a body; neither are the approaches in this matter of the world's creation closed, or even made hard to us: so that we should not be able to explain what is written, as we did when we showed that God hath no body, nay, peradventure, we could explain and make fast the doctrine of the world's eternity more easily than we did away with the doctrines that God hath a beatified body. Yet two things hinder me from doing as I have said, and believing that the world is eternal. As it hath been clearly shown that God hath not a body, we must perforce explain all those passages whereof the literal sense agreeth not with the demonstration, for sure it is that they can be so explained. But the eternity of the world hath not been so demonstrated, therefore it is not necessary to do violence to Scripture in support of some common opinion, whereof we might, at the bidding of reason, embrace the contrary."

Such are the words of Maimonides, and they are evidently sufficient to establish our point: for if he had been convinced by reason that the world is eternal, he would not have hesitated to twist and explain away the words of Scripture till he made them appear to teach this doctrine. He would have felt quite sure that Scripture, though everywhere plainly denying the eternity of the world, really intends to teach it. So that, however clear the meaning of Scripture may be, he would not feel certain of having grasped it, so long as he remained doubtful of the truth of what was written. For we are in doubt whether a thing is in conformity with reason, or contrary thereto, so long as we are uncertain of its truth, and, consequently, we cannot be sure whether the literal meaning of a passage be true or false.

If such a theory as this were sound, I would certainly grant that some faculty beyond the natural reason is required for interpreting Scripture. For nearly all things that we find in Scripture cannot be inferred from known principles of the natural reason, and therefore, we should be unable to come to any conclusion about their truth, or about the real meaning and intention of Scripture, but should stand in need of some further assistance.

Further, the truth of this theory would involve that the masses, having generally no comprehension of, nor leisure for, detailed proofs, would be reduced to receiving all their knowledge of Scripture on the authority and testimony of philosophers, and consequently, would be compelled to suppose that the interpretations given by philosophers were infallible.

Truly this would be a new form of ecclesiastical authority, and a new sort of priests or pontiffs, more likely to excite men's ridicule than their veneration. Certainly our method demands a knowledge of Hebrew for which the masses have no leisure; but no such objection as the foregoing can be brought against us. For the ordinary Jews or Gentiles, to whom the prophets and apostles preached and wrote, understood the language, and consequently, the intention of the prophet or apostle addressing them; but they did not grasp the intrinsic reason of what was preached, which, according to Maimonides, would be necessary for an understanding of it.

There is nothing, then, in our method which renders it necessary that the masses should follow the testimony of commentators, for I point to a set of unlearned people who understood the language of the prophets and apostles; whereas Maimonides could not point to any such who could arrive at the prophetic or apostolic meaning through their knowledge of the causes of things.

As to the multitude of our own time [we shall show] that whatsoever is necessary to salvation, though its reasons may be unknown, can easily be understood in any language, because it is thoroughly ordinary and usual; it is in such understanding as this that the masses acquiesce, not in the testimony of commentators; with regard to other questions, the ignorant and the learned fare alike.

But let us return to the opinion of Maimonides, and examine it more closely. In the first place, he supposes that the prophets were in entire agreement one with another, and that they were consummate philosophers and theologians; for he would have them to have based their conclusions on the absolute truth. Further, he supposes that the sense of Scripture cannot be made plain from Scripture itself, for the truth of things is not made plain therein (in that it does not prove anything, nor teach the matters of which it speaks through their definitions and first causes), therefore, according to Maimonides, the true sense of Scripture cannot be made plain from itself, and must not be there sought.

The falsity of such a doctrine is shown in this very chapter, for we have shown both by reason and examples that the meaning of Scripture is only made plain through Scripture itself, and even in questions deducible from ordinary knowledge should be looked for from no other source.

Lastly, such a theory supposes that we may explain the words of Scripture according to our preconceived opinions, twisting them about, and reversing or completely changing the literal sense, however plain it may be. Such license is utterly opposed to the teaching of this and the [succeeding] chapters, and moreover, will be evident to everyone as rash and excessive.

But if we grant all this license, what can it effect after all? Absolutely nothing. Those things which cannot be demonstrated, and which make up the greater part of Scripture, cannot be examined by reason, and cannot therefore be explained or interpreted by this rule; whereas, on the contrary, by following our own method, we can explain many questions of this nature, and discuss them on a sure basis, as we have already shown, by reason and example. Those matters which are by their nature comprehensible we can easily explain, as has been pointed out, simply by means of the context.

Therefore, the method of Maimonides is clearly useless: to which we may add, that it does away with all the certainty which the masses acquire by candid reading, or which is gained by any other persons in any other way. In conclusion, then, we dismiss Maimonides' theory as harmful, useless, and absurd.

As to the tradition of the Pharisees, we have already shown[3] that it is not consistent, while the authority of the popes of Rome stands in need of more credible evidence; the latter, indeed, I reject simply on this ground, for if the popes could point out to us the meaning of Scripture as surely as did the high priests of the Jews, I should not be deterred by the fact that there have been heretic and impious Roman pontiffs; for among the Hebrew high-priests of old there were also heretics and impious men who gained the high-priesthood by improper means, but who, nevertheless, had Scriptural sanction for their supreme power of interpreting the law. (See Deut. xvii. 11, 12, and xxxviii. 10, also Malachi ii. 8).

However, as the popes can show no such sanction, their authority remains open to very grave doubt, nor should any one be deceived by the example of the Jewish high-priests and think that the Catholic religion also stands in need of a pontiff; he should bear in mind that the laws of Moses being also the ordinary laws of the country, necessarily required some public authority to insure their observance; for, if everyone were free to interpret the laws of his country as he pleased, no state could stand, but would for that very reason be dissolved at once, and public rights would become private rights.

With religion the case is widely different. Inasmuch as it consists not so much in outward actions as in simplicity and truth of character, it stands outside the sphere of law and public authority. Simplicity and truth of character are not produced by the constraint of laws, nor by the authority of the state, no one the whole world over can be forced or legislated into a state of blessedness; the means required for such a consummation are faithful and brotherly admonition, sound education, and above all, free use of the individual judgment.

Therefore, as the supreme right of free thinking, even on religion, is in every man's power, and as it is inconceivable that such power could be alienated, it is also in every man's power to wield the supreme right and authority of free judgment in this behalf, and to explain and interpret religion for himself. The only reason for vesting the supreme authority in the interpretation of law, and judgment on public affairs in the hands of the magistrates, is that it concerns questions of public right. Similarly the supreme authority in explaining religion, and in passing judgment thereon, is lodged with the individual because it concerns questions of individual right. So far, then, from the authority of the Hebrew high-priests telling in confirmation of the authority of the Roman pontiffs to interpret religion, it would rather tend to establish individual freedom of judgment. Thus in this way, also, we have shown that our method of interpreting Scripture is the best. For as the highest power of Scriptural interpretation belongs to every man, the rule for such interpretation should be nothing but the natural light of reason which is common to all—not any supernatural light nor any external authority; moreover, such a rule ought not to be so difficult that it can only be applied by very skillful philosophers, but should be adapted to the natural and ordinary faculties and capacity of mankind. And such I have shown our method to be, for such difficulties as it has arise from men's carelessness, and are no part of its nature.

FOOTNOTES:

[2] From the *Tr. Th.-P.*, ch. vii, same title.

[3] The detailed discussion of this point has been omitted.—ED.

_____

CHAPTER III

OF PROPHETS AND PROPHECY[4]

I

Prophecy, or revelation, is sure knowledge revealed by God to man. A prophet is one who interprets the revelations of God to those who are unable to attain to sure knowledge of the matters revealed, and therefore can only apprehend them by simple faith.

The Hebrew word for prophet is "*nabi*," *i.e.*, speaker or interpreter, but in Scripture its meaning is restricted to interpreter of God, as we may learn from Exodus vii. 1, where God says to Moses, "See, I have made thee a god to Pharaoh, and Aaron thy brother shall be thy prophet;" implying that, since in interpreting Moses' words to Pharaoh, Aaron acted the part of a prophet, Moses would be to Pharaoh as a god, or in the attitude of a god....

Now it is evident, from the definition above given, that prophecy really includes ordinary knowledge; for the knowledge which we acquire by our natural faculties depends on our knowledge of God and His eternal laws; but ordinary knowledge is common to all men as men, and rests on foundations which all share, whereas the multitude always strains after rarities and exceptions, and thinks little of the gifts of nature; so that, when prophecy is talked of, ordinary knowledge is not supposed to be included. Nevertheless it has as much right as any other to be called Divine, for God's nature, in so far as we share therein, and God's laws, dictate it to us; nor does it suffer from that to which we give the pre-eminence, except in so far as the latter transcends its limits and cannot be accounted for by natural laws taken in themselves. In respect to the certainty it involves, and the source from which it is derived, *i.e.*, God, ordinary knowledge is no whit inferior to prophetic, unless indeed we believe, or rather dream, that the prophets had human bodies but superhuman minds, and therefore that their sensations and consciousness were entirely different from our own.

But, although ordinary knowledge is Divine, its professors cannot be called prophets, for they teach what the rest of mankind could perceive and apprehend, not merely by simple faith, but as surely and honorably as themselves.

Seeing then that our mind subjectively contains in itself and partakes of the nature of God, and solely from this cause is enabled to form notions explaining natural phenomena and inculcating morality, it follows that we may rightly assert the nature of the human mind (in so far as it is thus conceived) to be a primary cause of Divine revelation. All that we clearly and distinctly understand is dictated to us, as I have just pointed out, by the idea and nature of God; not indeed through words, but in a way far more excellent and agreeing perfectly with the nature of the mind, as all who have enjoyed intellectual certainty will doubtless attest. Here, however, my chief purpose is to speak of matters having reference to Scripture, so these few words on the light of reason will suffice.

I will now pass on to, and treat more fully, the other ways and means by which God makes revelations to mankind, both of that which transcends ordinary knowledge and of that within its scope; for there is no reason why God should not employ other means to communicate what we know already by the power of reason.

Our conclusions on the subject must be drawn solely from Scripture; for what can we affirm about matters transcending our knowledge except what is told us by the words or writings of prophets? And since there are, so far as I know, no prophets now alive, we have no alternative but to read the books of prophets departed, taking care the while not to reason from metaphor or to ascribe anything to our authors which they do not themselves distinctly state. I must further premise that the Jews never make any mention or account of secondary, or particular causes, but in a spirit of religion, piety, and what is commonly called godliness, refer all things directly to the Deity. For instance, if they make money by a transaction, they say God gave it to them; if they desire anything, they say God has disposed their hearts towards it; if they think anything, they say God told them. Hence we must not suppose that everything is prophecy or revelation which is described in Scripture as told by God to anyone, but only such things as are expressly announced as prophecy or revelation, or are plainly pointed to as such by the context.

A perusal of the sacred books will show us that all God's revelations to the prophets were made through words or appearances, or a combination of the two. These words and appearances were of two kinds; (1) *real* when external to the mind of the prophet who heard or saw them, (2) *imaginary* when the imagination of the prophet was in a state which led him distinctly to suppose that he heard or saw them.

With a real voice God revealed to Moses the laws which He wished to be transmitted to the Hebrews, as we may see from Exodus xxv. 22, where God says, "And there I will meet with thee and I will commune with thee from the mercy seat which is between the Cherubim." Some sort of real voice must necessarily have been employed, for Moses found God ready to commune with him at any time. This is the only instance of a real voice.

... Some of the Jews believe that the actual words of the Decalogue were not spoken by God, but that the Israelites heard a noise only, without any distinct words, and during its continuance apprehend the Ten Commandments by pure intuition; to this opinion I myself once inclined, seeing that the words of the Decalogue in Exodus are different from the words of the Decalogue in Deuteronomy, for the discrepancy seemed to imply (since God only spoke once) that the Ten Commandments were not intended to convey the actual words of the Lord, but only His meaning. However, unless we would do violence to Scripture, we must certainly admit that the Israelites heard a real voice, for Scripture expressly says (Deut. v. 4), "God spake with you face to face," *i.e.*, as two men ordinarily interchange ideas through the instrumentality of their two bodies; and therefore it seems more consonant with Holy Writ to suppose that God really did create a voice of some kind with which the Decalogue was revealed....

Yet not even thus is all difficulty removed, for it seems scarcely reasonable to affirm that a created thing, depending on God in the same manner as other created things, would be able to express or explain the nature of God either verbally or really by means of its individual organism: for instance, by declaring in the first person, "I am the Lord your God."

Certainly when any one says his mouth, "I understand," we do not attribute the understanding to the mouth, but to the mind of the speaker; yet this is because the mouth is the natural organ of a man speaking, and the hearer, knowing what understanding is, easily comprehends, by a comparison with himself, that the speaker's mind is meant; but if we knew nothing of God beyond the mere name and wished to commune with Him, and be assured of His existence, I fail to see how our wish would be satisfied by the declaration of a created thing (depending on God neither more nor less than ourselves), "I am the Lord." If God contorted the lips of Moses, or, I will not say Moses, but some beast, till they pronounced the words, "I am the Lord," should we apprehend the Lord's existence therefrom?

Scripture seems clearly to point to the belief that God spoke Himself, having descended from heaven to Mount Sinai for the purpose—and not only that the Israelites heard Him speaking, but that their chief men beheld Him (Ex. xxiv.). Further, the laws of Moses which might neither be added to nor curtailed, and which was set up as a national standard of right, nowhere prescribed the belief that God is without body, or even without form or figure, but only ordained that the Jews should believe in His existence and worship Him alone: it forbade them to invent or fashion any likeness of the Deity, but this was to insure purity of service; because, never having seen God, they could not by means of images recall the likeness of God, but only the likeness of some created thing which might thus gradually take the place of God as the object of their adoration. Nevertheless, the Bible clearly implies that God has a form, and that Moses when he heard God speaking was permitted to behold it, or at least its hinder parts.

Doubtless some mystery lurks in this question which we will discuss more fully below. For the present I will call attention to the passages in Scripture indicating the means by which God has revealed His laws to man.

Revelation may be through figures only (as in 1 Chron. xxii.), where God displays his anger to David by means of an angel bearing a sword, and also in the story of Balaam.

Maimonides and others do indeed maintain that these and every other instance of angelic apparitions (*e.g.*, to Manoah and to Abraham offering up Isaac) occurred during sleep, for that no one with his eyes open ever could see an angel, but this is mere nonsense. The sole object of such commentators seemed to be to extort from Scripture confirmations of Aristotelian quibbles and their own inventions, a proceeding which I regard as the acme of absurdity.

In figures, not real but existing only in the prophet's imagination, God revealed to Joseph his future lordship, and in words and figures He revealed to Joshua that He would fight for the Hebrews, causing to appear an angel, as it were the captain of the Lord's host, bearing a sword, and by this means communicating verbally. The forsaking of Israel by Providence was portrayed to Isaiah by a vision of the Lord, the thrice Holy, sitting on a very lofty throne, and the Hebrews, stained with the mire of their sins, sunk, as it were, in uncleanness, and thus as far as possible distant from God. The wretchedness of the people at the time was thus revealed, while future calamities were foretold in words. I could cite from Holy Writ many similar examples, but I think they are sufficiently well known already....

We may be able quite to comprehend that God can communicate immediately with man, for without the intervention of bodily means He communicates to our minds His essence; still, a man who can by pure intuition comprehend ideas which are neither contained in nor deducible from the foundations of our natural knowledge, must necessarily possess a mind far superior to those of his fellow men, nor do I believe that any have been so endowed save Christ. To Him the ordinances of God leading men to salvation were revealed directly without words or visions, so that God manifested Himself to the Apostles through the mind of Christ as He formerly did to Moses through the supernatural voice. In this sense the voice of Christ, like the voice which Moses heard, may be called the voice of God, and it may be said that the wisdom of God (*i.e.*, wisdom more than human) took upon itself in Christ human nature, and that Christ was the way of salvation. I must at this juncture declare that those doctrines which certain churches put forward concerning Christ, I neither affirm nor deny, for I freely confess that I do not understand them. What I have just stated I gather from Scripture, where I never read that God appeared to Christ, or spoke to Christ, but that God was revealed to the Apostles through Christ; that Christ was the Way of Life, and that the old law was given through an angel, and not immediately by God; whence it follows that if Moses spoke with God face to face as a man speaks with his friend (*i.e.*, by means of their two bodies) Christ communed with God mind to mind.[5]

Thus we may conclude that no one except Christ received the revelations of God without the aid of imagination, whether in words or vision. Therefore the power of prophecy implies not a peculiarly perfect mind, but a peculiarly vivid imagination....

If the Jews were at a loss to understand any phenomenon, or were ignorant of its cause, they referred it to God. Thus a storm was termed the chiding of God, thunder and lightning the arrows of God, for it was thought that God kept the winds confined in caves, His treasuries; thus differing merely in name from the Greek wind-god Eolus. In like manner miracles were called works of God, as being especially marvelous; though in reality, of course, all natural events are the works of God, and take place solely by His power. The Psalmist calls the miracles in Egypt the works of God, because the Hebrews found in them a way of safety which they had not looked for, and therefore especially marveled at.

As, then, unusual natural phenomena are called works of God, and trees of unusual size are called trees of God, we cannot wonder that very strong and tall men, though impious robbers and whoremongers, are in Genesis called sons of God.

This reference of things wonderful to God was not peculiar to the Jews. Pharaoh, on hearing the interpretation of his dream, exclaimed that the mind of the gods was in Joseph. Nebuchadnezzar told Daniel that he possessed the mind of the holy gods; so also in Latin anything well made is often said to be wrought with Divine hands, which is equivalent to the Hebrew phrase, wrought with the hand of God.

... We find that the Scriptural phrases, "The Spirit of the Lord was upon a prophet," "The Lord breathed His Spirit into men," "Men were filled with the Spirit of God, with the Holy Spirit," etc., are quite clear to us, and mean that the prophets were endowed with a peculiar and extraordinary power, and devoted themselves to piety with especial constancy; that thus they perceived the mind or the thought of God, for we have shown [elsewhere] that God's spirit signifies in Hebrew God's mind or thought, and that the law which shows His mind and thought is called His Spirit; hence that the imagination of the prophets, inasmuch as through it were revealed the decrees of God, may equally be called the mind of God, and the prophets be said to have possessed the mind of God. On our minds also the mind of God and His eternal thoughts are impressed; but this being the same for all men is less taken into account, especially by the Hebrews, who claimed a pre-eminence, and despised other men and other men's knowledge.

[Also] the prophets were said to possess the Spirit of God because men knew not the cause of prophetic knowledge, and in their wonder referred it with other marvels directly to the Deity, styling it Divine knowledge.

We need no longer scruple to affirm that the prophets only perceived God's revelation by the aid of imagination, that is, by words and figures either real or imaginary. We find no other means mentioned in Scripture, and therefore must not invent any. As to the particular law of Nature by which the communications took place, I confess my ignorance. I might, indeed, say as others do, that they took place by the power of God; but this would be mere trifling, and no better than explaining some unique specimen by a transcendental term. Everything takes place by the power of God. Nature herself is the power of God under another name, and our ignorance of the power of God is co-extensive with our ignorance of Nature. It is absolutely folly, therefore, to ascribe an event to the power of God when we know not its natural cause, which is the power of God.

However, we are not now inquiring into the causes of prophetic knowledge. We are only attempting, as I have said, to examine the Scriptural documents, and to draw our conclusions from them as from ultimate natural facts; the causes of the documents do not concern us.

As the prophets perceived the revelations of God by the aid of imagination, they could indisputably perceive much that is beyond the boundary of the intellect, for many more ideas can be constructed from words and figures than from the principles and notions on which the whole fabric of reasoned knowledge is reared.

Thus we have a clue to the fact that the prophets perceived nearly everything in parables and allegories, and clothed spiritual truths in bodily forms, for such is the usual method of imagination. We need no longer wonder that Scripture and the prophets speak so strangely and obscurely of God's Spirit or Mind (cf. Numbers xi. 17, 1 Kings xxii, 21, etc.), that the Lord was seen by Micah as sitting, by Daniel as an old man clothed in white, by Ezekiel as a fire, that the Holy Spirit appeared to those with Christ as a descending dove, to the apostles as fiery tongues, to Paul on his conversion as a great light. All these expressions are plainly in harmony with the current ideas of God and spirits.

Inasmuch as imagination is fleeting and inconstant, we find that the power of prophecy did not remain with a prophet for long, nor manifest itself frequently, but was very rare; manifesting itself only in a few men, and in them not often.

We must necessarily inquire how the prophets became assured of the truth of what they perceived by imagination, and not by sure mental laws; but our investigation must be confined to Scripture, for the subject is one on which we cannot acquire certain knowledge, and which we cannot explain by the immediate causes.

II

... As I have said, the prophets were endowed with unusually vivid imaginations, and not with unusually perfect minds. This conclusion is amply sustained by Scripture, for we are told that Solomon was the wisest of men, but had no special faculty of prophecy. Heman, Calcol, and Dara, though men of great talent, were not prophets, whereas uneducated countrymen, nay, even women, such as Hagar, Abraham's handmaid, were thus gifted. Nor is this contrary to ordinary experience and reason. Men of great imaginative power are less fitted for abstract reasoning, whereas those who excel in intellect and its use keep their imagination more restrained and controlled, holding it in subjection, so to speak, lest it should usurp the place of reason.

Thus to suppose that knowledge of natural and spiritual phenomena can be gained from the prophetic books, is an utter mistake, which I shall endeavor to expose, as I think philosophy, the age, and the question itself demand. I care not for the girdings of superstition, for superstition is the bitter enemy of all true knowledge and true morality. Yes; it has come to this! Men who openly confess that they can form no idea of God, and only know Him through created things, of which they know not the causes, can unblushingly accuse philosophers of Atheism.

Treating the question methodically, I will show that prophecies varied, not only according to the imagination and physical temperament of the prophet, but also according to his particular opinions; and further that prophecy never rendered the prophet wiser than he was before. But I will first discuss the assurance of truth which the prophets received, for this is akin to the subject-matter of the chapter, and will serve to elucidate somewhat our present point.

Imagination does not, in its own nature, involve any certainty of truth, such as is implied in every clear and distinct idea, but requires some extrinsic reason to assure us of its objective reality: hence prophecy cannot afford certainty, and the prophets were assured of God's revelation by some sign, and not by the fact of revelation, as we may see from Abraham, who, when he had heard the promise of God, demanded a sign, not because he did not believe in God but because he wished to be sure that it was God Who made the promise. The fact is still more evident in the case of Gideon: "Show me," he says to God, "show me a sign, that I may know that it is Thou that talkest with me." God also says to Moses: "And let this be a sign that I have sent thee." Hezekiah, though he had long known Isaiah to be a prophet, none the less demanded a sign of the cure which he predicted. It is thus quite evident that the prophets always received some sign to certify them of their prophetic imaginings; and for this reason Moses bids the Jews (Deut. xviii.) ask of the prophets a sign, namely, the prediction of some coming event. In this respect, prophetic knowledge is inferior to natural knowledge, which needs no sign, and in itself implies certitude. Moreover, Scripture warrants the statement that the certitude of the prophets was not mathematical, but moral. Moses lays down the punishment of death for the prophet who preaches new gods, even though he confirm his doctrine by signs and wonders (Deut. xiii.); "For," he says, "the Lord also worketh signs and wonders to try His people." And Jesus Christ warns His disciples of the same thing (Matt. xxiv. 24). Furthermore, Ezekiel (xiv. 9) plainly states that God sometimes deceives men with false revelations; and Micaiah bears like witness in the case of the prophets of Ahab.

Although these instances go to prove that revelation is open to doubt, it nevertheless contains, as we have said, a considerable element of certainty, for God never deceives the good, nor His chosen, but (according to the ancient proverb and as appears in the history of Abigail and her speech), God uses the good as instruments of goodness, and the wicked as means to execute His wrath. This may be seen from the cases of Micaiah above quoted; for although God had determined to deceive Ahab, through prophets, He made use of lying prophets; to the good prophet He revealed the truth, and did not forbid his proclaiming it.

Still the certitude of prophecy remains, as I have said, merely moral; for no one can justify himself before God, nor boast that he is an instrument for God's goodness. Scripture itself teaches and shows that God led away David to number the people, though it bears ample witness to David's piety.

The whole question of the certitude of prophecy was based on these three considerations:—

1. That the things revealed were imagined very vividly, affecting the prophets in the same way as things seen when awake;

2. The presence of a sign;

3. Lastly and chiefly, that the mind of the prophet was given wholly to what was right and good.

Although Scripture does not always make mention of a sign, we must nevertheless suppose that a sign was always vouchsafed; for Scripture does not always relate every condition and circumstance (as many have remarked), but rather takes them for granted. We may, however, admit that no sign was needed when the prophecy declared nothing that was not already contained in the law of Moses, because it was confirmed by that law. For instance, Jeremiah's prophecy of the destruction of Jerusalem was confirmed by the prophecies of other prophets, and by the threats in the law, and therefore it needed no sign; whereas Hananiah, who, contrary to all the prophets, foretold the speedy restoration of the state, stood in need of a sign, or he would have been in doubt as to the truth of his prophecy, until it was confirmed by facts. "The prophet which prophesieth of peace, when the word of the prophet shall come to pass, then shall the prophet be known that the Lord hath truly sent him."

As, then, the certitude afforded to the prophet by signs was not mathematical (*i.e.*, did not necessarily follow from the perception of the thing perceived or seen), but only moral, and as the signs were only given to convince the prophet, it follows that such signs were given according to the opinions and capacity of each prophet, so that a sign which would convince one prophet would fall far short of convincing another who was imbued with different opinions. Therefore the signs varied according to the individual prophet.

So also did the revelation vary, as we have stated, according to individual disposition and temperament, and according to the opinions previously held.

It varied according to disposition, in this way: if a prophet was cheerful, victories, peace, and events which make men glad, were revealed to him; in that he was naturally more likely to imagine such things. If, on the contrary, he was melancholy, wars, massacres, and calamities were revealed; and so, according as a prophet was merciful, gentle, quick to anger, or severe, he was more fitted for one kind of revelation than another. It varied according to the temper of imagination in this way: if a prophet was cultivated he perceived the mind of God in a cultivated way, if he was confused he perceived it confusedly. And so with revelations perceived through visions. If a prophet was a countryman he saw visions of oxen, cows, and the like; if he was a soldier, he saw generals and armies; if a courtier, a royal throne, and so on.

Lastly, prophecy varied according to the opinions held by the prophets; for instance, to the Magi, who believed in the follies of astrology, the birth of Christ was revealed through the vision of a star in the East. To the augurs of Nebuchadnezzar the destruction of Jerusalem was revealed through entrails, whereas the king himself inferred it from oracles and the direction of arrows which he shot into the air. To prophets who believed that man acts from free choice and by his own power, God was revealed as standing apart from and ignorant of future human actions. All of which we will illustrate from Scripture....

The style of the prophecy also varied according to the eloquence of the individual prophet. The prophecies of Ezekiel and Amos are not written in a cultivated style like those of Isaiah and Nahum, but more rudely. Any Hebrew scholar who wishes to inquire into this point more closely, and compares chapters of the different prophets treating of the same subject, will find that God has no particular style in speaking, but, according to the learning and capacity of the prophet, is cultivated, compressed, severe, untutored, prolixed or obscure....

Everyone has been strangely hasty in affirming that the prophets knew everything within the scope of human intellect; and, although certain passages of

Scripture plainly affirm that the prophets were in certain respects ignorant, such persons would rather say that they do not understand the passages than admit that there was anything which the prophets did not know; or else they try to wrest the Scriptural words away from their evident meaning.

If either of these proceedings is allowable we may as well shut our Bibles, for vainly shall we attempt to prove anything from them if their plainest passages may be classed among obscure and impenetrable mysteries, or if we may put any interpretation on them which we fancy. For instance, nothing is more clear in the Bible than that Joshua, and perhaps also the author who wrote his history, thought that the sun revolves round the earth, and that the earth is fixed, and further that the sun for a certain period remained still. Many, who will not admit any movement in the heavenly bodies, explain away the passage till it seems to mean something quite different; others, who have learned to philosophize more correctly, and understand that the earth moves while the sun is still, or at any rate does not revolve round the earth, try with all their might to wrest this meaning from Scripture, though plainly nothing of the sort is intended. Such quibblers excite my wonder! Are we, forsooth, bound to believe that Joshua the soldier was a learned astronomer? or that a miracle could not be revealed to him, or that the light of the sun could not remain longer than usual above the horizon, without his knowing the cause? To me both alternatives appear ridiculous, and therefore I would rather say that Joshua was ignorant of the true cause of the lengthened day, and that he and the whole host with him thought that the sun moved round the earth every day, and that on that particular occasion it stood still for a time, thus causing the light to remain longer; and I would say that they did not conjecture that, from the amount of snow in the air (see Josh. x. 11), the refraction may have been greater than usual, or that there may have been some other cause which we will not now inquire into.

So also the sign of the shadow going back was revealed to Isaiah according to his understanding; that is, as proceeding from a going backwards of the sun; for he, too, thought that the sun moves and that the earth is still; of parhelia he perhaps never even dreamed. We may arrive at this conclusion without any scruple, for the sign could really have come to pass, and have been predicted by Isaiah to the king, without the prophet being aware of the real cause.

With regard to the building of the Temple by Solomon, if it was really dictated by God we must maintain the same doctrine: namely, that all the measurements were revealed according to the opinions and understanding of the king; for as we are not bound to believe that Solomon was a mathematician, we may affirm that he was ignorant of the true ratio between the circumference and the diameter of a circle, and that, like the generality of workmen, he thought that it was as three to one. But if it is allowable to declare that we do not understand the passage, in good sooth I know nothing in the Bible that we can understand; for the process of building is there narrated simply and as a mere matter of history. If, again, it is permitted to pretend that the passage has another meaning, and was written as it is from some reason unknown to us, this is no less than a complete subversal of the Bible; for every absurd and evil invention of human perversity could thus, without detriment to Scriptural authority, be defended and fostered. Our conclusion is in no wise impious, for though Solomon, Isaiah, Joshua, etc., were prophets, they were none the less men, and as such not exempt from human shortcomings.

According to the understanding of Noah it was revealed to him that God was about to destroy the whole human race, for Noah thought that beyond the limits of Palestine the world was not inhabited.

Not only in matters of this kind, but in others more important, the prophets could be, and in fact were, ignorant; for they taught nothing special about the Divine attributes, but held quite ordinary notions about God, and to these notions their revelations were adapted, as I will demonstrate by ample Scriptural testimony; from all which one may easily see that they were praised and commended, not so much for the sublimity and eminence of their intellect as for their piety and faithfulness.

Adam, the first man to whom God was revealed, did not know that He is omnipotent and omniscient; for he hid himself from Him, and attempted to make excuses for his fault before God, as though he had had to do with a man; therefore to him also was God revealed according to his understanding—that is, as being unaware of his situation or his sin, for Adam heard, or seemed to hear, the Lord walking in the garden, calling him and asking him where he was; and then, on seeing his shamefacedness, asking him whether he had eaten of the forbidden fruit. Adam evidently only knew the Deity as the Creator of all things. To Cain also God was revealed, according to his understanding, as ignorant of human affairs, nor was a higher conception of the Deity required for repentance of his sin.

To Laban the Lord revealed Himself as the God of Abraham, because Laban believed that each nation had its own special divinity (see Gen. xxxi. 29). Abraham also knew not that God is omnipresent, and has foreknowledge of all things; for when he heard the sentence against the inhabitants of Sodom, he prayed that the Lord should not execute it till He had ascertained whether they all merited such punishment; for he said (see Gen. xviii. 24), "Peradventure there be fifty righteous within the city," and in accordance with this belief God was revealed to him; as Abraham imagined, He spake thus: "I will go down now, and see whether they have done altogether according to the cry of it which is come unto Me; and if not I will know." Further, the Divine testimony concerning Abraham asserts nothing but that he was obedient, and that he "commanded his household after him that they should keep the way of the Lord" (Gen. xviii. 19); it does not state that he held sublime conceptions of the Deity.

Moses, also, was not sufficiently aware that God is omniscient, and directs human actions by His sole decree, for although God himself says that the Israelites should hearken to Him, Moses still considered the matter doubtful and repeated, "But if they will not believe me, nor hearken unto my voice." To him in like manner God was revealed as taking no part in, and as being ignorant of, future human actions: the Lord gave him two signs and said, "And it shall come to pass that if they will not believe thee, neither hearken to the voice of the first sign, that they will believe the voice of the latter sign; but if not, thou shalt take of the water of the river," etc. Indeed, if any one considers without prejudice the recorded opinions of Moses, he will plainly see that Moses conceived the Deity as a Being Who has always existed, does exist, and always will exist, and for this cause he calls Him by the name Jehovah, which in Hebrew signifies these three phases of existence: as to His nature, Moses only taught that He is merciful, gracious, and exceeding jealous, as appears from many passages in the Pentateuch. Lastly, he believed and taught that this Being was so different from all other beings, that He could not be expressed by the image of any visible thing; also, that He could not be looked upon, and that not so much from inherent impossibility as from human infirmity; further, that by reason of His power He was without equal and unique. Moses admitted, indeed, that there were beings (doubtless by the plan and command of the Lord) who acted as God's vicegerents—that is, beings to whom God had given the right, authority, and power to direct nations, and to provide and care for them; but he taught that this Being Whom they were bound to obey was the highest and Supreme God, (or to use the Hebrew phrase) God of gods, and thus in the song (Exod. xv. 11) he exclaims, "Who is like unto Thee, O Lord, among the gods?" and Jethro says (Exod. xviii. 11), "Now I know that the Lord is greater than all gods." That is to say, "I am at length compelled to admit to Moses that Jehovah is greater than all gods, and that His power is unrivalled." We must remain in doubt whether Moses thought that these beings who acted as God's vicegerents were created by Him, for he has stated nothing, so far as we know, about their creation and origin. He further taught that this Being had brought the visible world into order from Chaos, and had given Nature her germs, and therefore that He possesses supreme right and power over all things; further, that by reason of this supreme right and power He had chosen for Himself alone the Hebrew nation and a certain strip of territory, and had handed over to the care of other gods substituted by Himself the rest of the nations and territories, and that therefore He was called the God of Israel and the God of Jerusalem, whereas the other gods were called the gods of the Gentiles. For this reason the Jews believed that the strip of territory which God had chosen for Himself, demanded a Divine worship quite apart and different from the worship which obtained elsewhere, and that the Lord would not suffer the worship of other gods adapted to other countries. Thus they thought that the people whom the king of Assyria had brought into Judæa were torn in pieces by lions because they knew not the worship of the National Divinity (2 Kings xvii. 25)....

If we now examine the revelations to Moses, we shall find that they were accommodated to these opinions; as he believed that the Divine Nature was subject to the conditions of mercy, graciousness, etc., so God was revealed to him in accordance with his idea and under these attributes (see Exodus xxxiv. 6, 7, and the second commandment). Further it is related (Ex. xxxiii. 18) that Moses asked of God that he might behold Him, but as Moses (as we have said) had formed no mental image of God, and God (as I have shown) only revealed Himself to the prophets in accordance with the disposition of their imagination, He did not reveal Himself in any form. This, I repeat, was because the imagination of Moses was unsuitable, for other prophets bear witness that they saw the Lord; for instance, Isaiah, Ezekiel, Daniel, etc. For this reason God answered Moses, "Thou canst not see My face;" and inasmuch as Moses believed that God can be looked upon—that is, that no contradiction of the Divine nature is therein involved (for otherwise he would never have preferred his request)—it is added, "For no one shall look on Me and live," thus giving a reason in accordance with Moses' idea, for it is not stated that a contradiction of the Divine nature would be involved, as was really the case, but that the thing would not come to pass because of human infirmity....

Lastly, as Moses believed that God dwelt in the heavens, God was revealed to him as coming down from heaven on to a mountain, and in order to talk with the Lord Moses went up the mountain, which he certainly need not have done if he could have conceived of God as omnipresent.

The Israelites knew scarcely anything of God, although He was revealed to them; and this is abundantly evident from their transferring, a few days afterwards, the honor and worship due to Him to a calf, which they believed to be the god who had brought them out of Egypt. In truth, it is hardly likely that men accustomed to the superstitions of Egypt, uncultivated and sunk in most abject slavery, should have held any sound notions about the Deity, or that Moses should have taught them anything beyond a rule of right living; inculcating it not like a philosopher, as the result of freedom, but like a lawgiver compelling them to be moral by legal authority. Thus the rule of right living, the worship and love of God, was to them rather a bondage than the true liberty, the gift and grace of the Deity. Moses bid them love God and keep His law, because they had in the past received benefits from Him (such as the deliverance from slavery in Egypt), and further terrified them with threats if they transgressed His commands, holding out many promises of good if they should observe them; thus treating them as parents treat irrational children. It is, therefore, certain that they knew not the excellence of virtue and the true happiness.

Jonah thought that he was fleeing from the sight of God, which seems to show that he too held that God had entrusted the care of the nations outside Judæa to other substituted powers. No one in the whole of the Old Testament speaks more rationally of God than Solomon, who in fact surpassed all the men of his time in natural ability. Yet he considered himself above the law (esteeming it only to have been given for men without reasonable and intellectual grounds for their actions), and made small account of the laws concerning kings, which are mainly three: nay, he openly violated them (in this he did wrong, and acted in a manner unworthy of a philosopher, by indulging in sensual pleasure), and taught that all Fortune's favors to mankind are vanity, that humanity has no nobler gift than wisdom, and no greater punishment than folly. (See Proverbs xvi. 22, 23.)

... God adapted revelations to the understanding and opinions of the prophets, and ... in matters of theory without bearing on charity or morality, the prophets could be, and, in fact, were ignorant, and held conflicting opinions. It therefore follows that we must by no means go to the prophets for knowledge, either of natural or of spiritual phenomena.

We have determined, then, that we are only bound to believe in the prophetic writings, the object and substance of the revelation; with regard to the details, everyone may believe or not, as he likes.

For instance, the revelation to Cain only teaches us that God admonished him to lead the true life, for such alone is the object and substance of the revelation, not doctrines concerning free will and philosophy. Hence, though the freedom of the will is clearly implied in the words of the admonition, we are at liberty to hold a contrary opinion, since the words and reasons were adapted to the understanding of Cain.

So, too, the revelation to Micaiah would only teach that God revealed to him the true issue of the battle between Ahab and Aram; and this is all we are bound to believe. Whatever else is contained in the revelation concerning the true and the false Spirit of God, the army of heaven standing on the right hand and on the left, and all the other details, does not affect us at all. Everyone may believe as much of it as his reason allows.

The reasonings by which the Lord displayed His power to Job (if they really were a revelation, and the author of the history is narrating, and not merely, as some suppose, rhetorically adorning his own conceptions), would come under the same category—that is, they were adapted to Job's understanding, for the purpose of convincing him, and are not universal, or for the convincing of all men.

We can come to no different conclusion with respect to the reasonings of Christ, by which He convicted the Pharisees of pride and ignorance, and exhorted His disciples to lead the true life. He adapted them to each man's opinions and principles. For instance, when He said to the Pharisees (Matt. xii. 26), "And if Satan cast out devils, his house is divided against itself, how then shall his kingdom stand?" He only wished to convince the Pharisees according to their own principles, not to teach that there are devils, or any kingdom of devils. So, too, when He said to His disciples (Matt. viii. 10), "See that ye despise not one of these little ones, for I say unto you that their angels," etc., He merely desired to warn them against pride and despising any of their fellows, not to insist on the actual reason given, which was simply adopted in order to persuade them more easily.

Lastly, we should say exactly the same of the apostolic signs and reasonings, but there is no need to go further into the subject. If I were to enumerate all the passages of Scripture addressed only to individuals, or to a particular man's understanding, and which cannot, without great danger to philosophy, be defended as Divine doctrines, I should go far beyond the brevity at which I aim. Let it suffice then, to have indicated a few instances of general application, and let the curious reader consider others by himself. Although the points we have just raised concerning prophets and prophecy are the only ones which have any direct bearing on the end in view, namely, the separation of Philosophy from Theology, still, as I have touched on the general question, I may here inquire whether the gift of prophecy was peculiar to the Hebrews, or whether it was common to all nations. I must then come to a conclusion about the vocation of the Hebrews, all of which I shall do in the ensuing chapter.

FOOTNOTES:

[4] From the *Tr. Th.-P.* ch. i *Of Prophecy*; and ch. ii of *Of Prophets*.

[5] ... I will tell you that I do not think it necessary for salvation to know Christ according to the flesh; but with regard to the Eternal Son of God, that is the Eternal Wisdom of God, which has manifested itself in all things and especially in the human mind, and above all in Christ Jesus, the case is far otherwise. For without this no one can come to a state of blessedness, inasmuch as it alone teaches what is true or false, good or evil. And, inasmuch as this wisdom was made especially manifest through Jesus Christ, as I have said, His disciples preached it, in so far as it was revealed to them through Him, and thus showed that they could rejoice in that spirit of Christ more than the rest of mankind. The doctrines added by certain churches, such as that God took upon Himself human nature, I have expressly said that I do not understand. In fact, to speak the truth, they seem to me no less absurd than would a statement that a circle had taken upon itself the nature of a square. This I think will be sufficient explanation of my opinion.... Whether it will be satisfactory to Christians you will know better than I. Farewell. *From a letter to Henry Oldenburg* (Nov. 1675).

... For the rest, I accept Christ's passion, death, and burial literally, as you do, but His resurrection I understand allegorically. I admit, that it is related by the Evangelists in such detail that we cannot deny that they themselves believed Christ's body to have risen from the dead and ascended to heaven in order to sit at the right hand of God, or that they believed that Christ might have been seen by unbelievers, if they had happened to be at hand, in the places where He appeared to His disciples; but in these matters they might, without injury to Gospel teaching, have been deceived, as was the case with other prophets.... But Paul, to whom Christ afterwards appeared, rejoices that he knew Christ, not after the flesh, but after the spirit. *From a letter to Henry Oldenburg* (Jan. 1676).

CHAPTER IV

OF THE VOCATION OF THE HEBREWS[6]

Every man's true happiness and blessedness consist solely in the enjoyment of what is good, not in the pride that he alone is enjoying it, to the exclusion of others. He who thinks himself the more blessed because he is enjoying benefits which others are not, or because he is more blessed or more fortunate than his fellows, is ignorant of true happiness and blessedness, and the joy which he feels is either childish or envious and malicious. For instance, a man's true happiness consists only in wisdom, and the knowledge of the truth, not at all in the fact that he is wiser than others, or that others lack such knowledge: such considerations do not increase his wisdom or true happiness.

Whoever, therefore, rejoices for such reasons, rejoices in another's misfortune, and is, so far, malicious and bad, knowing neither true happiness nor the peace of the true life.

When Scripture, therefore, in exhorting the Hebrews to obey the law, says that the Lord has chosen them for Himself before other nations (Deut. x. 15); that He is near them, but not near others (Deut. iv. 7); that to them alone He has given just laws (Deut. iv. 8); and, lastly, that He has marked them out before others (Deut. iv. 32); it speaks only according to the understanding of its hearers, who, as we have shown in the last chapter, and as Moses also testified (Deut. ix. 6, 7), knew not true blessedness. For in good sooth they would have been no less blessed if God had called all men equally to salvation, nor would God have been less present to them for being equally present to others; their laws would have been no less just if they had been ordained for all, and they themselves would have been no less wise. The miracles would have shown God's power no less by being wrought for other nations also; lastly, the Hebrews would have been just as much bound to worship God if He had bestowed all these gifts equally on all men.

When God tells Solomon (1 Kings iii. 12) that no one shall be as wise as he in time to come, it seems to be only a manner of expressing surpassing wisdom; it is little to be believed that God would have promised Solomon, for his greater happiness, that He would never endow any one with so much wisdom in time to come; this would in no wise have increased Solomon's intellect, and the wise king would have given equal thanks to the Lord if everyone had been gifted with the same faculties.

Still, though we assert that Moses, in the passages of the Pentateuch just cited, spoke only according to the understanding of the Hebrews, we have no wish to deny that God ordained the Mosaic law for them alone, nor that He spoke to them alone, nor that they witnessed marvels beyond those which happened to any other nation; but we wish to emphasize that Moses desired to admonish the Hebrews in such a manner and with such reasonings as would appeal most forcibly to their childish understanding and constrain them to worship the Deity. Further, we wished to show that the Hebrews did not surpass other nations in knowledge, or in piety, but evidently in some attribute different from these; or (to speak like the Scriptures, according to their understanding), that the Hebrews were not chosen by God before others for the sake of the true life and sublime ideas, though they were often thereto admonished, but with some other object. What that object was I will duly show.

But before I begin, I wish in a few words to explain what I mean by the guidance of God, by the help of God, external and inward, and lastly, what I understand by fortune.

By the help of God, I mean the fixed and unchangeable order of nature or the chain of natural events: for I have said before and shown elsewhere that the universal laws of nature, according to which all things exist and are determined, are only another name for the eternal decrees of God, which always involve eternal truth and necessity.

So that to say that everything happens according to natural laws, and to say that everything is ordained by the decree and ordinance of God, is the same thing. Now since the power in Nature is identical with the power of God, by which alone all things happen and are determined, it follows that whatsoever man, as a part of Nature, provides himself with to aid and preserve his existence, or whatsoever Nature affords him without his help, is given to him solely by the Divine power, acting either through human nature or through external circumstance. So whatever human nature can furnish itself with by its own efforts to preserve its existence, may be fitly called the inward aid of God, whereas whatever else accrues to man's profit from outward causes may be called the external aid of God.

We can now easily understand what is meant by the election of God. For since no one can do anything save by the predetermined order of Nature, that is by

God's eternal ordinance and decree, it follows that no one can choose a plan of life for himself, or accomplish any work save by God's vocation choosing him for the work or the plan of life in question, rather than any other. Lastly, by fortune, I mean the ordinance of God in so far as it directs human life through external and unexpected means. With these preliminaries I return to my purpose of discovering the reason why the Hebrews were said to be elected by God before other nations, and with the demonstration I thus proceed.

All objects of legitimate desire fall, generally speaking, under one of these three categories:—

1. The knowledge of things through their primary causes.

2. The government of the passions, or the acquirement of the habit of virtue.

3. Secure and healthy life.

The means which most directly conduce towards the first two of these ends, and which may be considered their proximate and efficient causes are contained in human nature itself, so that their acquisition hinges only on our own power, and on the laws of human nature. It may be concluded that these gifts are not peculiar to any nation, but have always been shared by the whole human race, unless, indeed, we would indulge the dream that Nature formerly created men of different kinds. But the means which conduce to security and health are chiefly in external circumstance, and are called the gifts of fortune because they depend chiefly on objective causes of which we are ignorant; for a fool may be almost as liable to happiness or unhappiness as a wise man. Nevertheless, human management and watchfulness can greatly assist towards living in security and warding off the injuries of our fellow men, and even of beasts. Reason and experience show no more certain means of attaining this object than the formation of a society with fixed laws, the occupation of a strip of territory, and the concentration of all forces, as it were, into one body, that is the social body. Now for forming and preserving a society, no ordinary ability and care is required: that society will be most secure, most stable, and least liable to reverses, which is founded and directed by far-seeing and careful men; while, on the other hand, a society constituted by men without trained skill, depends in a great measure on fortune, and is less constant. If, in spite of all, such a society lasts a long time, it is owing to some other directing influence than its own; if it overcomes great perils and its affairs prosper, it will perforce marvel at and adore the guiding Spirit of God (in so far, that is, as God works through hidden means, and not through the nature and mind of man), for everything happens to it unexpectedly and contrary to anticipation, it may even be said and thought to be by miracle. Nations, then, are distinguished from one another in respect to the social organization and the laws under which they live and are governed; the Hebrew nation was not chosen by God in respect to its wisdom nor its tranquillity of mind, but in respect to its social organization and the good fortune with which it obtained supremacy and kept it so many years. This is abundantly clear from Scripture. Even a cursory perusal will show us that the only respects in which the Hebrews surpassed other nations, are in their successful conduct of matters relating to government, and in their surmounting great perils solely by God's external aid; in other ways they were on a par with their fellows, and God was equally gracious to all. For in respect to intellect (as we have shown in the last chapter) they held very ordinary ideas about God and Nature, so that they cannot have been God's chosen in this respect; nor were they so chosen in respect of virtue and the true life, for here again they, with the exception of a very few elect, were on an equality with other nations: therefore their choice and vocation consisted only in the temporal happiness and advantages of independent rule. In fact, we do not see that God promised anything beyond this to the patriarchs or their successors; in the law no other reward is offered for obedience than the continual happiness of an independent commonwealth and other goods of this life; while, on the other hand, against contumacy and the breaking of the covenant is threatened the downfall of the commonwealth and great hardships. Nor is this to be wondered at; for the ends of every social organization and commonwealth are (as appears from what we have said, and as we will explain more at length hereafter) security and comfort; a commonwealth can only exist by the laws being binding on all. If all the members of a state wish to disregard the law, by that very fact they dissolve the state and destroy the commonwealth. Thus, the only reward which could be promised to the Hebrews for continued obedience to the law was security and its attendant advantages, while no surer punishment could be threatened for disobedience, than the ruin of the state and the evils which generally follow therefrom, in addition to such further consequences as might accrue to the Jews in particular from the ruin of their especial state. But there is no need here to go into this point at more length. I will only add that the laws of the Old Testament were revealed and ordained to the Jews only, for as God chose them in respect to the special constitution of their society and government, they must, of course, have had special laws. Whether God ordained special laws for other nations also, and revealed Himself to their lawgivers prophetically, that is, under the attributes by which the latter were accustomed to imagine Him, I cannot sufficiently determine. It is evident from Scripture itself that other nations acquired supremacy and particular laws by the external aid of God.

If any one wishes to maintain that the Jews ... have been chosen by God for ever, I will not gainsay him if he will admit that this choice, whether temporary or eternal, has no regard, in so far as it is peculiar to the Jews, to aught but dominion and physical advantages (for by such alone can one nation be distinguished from another), whereas in regard to intellect and true virtue, every nation is on a par with the rest, and God has not in these respects chosen one people rather than another.

FOOTNOTES:

[6] From the *Tr. Th.-P.*, ch. iii, same title.

CHAPTER V

OF THE DIVINE LAW[7]

The word law, taken in the abstract means that by which an individual, or all things, or as many things as belong to a particular species, act in one and the same fixed and definite manner, which manner depends either on natural necessity or on human decree. A law which depends on natural necessity is one which necessarily follows from the nature, or from the definition of the thing in question; a law which depends on human decree, and which is more correctly called an ordinance, is one which men have laid down for themselves and others in order to live more safely or conveniently, or from some similar reason.

For example, the law that all bodies impinging on lesser bodies, lose as much of their own motion as they communicate to the latter is a universal law of all bodies, and depends on natural necessity. So, too, the law that a man in remembering one thing, straightway remembers another either like it, or which he had perceived simultaneously with it, is a law which necessarily follows from the nature of man. But the law that men must yield, or be compelled to yield, somewhat of their natural right, and that they bind themselves to live in a certain way, depends on human decree. Now, though I freely admit that all things are predetermined by universal natural laws to exist and operate in a given, fixed, and definite manner, I still assert that the laws I have just mentioned depend on human decree.

(1.) Because man, in so far as he is a part of Nature, constitutes a part of the power of Nature. Whatever, therefore, follows necessarily from the necessity of human nature (that is, from Nature herself, in so far as we conceive of her as acting through man) follows, even though it be necessarily, from human power. Hence the sanction of such laws may very well be said to depend on man's decree, for it principally depends on the power of the human mind; so that the human mind in respect to its perception of things as true and false, can readily be conceived as without such laws, but not without necessary law as we have just defined it.

(2.) I have stated that these laws depend on human decree because it is well to define and explain things by their proximate causes. The general consideration of fate and the concatenation of causes would aid us very little in forming and arranging our ideas concerning particular questions. Let us add that as to the actual co-ordination and concatenation of things, that is how things are ordained and linked together, we are obviously ignorant; therefore, it is more profitable for right living, nay, it is necessary for us to consider things as contingent. So much about law in the abstract.

Now the word law seems to be only applied to natural phenomena by analogy, and is commonly taken to signify a command which men can either obey or neglect, inasmuch as it restrains human nature within certain originally exceeded limits, and therefore lays down no rule beyond human strength. Thus it is expedient to define law more particularly as a plan of life laid down by man for himself or others with a certain object.

However, as the true object of legislation is only perceived by a few, and most men are almost incapable of grasping it, though they live under its conditions, legislators, with a view to exacting general obedience, have wisely put forward another object, very different from that which necessarily follows from the nature of law: they promise to the observers of the law that which the masses chiefly desire, and threaten its violators with that which they chiefly fear: thus endeavoring to restrain the masses, as far as may be, like a horse with a curb; whence it follows that the word law is chiefly applied to the modes of life enjoined on men by the sway of others; hence those who obey the law are said to live under it and to be under compulsion. In truth, a man who renders everyone their due because he fears the gallows, acts under the sway and compulsion of others, and cannot be called just. But a man who does the same from a knowledge of the true reason for laws and their necessity, acts from a firm purpose and of his own accord, and is therefore properly called just. This, I take it, is Paul's meaning when he says, that those who live under the law cannot be justified through the law, for justice, as commonly defined, is the constant and perpetual will to render every man his due. Thus Solomon says (Prov. xxi. 15), "It is a joy to the just to do judgment," but the wicked fear.

Law, then, being a plan of living which men have for a certain object laid down for themselves or others, may, as it seems, be divided into human law and Divine law.

By human law I mean a plan of living which serves only to render life and the state secure.

By Divine law I mean that which only regards the highest good, in other words, the true knowledge of God and love.

I call this law Divine because of the nature of the highest good, which I will here shortly explain as clearly as I can.

Inasmuch as the intellect is the best part of our being, it is evident that we should make every effort to perfect it as far as possible if we desire to search for what is really profitable to us. For in intellectual perfection the highest good should consist. Now, since all our knowledge, and the certainty which removes every doubt, depend solely on the knowledge of God;—firstly, because without God nothing can exist or be conceived; secondly, because so long as we have no clear and distinct idea of God we may remain in universal doubt—it follows that our highest good and perfection also depend solely on the knowledge of God. Further, since without God nothing can exist or be conceived, it is evident that all natural phenomena involve and express the conception of God as far as their essence and perfection extend, so that we have greater and more perfect knowledge of God in proportion to our knowledge of natural phenomena: conversely (since the knowledge of an effect through its cause is the same thing as the knowledge of a particular property of a cause) the greater our knowledge of natural phenomena, the more perfect is our knowledge of the essence of God (which is the cause of all things). So, then, our highest good not only depends on the knowledge of God, but wholly consists therein; and it further follows that man is perfect or the reverse in proportion to the nature and perfection of the object of his special desire; hence the most perfect and the chief sharer in the highest blessedness is he who prizes above all else, and takes especial delight in the intellectual knowledge of God, the most perfect Being.

Hither, then, our highest good and our highest blessedness aim—namely, to the knowledge and love of God; therefore the means demanded by this aim of all human actions, that is, by God in so far as the idea of him is in us, may be called the commands of God, because they proceed, as it were, from God Himself, inasmuch as He exists in our minds, and the plan of life which has regard to this aim may be fitly called the law of God.

The nature of the means, and the plan of life which this aim demands, how the foundations of the best states follow its lines, and how men's life is conducted, are questions pertaining to general ethics. Here I only proceed to treat of the Divine law in a particular application.

As the love of God is man's highest happiness and blessedness, and the ultimate end and aim of all human actions, it follows that he alone lives by the Divine law who loves God not from fear of punishment, or from love of any other object, such as sensual pleasure, fame, or the like; but solely because he has knowledge of God, or is convinced that the knowledge and love of God is the highest good. The sum and chief precept, then, of the Divine law is to love

God as the highest good, namely, as we have said, not from fear of any pains and penalties or from the love of any other object in which we desire to take pleasure. The idea of God lays down the rule that God is our highest good—in other words, that the knowledge and love of God is the ultimate aim to which all our actions should be directed. The worldling cannot understand these things, they appear foolishness to him, because he has too meager a knowledge of God, and also because in this highest good he can discover nothing which he can handle or eat, or which affects the fleshly appetites wherein he chiefly delights, for it consists solely in thought and the pure reason. They, on the other hand, who know that they possess no greater gift than intellect and sound reason, will doubtless accept what I have said without question.

We have now explained that wherein the Divine law chiefly consists, and what are human laws, namely, all those which have a different aim unless they have been ratified by revelation, for in this respect also things are referred to God (as we have shown above) and in this sense the law of Moses, although it was not universal, but entirely adapted to the disposition and particular preservation of a single people, may yet be called a law of God or Divine law, inasmuch as we believe that it was ratified by prophetic insight. If we consider the nature of natural Divine law as we have just explained it, we shall see

I. That it is universal or common to all men, for we have deduced it from universal human nature.

II. That it does not depend on the truth of any historical narrative whatsoever, for inasmuch as this natural Divine law is comprehended solely by the consideration of human nature, it is plain that we can conceive it as existing as well in Adam as in any other man, as well in a man living among his fellows as in a man who lives by himself.

The truth of a historical narrative, however assured, cannot give us the knowledge nor consequently the love of God, for love of God springs from knowledge of Him, and knowledge of Him should be derived from general ideas, in themselves certain and known, so that the truth of a historical narrative is very far from being a necessary requisite for our attaining our highest good.

Still, though the truth of histories cannot give us the knowledge and love of God, I do not deny that reading them is very useful with a view to life in the world, for the more we have observed and known of men's customs and circumstances, which are best revealed by their actions, the more warily we shall be able to order our lives among them, and so far as reason dictates to adapt our actions to their dispositions.

III. We see that this natural Divine law does not demand the performance of ceremonies—that is, actions in themselves indifferent, which are called good from the fact of their institution, or actions symbolizing something profitable for salvation, or (if one prefers this definition) actions of which the meaning surpasses human understanding. The natural light of reason does not demand anything which it is itself unable to supply, but only such as it can very clearly show to be good, or a means to our blessedness. Such things as are good simply because they have been commanded or instituted, or as being symbols of something good, are mere shadows which cannot be reckoned among actions that are the offspring, as it were, or fruit of a sound mind and of intellect. There is no need for me to go into this now in more detail.

IV. Lastly, we see that the highest reward of the Divine law is the law itself, namely, to know God and to love Him of our free choice, and with an undivided and fruitful spirit; while its penalty is the absence of these things, and being in bondage to the flesh—that is, having an inconstant and wavering spirit.

These points being noted, I must now inquire

I. Whether by the natural light of reason we can conceive of God as a lawgiver or potentate ordaining laws for men?

II. What is the teaching of Holy Writ concerning this natural light of reason and natural law?

III. With what objects were ceremonies formerly instituted?

IV. Lastly, what is the good gained by knowing the sacred histories and believing them?

Of the first two I will treat in this chapter, of the remaining two in the following one.

Our conclusion about the first is easily deduced from the nature of God's will, which is only distinguished from His understanding in relation to our intellect—that is, the will and the understanding of God are in reality one and the same, and are only distinguished in relation to our thoughts which we form concerning God's understanding. For instance, if we are only looking to the fact that the nature of a triangle is from eternity contained in the Divine nature as an eternal verity, we say that God possesses the idea of a triangle, or that He understands the nature of a triangle; but if afterwards we look to the fact that the nature of a triangle is thus contained in the Divine nature, solely by the necessity of the Divine nature, and not by the necessity of the nature and essence of a triangle—in fact, that the necessity of a triangle's essence and nature, in so far as they are conceived of as eternal verities, depends solely on the necessity of the Divine nature and intellect, we then style God's will or decree, that which before we styled His intellect. Wherefore we make one and the same affirmation concerning God when we say that He has from eternity decreed that three angles of a triangle are equal to two right angles, as when we say that He has understood it.

Hence the affirmations and the negations of God always involve necessity or truth; so that, for example, if God said to Adam that He did not wish him to eat of the tree of knowledge of good and evil, it would have involved a contradiction that Adam should have been able to eat of it, and would therefore have been impossible that he should have so eaten, for the Divine command would have involved an eternal necessity and truth. But since Scripture nevertheless narrates that God did give this command to Adam, and yet that none the less Adam ate of the tree, we must perforce say that God revealed to Adam the evil which would surely follow if he should eat of the tree, but did not disclose that such evil would of necessity come to pass. Thus it was that Adam took the revelation to be not an eternal and necessary truth, but a law—that is, an ordinance followed by gain or loss, not depending necessarily on the nature of the act performed, but solely on the will and absolute power of some potentate, so that the revelation in question was solely in relation to Adam, and solely through his lack of knowledge a law, and God was, as it were, a lawgiver and potentate. From the same cause, namely, from lack of knowledge, the Decalogue in relation to the Hebrews was a law, for since they knew not the existence of God as an eternal truth, they must have taken as a law that which was revealed to them in the Decalogue, namely, that God exists, and that God only should be worshiped. But if God had spoken to them without the intervention of any bodily means, immediately they would have perceived it not as a law but as an eternal truth.

What we have said about the Israelites and Adam applies also to all the prophets who wrote laws in God's name—they did not adequately conceive God's decrees as eternal truths. For instance, we must say of Moses that from revelation, from the basis of what was revealed to him, he perceived the method by which the Israelitish nation could best be united in a particular territory, and could form a body politic or state, and further that he perceived the method by which that nation could best be constrained to obedience; but he did not perceive, nor was it revealed to him, that this method was absolutely the best, nor that the obedience of the people in a certain strip of territory would necessarily imply the end he had in view. Wherefore he perceived these things not as eternal truths, but as precepts and ordinances, and he ordained them as laws of God, and thus it came to be that he conceived God as a ruler, a legislator, a king, as merciful, just, etc., whereas such qualities are simply attributes of human nature, and utterly alien from the nature of the Deity. Thus much we may affirm of the prophets who wrote laws in the name of God; but we must not affirm it of Christ, for Christ, although He too seems to have written laws in the name of God, must be taken to have had a clear and adequate perception, for Christ was not so much a prophet as the mouthpiece of God. For God made revelations to mankind through Christ as He had before done through angels—that is, a created voice, visions, etc. It would be as unreasonable to say that God had accommodated His revelations to the opinions of Christ as that He had before accommodated them to the opinions of angels (that is, of a created voice or visions) as matters to be revealed to the prophets, a wholly absurd hypothesis. Moreover, Christ was sent to teach not only the Jews but the whole human race, and therefore it was not enough that His mind should be accommodated to the opinions of the Jews alone, but also to the opinion and fundamental teaching common to the whole human race—in other words, to ideas universal and true. Inasmuch as God revealed Himself to Christ, or to Christ's mind immediately, and not as to the prophets through words and symbols, we must needs suppose that Christ perceived truly what was revealed, in other words, He understood it, for a matter is understood when it is perceived simply by the mind without words or symbols.

Christ, then, perceived (truly and adequately) what was revealed, and if He ever proclaimed such revelations as laws, He did so because of the ignorance and obstinacy of the people, acting in this respect the part of God; inasmuch as He accommodated Himself to the comprehension of the people, and though He spoke somewhat more clearly than the other prophets, yet He taught what was revealed obscurely, and generally through parables, especially when He was speaking to those to whom it was not yet given to understand the kingdom of heaven. (See Matt. xiii. 10, etc.) To those to whom it was given to understand the mysteries of heaven, He doubtless taught His doctrines as eternal truths and did not lay them down as laws, thus freeing the minds of His hearers from the bondage of that law which He further confirmed and established. Paul apparently points to this more than once (*e.g.*, Rom. vii. 6, and iii. 28), though he never himself seems to wish to speak openly, but, to quote his own words (Rom. iii. 5, and vi. 19), "merely humanly." This he expressly states when he calls God just, and it was doubtless in concession to human weakness that he attributes mercy, grace, anger, and similar qualities to God, adapting his language to the popular mind, or, as he puts it (1 Cor. iii. 1, 2), to carnal men. In Rom. ix. 18, he teaches undisguisedly that God's anger and mercy depend not on the actions of men, but on God's own nature or will; further, that no one is justified by the works of the law, but only by faith, which he seems to identify with the full assent of the soul; lastly, that no one is blessed unless he have in him the mind of Christ (Rom. viii. 9), whereby he perceives the laws of God as eternal truths. We conclude, therefore, that God is described as a lawgiver or prince, and styled just, merciful, etc., merely in concession to popular understanding, and the imperfection of popular knowledge; that in reality God acts and directs all things simply by the necessity of His nature and perfection, and that His decrees and volitions are eternal truths, and always involve necessity. So much for the first point which I wished to explain and demonstrate.

Passing on to the second point, let us search the sacred pages for their teaching concerning the light of nature and this Divine law. The first doctrine we find in the history of the first man, where it is narrated that God commanded Adam not to eat of the fruit of the tree of the knowledge of good and evil; this seems to mean that God commanded Adam to do and to seek after righteousness because it was good, not because the contrary was evil: that is, to seek the good for its own sake, not from fear of evil. We have seen that he who acts rightly from the true knowledge and love of right, acts with freedom and constancy, whereas he who acts from fear of evil, is under the constraint of evil, and acts in bondage under external control. So that this commandment of God to Adam comprehends the whole Divine natural law, and absolutely agrees with the dictates of the light of nature; nay, it would be easy to explain on this basis the whole history or allegory of the first man. But I prefer to pass over the subject in silence, because, in the first place, I cannot be absolutely certain that my explanation would be in accordance with the intention of the sacred writer; and, secondly, because many do not admit that this history is an allegory, maintaining it to be a simple narrative of facts. It will be better, therefore, to adduce other passages of Scripture, especially such as were written by him, who speaks with all the strength of his natural understanding, in which he surpassed all his contemporaries, and whose sayings are accepted by the people as of equal right with those of the prophets. I mean Solomon, whose prudence and wisdom are commended in Scripture rather than his piety and gift of prophecy. He, in his proverbs, calls the human intellect the well-spring of true life, and declares that misfortune is made up of folly. "Understanding is a well-spring of life to him that hath it; but the instruction of fools is folly" (Prov. xvi. 22). Life being taken to mean the true life (as is evident from Deut. xxx. 19), the fruit of the understanding consists only in the true life, and its absence constitutes punishment. All this absolutely agrees with what was set out in our fourth point concerning natural law. Moreover, our position that it is the well-spring of life, and that the intellect alone lays down laws for the wise, is plainly taught by the sage, for he says (Prov. xiii. 14): "The law of the wise is a fountain of life"—that is, as we gather from the preceding text, the understanding. In chap. iii. 13, he expressly teaches that the understanding renders man blessed and happy, and gives him true peace of mind. "Happy is the man that findeth wisdom, and the man that getteth understanding," for "Wisdom gives length of days, and riches and honour; her ways are ways of pleasantness, and all her paths peace" (Prov xiii. 16, 17). According to Solomon, therefore, it is only the wise who live in peace and equanimity, not like the wicked whose minds drift hither and thither, and (as Isaiah says, chap. lvii. 20) "are like the troubled sea, for them there is no peace."

Lastly, we should especially note the passage in chap. ii. of Solomon's proverbs which most clearly confirms our contention: "If thou criest after knowledge, and liftest up thy voice for understanding ... then shalt thou understand the fear of the Lord, and find the knowledge of God; for the Lord giveth wisdom; out of His mouth cometh knowledge and understanding." These words clearly enunciate (1), that wisdom or intellect alone teaches us to fear God wisely—that is, to worship Him truly; (2), that wisdom and knowledge flow from God's mouth, and that God bestows on us this gift; this we have already shown in proving that our understanding and our knowledge depend on, spring from, and are perfected by the idea or knowledge of God, and nothing else. Solomon goes on to say in so many words that this knowledge contains and involves the true principles of ethics and politics: "When wisdom entereth into thy heart, and knowledge is pleasant to thy soul, discretion shall preserve thee, understanding shall keep thee, then shalt thou understand righteousness, and judgment, and equity, yea every good path." All of which is in obvious agreement with natural knowledge: for after we have come to the understanding of things, and have tasted the excellence of knowledge, she teaches us ethics and true virtue.

Thus the happiness and the peace of him who cultivates his natural understanding lies, according to Solomon also, not so much under the dominion of fortune (or God's external aid) as in inward personal virtue (or God's internal aid), for the latter can to a great extent be preserved by vigilance, right action, and thought.

Lastly, we must by no means pass over the passage in Paul's Epistle to the Romans (i. 20), in which he says: "For the invisible things of God from the creation of the world are clearly seen, being understood by the things that are made, even His eternal power and Godhead; so that they are without excuse, because, when they knew God, they glorified Him not as God, neither were they thankful." These words clearly show that everyone can by the light of nature clearly understand the goodness and the eternal divinity of God, and can thence know and deduce what they should seek for and what avoid; wherefore the Apostle says that they are without excuse and cannot plead ignorance, as they certainly might if it were a question of supernatural light and the incarnation, passion, resurrection of Christ. "Wherefore," he goes on to say (*ib.* 24), "God gave them up to uncleanness through the lusts of their own hearts;" and so on, through the rest of the chapter, he describes the vices of ignorance, and sets them forth as the punishment of ignorance. This obviously agrees with the verse of Solomon, already quoted, "The instruction of fools is folly," so that it is easy to understand why Paul says that the wicked are without excuse. As every man sows so shall he reap: out of evil, evils necessarily spring, unless they be wisely counteracted.

Thus we see that Scripture literally approves of the light of natural reason and the natural Divine law, and I have fulfilled the promises made at the beginning of this chapter.

FOOTNOTES:

[7] From the *Tr. Th.-P.*, ch. iv, same title.

CHAPTER VI

OF THE CEREMONIAL LAW[8]

In the foregoing chapter we have shown that the Divine law, which renders men truly blessed, and teaches them the true life, is universal to all men; nay, we have so intimately deduced it from human nature that it must be esteemed innate, and, as it were, ingrained in the human mind.

But with regard to the ceremonial observances which were ordained in the Old Testament for the Hebrews only, and were so adapted to their state that they could for the most part only be observed by the society as a whole and not by each individual, it is evident that they formed no part of the Divine law, and had nothing to do with blessedness and virtue, but had reference only to the election of the Hebrews, that is (as I have shown in Chapter IV), to their temporal bodily happiness and the tranquility of their kingdom, and that therefore they were only valid while that kingdom lasted. If in the Old Testament they are spoken of as the law of God, it is only because they were founded on revelation, or a basis of revelation. Still as reason, however sound, has little weight with ordinary theologians, I will adduce the authority of Scripture for what I here assert, and will further show, for the sake of greater clearness, why and how these ceremonials served to establish and preserve the Jewish kingdom. Isaiah teaches most plainly that the Divine law in its strict sense signifies that universal law which consists in a true manner of life, and does not signify ceremonial observances. In chapter i., verse 10, the prophet calls on his countrymen to hearken to the Divine law as he delivers it, and first excluding all kinds of sacrifices and all feasts, he at length sums up the law in these few words: "Cease to do evil, learn to do well: seek judgment, relieve the oppressed." Not less striking testimony is given in Psalm xl. 7-9, where the Psalmist addresses God: "Sacrifice and offering Thou didst not desire; mine ears hast Thou opened; burnt offering and sin-offering hast Thou not required; I delight to do Thy will, O my God; yea, Thy law is within my heart." Here the Psalmist reckons as the law of God only that which is inscribed in his heart, and excludes ceremonies therefrom, for the latter are good and inscribed on the heart only from the fact of their institution, and not because of their intrinsic value.

Other passages of Scripture testify to the same truth, but these two will suffice. We may also learn from the Bible that ceremonies are no aid to blessedness, but only have reference to the temporal prosperity of the kingdom; for the rewards promised for their observance are merely temporal advantages and de-

91

lights, blessedness being reserved for the universal Divine law. In all the five books commonly attributed to Moses nothing is promised, as I have said, beyond temporal benefits, such as honors, fame, victories, riches, enjoyments, and health. Though many moral precepts besides ceremonies are contained in these five books, they appear not as moral doctrines universal to all men, but as commands especially adapted to the understanding and character of the Hebrew people, and as having reference only to the welfare of the kingdom. For instance, Moses does not teach the Jews as a prophet not to kill or to steal, but gives these commandments solely as a lawgiver and judge; he does not reason out the doctrine, but affixes for its non-observance a penalty which may and very properly does vary in different nations. So, too, the command not to commit adultery is given merely with reference to the welfare of the state; for if the moral doctrine had been intended, with reference not only to the welfare of the state, but also to the tranquility and blessedness of the individual, Moses would have condemned not merely the outward act, but also the mental acquiescence, as is done by Christ, Who taught only universal moral precepts, and for this cause promises a spiritual instead of a temporal reward. Christ, as I have said, was sent into the world, not to preserve the state nor to lay down laws, but solely to teach the universal moral law, so we can easily understand that He wished in no wise to do away with the law of Moses, inasmuch as He introduced no new laws of His own—His sole care was to teach moral doctrines, and distinguish them from the laws of the state; for the Pharisees, in their ignorance, thought that the observance of the state law and the Mosaic law was the sum total of morality; whereas such laws merely had reference to the public welfare, and aimed not so much at instructing the Jews as at keeping them under constraint. But let us return to our subject, and cite other passages of Scripture which set forth temporal benefits as rewards for observing the ceremonial law, and blessedness as reward for the universal law.

None of the prophets puts the point more clearly than Isaiah. After condemning hypocrisy, he commends liberty and charity towards oneself and one's neighbors, and promises as a reward: "Then shall thy light break forth as the morning, and thy health shall spring forth speedily, thy righteousness shall go before thee, and the glory of the Lord shall be thy reward" (chap. lviii. 8). Shortly afterwards he commends the Sabbath, and for a due observance of it promises: "Then shalt thou delight thyself in the Lord, and I will cause thee to ride upon the high places of the earth, and feed thee with the heritage of Jacob thy father: for the mouth of the Lord has spoken it." Thus the prophet, for liberty bestowed and charitable works, promises a healthy mind in a healthy body, and the glory of the Lord even after death; whereas, for ceremonial exactitude, he only promises security of rule, prosperity, and temporal happiness.

... It remains to show why and how the ceremonial observances tended to preserve and confirm the Hebrew kingdom; and this I can very briefly do on grounds universally accepted.

The formation of society serves not only for defensive purposes, but is also very useful, and, indeed, absolutely necessary, as rendering possible the division of labor. If men did not render mutual assistance to each other, no one would have either the skill or the time to provide for his own sustenance and preservation: for all men are not equally apt for all work, and no one would be capable of preparing all that he individually stood in need of. Strength and time, I repeat, would fail, if everyone had in person to plow, to sow, to reap, to grind corn, to cook, to weave, to stitch and perform the other numerous functions required to keep life going; to say nothing of the arts and sciences which are also entirely necessary to the perfection and blessedness of human nature. We see that peoples living in uncivilized barbarism lead a wretched and almost animal life, and even they would not be able to acquire their few rude necessaries without assisting one another to a certain extent.

Now if men were so constituted by nature that they desired nothing but what is designated by true reason, society would obviously have no need of laws: it would be sufficient to inculcate true moral doctrines; and men would freely, without hesitation, act in accordance with their true interests. But human nature is framed in a different fashion: everyone, indeed, seeks his own interest, but does not do so in accordance with the dictates of sound reason, for most men's ideas of desirability and usefulness are guided by their fleshly instincts and emotions, which take no thought beyond the present and the immediate object. Therefore, no society can exist without government, and force, and laws to restrain and repress men's desires and immoderate impulses. Still human nature will not submit to absolute repression. Violent governments, as Seneca says, never last long; the moderate governments endure.

So long as men act simply from fear they act contrary to their inclinations, taking no thought for the advantages or necessity of their actions, but simply endeavoring to escape punishment or loss of life. They must needs rejoice in any evil which befalls their ruler, even if it should involve themselves; and must long for and bring about such evil by every means in their power. Again, men are especially intolerant of serving and being ruled by their equals. Lastly, it is exceedingly difficult to revoke liberties once granted.

From these considerations it follows, firstly, that authority should either be vested in the hands of the whole state in common, so that everyone should be bound to serve, and yet not be in subjection to his equals; or else, if power be in the hands of a few, or one man, that one man should be something above average humanity, or should strive to get himself accepted as such. Secondly, laws should in every government be so arranged that people should be kept in bounds by the hope of some greatly desired good, rather than by fear, for then everyone will do his duty willingly.

Lastly, as obedience consists in acting at the bidding of external authority, it would have no place in a state where the government is vested in the whole people, and where laws are made by common consent. In such a society the people would remain free, whether the laws were added to or diminished, inasmuch as it would not be done on external authority, but their own free consent. The reverse happens when the sovereign power is vested in one man, for all act at his bidding; and, therefore, unless they had been trained from the first to depend on the words of their ruler, the latter would find it difficult, in case of need, to abrogate liberties once conceded, and impose new laws.

From these universal considerations, let us pass on to the kingdom of the Jews. The Jews when they first came out of Egypt were not bound by any national laws, and were therefore free to ratify any laws they liked, or to make new ones, and were at liberty to set up a government and occupy a territory wherever they chose. However, they were entirely unfit to frame a wise code of laws and to keep the sovereign power vested in the community; they were all uncultivated and sunk in a wretched slavery, therefore the sovereignty was bound to remain vested in the hands of one man who would rule the rest and keep them under constraint, make laws and interpret them. This sovereignty was easily retained by Moses, because he surpassed the rest in virtue and persuaded the people of the fact, proving it by many testimonies (see Exod. chap. xiv., last verse, and chap. xix., verse 9). He then, by the Divine virtue he possessed, made laws and ordained them for the people, taking the greatest care that they should be obeyed willingly and not through fear, being specially induced to adopt this course by the obstinate nature of the Jews, who would not have submitted to be ruled solely by constraint; and also by the imminence of war, for it is always better to inspire soldiers with a thirst for glory than to terrify them with threats; each man will then strive to distinguish himself by valor and courage, instead of merely trying to escape punishment. Moses, therefore, by his virtue and the Divine command, introduced a religion so that the people might do their duty from devotion rather than fear. Further, he bound them over by benefits, and prophesied many advantages in the future; nor were his laws very severe, as any one may see for himself, especially if he remarks the number of circumstances necessary in order to procure the conviction of an accused person.

Lastly, in order that the people which could not govern itself should be entirely dependent on its ruler, he left nothing to the free choice of individuals (who had hitherto been slaves); the people could do nothing but remember the law, and follow the ordinances laid down at the good pleasure of their ruler; they were not allowed to plow, to sow, to reap, nor even to eat; to clothe themselves, to shave, to rejoice, or, in fact, to do anything whatever as they liked, but were bound to follow the directions given in the law; and not only this, but they were obliged to have marks on their doorposts, on their hands, and between their eyes to admonish them to perpetual obedience.

This, then, was the object of the ceremonial law, that men should do nothing of their own free will, but should always act under external authority, and should continually confess by their actions and thoughts that they were not their own masters, but were entirely under the control of others.

From all these considerations it is clearer than day that ceremonies have nothing to do with a state of blessedness, and that those mentioned in the Old Testament, *i.e.*, the whole Mosaic Law, had reference merely to the government of the Jews, and merely temporal advantages.

As for the Christian rites, such as baptism, the Lord's Supper, festivals, public prayers, and any other observances which are, and always have been, common to all Christendom, if they were instituted by Christ or His Apostles (which is open to doubt), they were instituted as external signs of the universal church, and not as having anything to do with blessedness, or possessing any sanctity in themselves. Therefore, though such ceremonies were not ordained for the sake of upholding a government, they were ordained for the preservation of a society, and accordingly he who lives alone is not bound by them: nay, those who live in a country where the Christian religion is forbidden, are bound to abstain from such rites, and can none the less live in a state of blessedness. We have an example of this in Japan, where the Christian religion is forbidden, and the Dutch who live there are enjoined by their East India Company not to practice any outward rites of religion. I need not cite other examples, though it would be easy to prove my point from the fundamental principles of the New Testament, and to adduce many confirmatory instances; but I pass on the more willingly, as I am anxious to proceed to my next proposition. I will now, therefore, pass on to what I proposed to treat of in the second part of this chapter, namely, what persons are bound to believe in the narratives contained in Scripture, and how far they are so bound. Examining this question by the aid of natural reason, I will proceed as follows:

If any one wishes to persuade his fellows for or against anything which is not self-evident, he must deduce his contention from their admissions, and convince them either by experience or by ratiocination; either by appealing to facts of natural experience, or to self-evident intellectual axioms. Now unless the experience be of such a kind as to be clearly and distinctly understood, though it may convince a man, it will not have the same effect on his mind and disperse the clouds of his doubt so completely as when the doctrine taught is deduced entirely from intellectual axioms—that is, by the mere power of the understanding and logical order, and this is especially the case in spiritual matters which have nothing to do with the senses.

But the deduction of conclusions from general truths *à priori*, usually requires a long chain of arguments, and, moreover, very great caution, acuteness, and self-restraint—qualities which are not often met with; therefore people prefer to be taught by experience rather than deduce their conclusion from a few axioms, and set them out in logical order. Whence it follows, that if any one wishes to teach a doctrine to a whole nation (not to speak of the whole human race), and to be understood by all men in every particular, he will seek to support his teaching with experience, and will endeavor to suit his reasonings and the definitions of his doctrines as far as possible to the understanding of the common people, who form the majority of mankind, and he will not set them forth in logical sequence nor adduce the definitions which serve to establish them. Otherwise he writes only for the learned—that is, he will be understood by only a small proportion of the human race.

All Scripture was written primarily for an entire people, and secondarily for the whole human race; therefore its contents must necessarily be adapted as far as possible to the understanding of the masses, and proved only by examples drawn from experience. We will explain ourselves more clearly. The chief speculative doctrines taught in Scripture are the existence of God, or a Being Who made all things, and Who directs and sustains the world with consummate wisdom; furthermore, that God takes the greatest thought for men, or such of them as live piously and honorably, while He punishes, with various penalties, those who do evil, separating them from the good. All this is proved in Scripture entirely through experience—that is, through the narratives there related. No definitions of doctrine are given, but all the sayings and reasonings are adapted to the understanding of the masses. Although experience can give no clear knowledge of these things, nor explain the nature of God, nor how He directs and sustains all things, it can nevertheless teach and enlighten men sufficiently to impress obedience and devotion on their minds.

It is not, I think, sufficiently clear what persons are bound to believe in the Scripture narratives, and in what degree they are so bound, for it evidently follows from what has been said that the knowledge of and belief in them is particularly necessary to the masses whose intellect is not capable of perceiving things clearly and distinctly. Further, he who denies them because he does not believe that God exists or takes thought for men and the world, may be accounted impious; but a man who is ignorant of them, and nevertheless shows by natural reason that God exists, as we have said, and has a true plan of life, is altogether blessed—yes, more blessed than the common herd of believers, because besides true opinions he possesses also a true and distinct conception. Lastly, he who is ignorant of the Scriptures and knows nothing by the light of reason, though he may not be impious or rebellious, is yet less than human and almost brutal, having none of God's gifts.

We must here remark that when we say that the knowledge of the sacred narrative is particularly necessary to the masses, we do not mean the knowledge of absolutely all the narratives in the Bible, but only of the principal ones, those which, taken by themselves, plainly display the doctrine we have just stated, and have most effect over men's minds.

If all the narratives in Scripture were necessary for the proof of this doctrine, and if no conclusion could be drawn without the general consideration of everyone of the histories contained in the sacred writings, truly the conclusion and demonstration of such doctrine would overtask the understanding and strength not only of the masses, but of humanity; who is there who could give attention to all the narratives at once, and to all the circumstances, and all the scraps of doctrine to be elicited from such a host of diverse histories? I cannot believe that the men who have left us the Bible as we have it were so abounding in talent that they attempted setting about such a method of demonstration, still less can I suppose that we cannot understand Scriptural doctrine till we have given heed to the quarrels of Isaac, the advice of Achitophel to Absalom, the civil war between Jews and Israelites, and other similar chronicles; nor can I think that it was more difficult to teach such doctrine by means of history to the Jews of early times, the contemporaries of Moses, than it was to the contemporaries of Esdras. But more will be said on this point hereafter, we may now only note that the masses are only bound to know those histories which can most powerfully dispose their mind to obedience and devotion. However, the masses are not sufficiently skilled to draw conclusions from what they read, they take more delight in the actual stories, and in the strange and un-looked-for issues of events than in the doctrines implied; therefore, besides reading these narratives, they are always in need of pastors or church ministers to explain them to their feeble intelligence.

But not to wander from our point, let us conclude with what has been our principal object—namely, that the truth of narratives, be they what they may, has nothing to do with the Divine law, and serves for nothing except in respect of doctrine, the sole element which makes one history better than another. The narratives in the Old and New Testaments surpass profane history, and differ among themselves in merit simply by reason of the salutary doctrines which they inculcate. Therefore, if a man were to read the Scripture narratives believing the whole of them, but were to give no heed to the doctrines they contain, and make no amendment in his life, he might employ himself just as profitably in reading the Koran or the poetic drama, or ordinary chronicles, with the attention usually given to such writings; on the other hand, if a man is absolutely ignorant of the Scriptures, and none the less has right opinions and a true plan of life, he is absolutely blessed and truly possesses in himself the spirit of Christ.

The Jews are of a directly contrary way of thinking, for they hold that true opinions and a true plan of life are of no service in attaining blessedness, if their possessors have arrived at them by the light of reason only, and not like the documents prophetically revealed to Moses. Maimonides ventures openly to make this assertion: "Every man who takes to heart the seven precepts and diligently follows them, is counted with the pious among the nations, and an heir of the world to come; that is to say, if he takes to heart and follows them because God ordained them in the law, and revealed them to us by Moses, because they were of aforetime precepts to the sons of Noah: but he who follows them as lead thereto by reason, is not counted as a dweller among the pious, nor among the wise of the nations." Such are the words of Maimonides, to which R. Joseph, the son of Shem Job, adds in his book, which he calls *Kebod Elohim, or God's Glory*, that although Aristotle (whom he considers to have written the best ethics and to be above everyone else) has not omitted anything that concerns true ethics, and which he has adopted in his own book, carefully following the lines laid down, yet this was not able to suffice for his salvation, inasmuch as he embraced his doctrines in accordance with the dictates of reason and not as Divine documents prophetically revealed.[9]

However, that these are mere figments and are not supported by Scriptural authority will, I think, be sufficiently evident to the attentive reader, so that an examination of the theory will be sufficient for its refutation. It is not my purpose here to refute the assertions of those who assert that the natural light of reason can teach nothing of any value concerning the true way of salvation. People who lay no claims to reason for themselves are not able to prove by reason this their assertion; and if they hawk about something superior to reason, it is a mere figment, and far below reason, as their general method of life sufficiently shows. But there is no need to dwell upon such persons. I will merely add that we can only judge of a man by his works. If a man abounds in the fruits of the Spirit, charity, joy, peace, long-suffering, kindness, goodness, faith, gentleness, chastity, against which, as Paul says (Gal. v. 22), there is no law, such an one, whether he be taught by reason only or by the Scripture only, has been in very truth taught by God, and is altogether blessed. Thus have I said all that I undertook to say concerning Divine law.

FOOTNOTES:

[8] From the *Tr. Th.-P.*, ch. v, same title.

[9] The Jews were not, of course, alone in holding this point of view. Dante consigned the ancient philosophers—including Aristotle—and even Vergil to Limbo, agreeing thus in doctrine with Maimonides and R. Joseph, the son of Shem Job.—ED.

CHAPTER VII

OF MIRACLES[110]

As men are accustomed to call Divine the knowledge which transcends human understanding, so also do they style Divine, or the work of God, anything of which the cause is not generally known: for the masses think that the power and providence of God are most clearly displayed by events that are extraordinary and contrary to the conception they have formed of Nature, especially if such events bring them any profit or convenience: they think that the clearest possible proof of God's existence is afforded when Nature, as they suppose, breaks her accustomed order, and consequently they believe that those who explain or endeavor to understand phenomena or miracles through their natural causes are doing away with God and His providence. They suppose, forsooth, that God is inactive so long as Nature works in her accustomed order, and *vice versa*, that the power of Nature and natural causes are idle so long as God is acting: thus they imagine two powers distinct one from the other, the power of God and the power of Nature, though the latter is in a sense determined by God, or (as most people believe now) created by Him. What they mean by either, and what they understand by God and Nature they do not know, except that they imagine the power of God to be like that of some royal potentate, and Nature's power to consist in force and energy.

The masses then style unusual phenomena "miracles," and partly from piety, partly for the sake of opposing the students of science, prefer to remain in ignorance of natural causes, and only to hear of those things which they know least, and consequently admire most. In fact, the common people can only adore God, and refer all things to His power by removing natural causes, and conceiving things happening out of their due course, and only admires the power of God when the power of Nature is conceived of as in subjection to it.

This idea seems to have taken its rise among the early Jews who saw the Gentiles round them worshiping visible gods, such as the sun, the moon, the earth, water, air, etc., and in order to inspire the conviction that such divinities were weak and inconstant, or changeable, told how they themselves were under the sway of an invisible God, and narrated their miracles, trying further to show that the God whom they worshiped arranged the whole of nature for their sole benefit. This idea was so pleasing to humanity that men go on to this day imagining miracles, so that they may believe themselves God's favorites and the final cause for which God created and directs all things.

What pretensions will not people in their folly advance! They have no single sound idea concerning either God or Nature, they confound God's decrees with human decrees, they conceive Nature as so limited that they believe man to be its chief part! I have spent enough space in setting forth these common ideas and prejudices concerning Nature and miracles, but in order to afford a regular demonstration I will show:

1. That Nature cannot be contravened, but that she preserves a fixed and immutable order, and at the same time I will explain what is meant by a miracle.

2. That God's nature and existence, and consequently His providence, cannot be known from miracles, but that they can all be much better perceived from the fixed and immutable order of Nature.

3. That by the decrees and volitions, and consequently the providence of God, Scripture (as I will prove by Scriptural examples) means nothing but Nature's order following necessarily from her eternal laws.

4. Lastly, I will treat of the method of interpreting Scriptural miracles, and the chief points to be noted concerning the narratives of them.

Such are the principal subjects which will be discussed in this chapter, and which will serve, I think, not a little to further the object of this treatise.

Our first point is easily proved from what we showed in Chapter V about Divine law—namely, that all that God wishes or determines involves eternal necessity and truth, for we demonstrated that God's understanding is identical with His will, and that it is the same thing to say that God wills a thing, as to say that He understands it; hence, as it follows necessarily from the Divine nature and perfection that God understands a thing as it is, it follows no less necessarily that He wills it as it is. Now, as nothing is necessarily true save only by Divine decree, it is plain that the universal laws of Nature are decrees of God following from the necessity and perfection of the Divine nature. Hence, any event happening in nature which contravened Nature's universal laws, would necessarily also contravene the Divine decree, nature, and understanding; or if any one asserted that God acts in contravention to the laws of Nature, he, *ipso facto*, would be compelled to assert that God acted against His own nature—an evident absurdity. One might easily show from the same premises that the power and efficiency of Nature are in themselves the Divine power and efficiency, and that the Divine power is the very essence of God, but this I gladly pass over for the present.

Nothing, then, comes to pass in Nature[11] in contravention to her universal laws, nay, everything agrees with them and follows from them, for whatsoever comes to pass, comes to pass by the will and eternal decree of God; that is, as we have just pointed out, whatever comes to pass, comes to pass according to laws and rules which involve eternal necessity and truth; Nature, therefore, always observes laws and rules which involve eternal necessity and truth, although they may not all be known to us, and therefore she keeps a fixed and immutable order. Nor is there any sound reason for limiting the power and efficacy of Nature, and asserting that her laws are fit for certain purposes, but not for all; for as the efficacy and power of Nature are the very efficacy and power of God, and as the laws and rules of Nature are the decrees of God, it is in every way to be believed that the power of Nature is infinite, and that her laws are broad enough to embrace everything conceived by the Divine intellect. The only alternative is to assert that God has created Nature so weak, and has ordained for her laws so barren, that He is repeatedly compelled to come afresh to her aid if He wishes that she should be preserved, and that things should happen as He desires: a conclusion, in my opinion, very far removed from reason. Further, as nothing happens in Nature which does not follow from her laws, and as her laws embrace everything conceived by the Divine intellect, and, lastly, as Nature preserves a fixed and immutable order, it most clearly follows that miracles are only intelligible as in relation to human opinions, and merely mean events of which the natural cause cannot be explained by a reference to any ordinary occurrence, either by us, or at any rate by the writer and narrator of the miracle.

We may, in fact, say that a miracle is an event of which the causes cannot be explained by the natural reason through a reference to ascertained workings of Nature; but since miracles were wrought according to the understanding of the masses, who are wholly ignorant of the workings of Nature, it is certain that the ancients took for a miracle whatever they could not explain by the method adopted by the unlearned in such cases, namely, an appeal to the memory, a recalling of something similar, which is ordinarily regarded without wonder; for most people think they sufficiently understand a thing when they have ceased to wonder at it. The ancients, then, and indeed most men up to the present day, had no other criterion for a miracle; hence we cannot doubt that many things are narrated in Scripture as miracles of which the causes could easily be explained by reference to ascertained workings of Nature. We have hinted as much in Chapter III, in speaking of the sun standing still in the time of Joshua, and going backwards in the time of Ahaz; but we shall soon have more to say on the subject when we come to treat of the interpretation of miracles later on in this chapter.

It is now time to pass on to the second point, and show that we cannot gain an understanding of God's essence, existence, or providence by means of miracles, but that these truths are much better perceived through the fixed and immutable order of Nature.

I thus proceed with the demonstration. As God's existence is not self-evident, it must necessarily be inferred from ideas so firmly and incontrovertibly true that no power can be postulated or conceived sufficient to impugn them. They ought certainly so to appear to us when we infer from them God's existence, if we wish to place our conclusion beyond the reach of doubt; for if we could conceive that such ideas could be impugned by any power whatsoever, we should doubt of their truth, we should doubt of our conclusion, namely, of God's existence, and should never be able to be certain of anything. Further, we know that nothing either agrees with or is contrary to Nature, unless it agrees with or is contrary to these primary ideas; wherefore if we would conceive that anything could be done in Nature by any power whatsoever which would be contrary to the laws of Nature, it would also be contrary to our primary ideas, and we should have either to reject it as absurd, or else to cast doubt (as just shown) on our primary ideas, and consequently on the existence of God, and on everything howsoever perceived. Therefore miracles, in the sense of events contrary to the laws of Nature, so far from demonstrating to us the existence of God, would, on the contrary, lead us to doubt it, where, otherwise, we might have been absolutely certain of it, as knowing that Nature follows a fixed and immutable order.

Let us take miracle as meaning that which cannot be explained through natural causes. This may be interpreted in two senses: either as that which has natural causes, but cannot be examined by the human intellect; or as that which has no cause save God and God's will. But as all things which come to pass through natural causes come to pass also solely through the will and power of God, it comes to this: that a miracle, whether it has natural causes or not, is a result which cannot be explained by its cause, that is a phenomenon which surpasses human understanding; but from such a phenomenon, and certainly from a result surpassing our understanding, we can gain no knowledge. For whatsoever we understand clearly and distinctly should be plain to us either in itself or by means of something else clearly and distinctly understood; wherefore from a miracle or a phenomenon which we cannot understand we can gain no knowledge of God's essence, or existence, or indeed anything about God or nature; whereas when we know that all things are ordained and ratified by God, that the operations of Nature follow from the essence of God, and that the laws of Nature are eternal decrees and volitions of God, we must perforce conclude that our knowledge of God and of God's will increases in proportion to our knowledge and clear understanding of Nature, as we see how she depends on her primal cause, and how she works according to eternal law. Wherefore so far as our understanding goes, those phenomena which we clearly and distinctly understand have much better right to be called works of God, and to be referred to the will of God than those about which we are entirely ignorant, although they appeal powerfully to the imagination, and compel men's admiration.

It is only phenomena that we clearly and distinctly understand which heighten our knowledge of God and most clearly indicate His will and decrees. Plainly, they are but triflers who, when they cannot explain a thing, run back to the will of God; this is, truly, a ridiculous way of expressing ignorance. Again, even supposing that some conclusion could be drawn from miracles, we could not possibly infer from them the existence of God; for a miracle being an event under limitations is the expression of a fixed and limited power, therefore we could not possibly infer from an effect of this kind the existence of a cause whose power is infinite, but at the utmost only of a cause whose power is greater than that of the said effect. I say at the utmost, for a phenomenon may be the result of many concurrent causes, and its power may be less than the power of the sum of such causes, but far greater than that of any one of them taken individually. On the other hand, the laws of nature, as we have shown, extend over infinity, and are conceived by us as, after a fashion, eternal, and Nature works in accordance with them in a fixed and immutable order; therefore, such laws indicate to us in a certain degree the infinity, the eternity and the immutability of God.

We may conclude, then, that we cannot gain knowledge of the existence and providence of God by means of miracles, but that we can far better infer them from the fixed and immutable order of Nature. By miracle I here mean an event which surpasses, or is thought to surpass, human comprehension: for in so far as it is supposed to destroy or interrupt the order of Nature or her laws, it not only can give us no knowledge of God, but, contrariwise, takes away that which we naturally have, and makes us doubt of God and everything else.

Neither do I recognize any difference between an event against the laws of Nature and an event beyond the laws of Nature (that is, according to some, an event which does not contravene Nature, though she is inadequate to produce or effect it), for a miracle is wrought in, and not beyond Nature, though it may be said in itself to be above Nature, and, therefore, must necessarily interrupt the order of Nature, which otherwise we conceive of as fixed and unchangeable, according to God's decrees. If therefore anything should come to pass in Nature which does not follow from her laws, it would also be in contravention to the order which God has established in Nature forever through universal natural laws. It would, therefore, be in contravention to God's nature and laws, and, consequently belief in it would throw doubt upon everything, and lead to Atheism.

I think I have now sufficiently established my second point, so that we can again conclude that a miracle, whether in contravention to, or beyond, Nature, is a mere absurdity; and therefore that what is meant in Scripture by a miracle can only be a work of Nature, which surpasses, or is believed to surpass, human comprehension. Before passing on to my third point, I will adduce Scriptural authority for my assertion that God cannot be known from miracles. Scripture nowhere states the doctrine openly, but it can readily be inferred from several passages. Firstly, that in which Moses commands (Deut. xiii.) that a false prophet should be put to death, even though he work miracles: "If there arise a prophet among you, and giveth thee a sign or wonder, and the sign or wonder come to pass, saying, Let us go after other gods ... thou shalt not hearken unto the voice of that prophet; for the Lord your God proveth you, and that prophet shall be put to death." From this it clearly follows that miracles could be wrought even by false prophets; and that, unless men are honestly endowed with the true knowledge and love of God, they may be as easily led by miracles to follow false gods as to follow the true God; for these words are added: "For the Lord your God tempts you, that He may know whether you love Him with all your heart and with all your mind."

Further, the Israelites, from all their miracles, were unable to form a sound conception of God, as their experience testified: for when they had persuaded themselves that Moses had departed from among them they petitioned Aaron to give them visible gods; and the idea of God they had formed as the result of all their miracles was a calf!...

I now go on to my *third* point, and show from Scripture that the decrees and mandates of God, and consequently His providence, are merely the order of Nature—that is, when Scripture describes an event as accomplished by God or

God's will, we must understand merely that it was in accordance with the law and order of Nature, not, as most people believe, that Nature had for a season ceased to act, or that her order was temporarily interrupted. But Scripture does not directly teach matters unconnected with its doctrine, wherefore it has no care to explain things by their natural causes, nor to expound matters merely speculative. Wherefore our conclusion must be gathered by inference from those Scriptural narratives which happen to be written more at length and circumstantially than usual. Of these I will cite a few.

In the first book of Samuel (ix. 15, 16), it is related that God revealed to Samuel that He would send Saul to him, yet God did not send Saul to Samuel as people are wont to send one man to another. His "sending" was merely the ordinary course of Nature. Saul was looking for the asses he had lost, and was meditating a return home without them, when, at the suggestion of his servant, he went to the Prophet Samuel, to learn from him where he might find them. From no part of the narrative does it appear that Saul had any command from God to visit Samuel beyond this natural motive....

But perhaps some one will insist that we find many things in Scripture which seem in nowise explicable by natural causes, as, for instance, that the sins of men and their prayers can be the cause of rain and of the earth's fertility, or that faith can heal the blind, and so on. But I think I have already made sufficient answer: I have shown that Scripture does not explain things by their secondary causes, but only narrates them in the order and the style which has most power to move men, and especially uneducated men, to devotion; and therefore it speaks inaccurately of God and of events, seeing that its object is not to convince the reason, but to attract and lay hold of the imagination. If the Bible were to describe the destruction of an empire in the style of political historians, the masses would remain unstirred, whereas the contrary is the case when it adopts the method of poetic description, and refers all things immediately to God. When, therefore, the Bible says that the earth is barren because of men's sins, or that the blind were healed by faith, we ought to take no more notice than when it says that God is angry at men's sins, that He is sad, that He repents of the good He has promised and done; or that on seeing a sign He remembers something He had promised, and other similar expressions, which are either thrown out poetically or related according to the opinion and prejudices of the writer.

We may then be absolutely certain that every event which is truly described in Scripture necessarily happened, like everything else, according to natural laws; and if anything is there set down which can be proved in set terms to contravene the order of Nature, or not to be deducible therefrom, we must believe it to have been foisted into the sacred writings by irreligious hands; for whatsoever is contrary to Nature is also contrary to reason, and whatsoever is contrary to reason is absurd, and, *ipso facto*, to be rejected.

There remain some points concerning the interpretation of miracles to be noted, or rather to be recapitulated, for most of them have been already stated. These I proceed to discuss in the fourth division of my subject, and I am led to do so lest any one should, by wrongly interpreting a miracle, rashly suspect that he has found something in Scripture contrary to human reason.

It is very rare for men to relate an event simply as it happened, without adding any element of their own judgment. When they hear or see anything new, they are, unless strictly on their guard, so occupied with their own preconceived opinions that they perceive something quite different from the plain facts seen or heard, especially if such facts surpass the comprehension of the beholder or hearer, and, most of all, if he is interested in their happening in a given way.

Thus men relate in chronicles and histories their own opinions rather than actual events, so that one and the same event is so differently related by two men of different opinions, that it seems like two separate occurrences; and, further, it is very easy from historical chronicles to gather the personal opinions of the historian.

I could cite many instances in proof of this from the writings both of natural philosophers and historians, but I will content myself with one only from Scripture, and leave the reader to judge of the rest.

In the time of Joshua the Hebrews held the ordinary opinion that the sun moves with a daily motion, and that the earth remains at rest; to this preconceived opinion they adapted the miracle which occurred during their battle with the five kings. They did not simply relate that that day was longer than usual, but asserted that the sun and moon stood still, or ceased from their motion—a statement which would be of great service to them at that time in convincing and proving by experience to the Gentiles, who worshiped the sun, that the sun was under the control of another deity who could compel it to change its daily course. Thus, partly through religious motives, partly through preconceived opinions, they conceived of and related the occurrence as something quite different from what really happened.

Thus in order to interpret the Scriptural miracles and understand from the narration of them how they really happened, it is necessary to know the opinions of those who first related them, and have recorded them for us in writing, and to distinguish such opinions from the actual impression made upon their senses, otherwise we shall confound opinions and judgments with the actual miracle as it really occurred; nay, further, we shall confound actual events with symbolical and imaginary ones. For many things are narrated in Scripture as real, and were believed to be real, which were in fact only symbolical and imaginary. As, for instance, that God came down from heaven (Exod. xix. 28, Deut. v. 28), and that Mount Sinai smoked because God descended upon it surrounded with fire; or, again, that Elijah ascended into heaven in a chariot of fire, with horses of fire; all these things were assuredly merely symbols adapted to the opinions of those who have handed them down to us as they were represented to them, namely, as real. All who have any education know that God has no right hand nor left; that He is not moved nor at rest, nor in a particular place, but that He is absolutely infinite and contains in Himself all perfections.

These things, I repeat, are known to whoever judges of things by the perception of pure reason, and not according as his imagination is affected by his outward senses,—following the example of the masses who imagine a bodily Deity, holding a royal court with a throne on the convexity of heaven, above the stars, which are believed to be not very far off from the earth.

To these and similar opinions very many narrations in Scripture are adapted, and should not, therefore, be mistaken by philosophers for realities.

Lastly, in order to understand, in the case of miracles, what actually took place, we ought to be familiar with Jewish phrases and metaphors; anyone who did not make sufficient allowance for these would be continually seeing miracles in Scripture where nothing of the kind is intended by the writer; he would thus miss the knowledge not only of what actually happened, but also of the mind of the writers of the sacred text. For instance, Zachariah, speaking of some future war, says (chap, xiv., verse 7): "It shall be one day which shall be known to the Lord, not day nor night; but at even time it shall be light." In these words he seems to predict a great miracle, yet he only means that the battle will be doubtful the whole day, that the issue will be known only to God, but that in the evening they will gain the victory. The prophets frequently used to predict victories and defeats of the nations in similar phrases. Thus Isaiah, describing the destruction of Babylon, says (chap. xiii.): "The stars of heaven, and the constellations thereof, shall not give their light; the sun shall be darkened in his going forth, and the moon shall not cause her light to shine." Now I suppose no one imagines that at the destruction of Babylon these phenomena actually occurred any more than that which the prophet adds, "For I will make the heavens to tremble, and remove the earth out of her place."

So, too, Isaiah in foretelling to the Jews that they would return from Babylon to Jerusalem in safety, and would not suffer from thirst on their journey, says: "And they thirsted not when He led them through the deserts; He caused the waters to flow out of the rocks for them; He clave the rocks, and the waters gushed out." These words merely mean that the Jews, like other people, found springs in the desert, at which they quenched their thirst; for when the Jews returned to Jerusalem with the consent of Cyrus, it is admitted that no similar miracles befell them.

In this way many occurrences in the Bible are to be regarded merely as Jewish expressions. There is no need for me to go through them in detail; but I will call attention generally to the fact that the Jews employed such phrases not only rhetorically, but also, and indeed chiefly, from devotional motives. Such is the reason for the substitution of "bless God" for "curse God" (in 1 Kings xxi. 10, and Job ii. 9), and for all things being referred to God, whence it appears that the Bible seems to relate nothing but miracles, even when speaking of the most ordinary occurrences, as in the examples given above.

Hence we must believe that when the Bible says that the Lord hardened Pharaoh's heart, it only means that Pharaoh was obstinate; when it says that God opened the windows of heaven, it only means that it rained very hard, and so on. When we reflect on these peculiarities, and also on the fact that most things are related very shortly, with very little detail, and almost in abridgments, we shall see that there is hardly anything in Scripture which can be proved contrary to natural reason, while, on the other hand, many things which before seemed obscure, will after a little consideration be understood and easily explained.

I think I have now very clearly explained all that I proposed to explain, but before I finish this chapter I would call attention to the fact that I have adopted a different method in speaking of miracles to that which I employed in treating of prophecy. Of prophecy I have asserted nothing which could not be inferred from premises revealed in Scripture, whereas in this chapter I have deduced my conclusions solely from the principles ascertained by the natural light of reason. I have proceeded in this way advisedly, for prophecy, in that it surpasses human knowledge, is a purely theological question; therefore, I knew that I could not make any assertions about it, nor learn wherein it consists, except through deductions from premises that have been revealed; therefore I was compelled to collate the history of prophecy, and to draw therefrom certain conclusions which would teach me, in so far as such teaching is possible, the nature and properties of the gift. But in the case of miracles, as our inquiry is a question purely philosophical (namely, whether anything can happen which contravenes, or does not follow from the laws of Nature), I was not under any such necessity: I therefore thought it wiser to unravel the difficulty through premises ascertained and thoroughly known by the natural light of reason. I say I thought it wiser, for I could also easily have solved the problem merely from the doctrines and fundamental principles of Scripture: in order that everyone may acknowledge this, I will briefly show how it could be done.

Scripture makes the general assertion in several passages that nature's course is fixed and unchangeable. (In Ps. cxlviii. 6, for instance, and Jer. xxxi. 35.) The wise man also (in Eccles. i. 10) distinctly teaches that "there is nothing new under the sun," and (in verses 11, 12), illustrating the same idea, he adds that although something occasionally happens which seems new, it is not really new, but "hath been already of old time, which was before us, whereof there is no remembrance, neither shall there be any remembrance of things that are to come with those that come after." Again (in chap. iii. 11), he says, "God hath made everything beautiful in his time," and immediately afterwards adds, "I know that whatsoever God doeth, it shall be forever; nothing can be put to it, nor anything taken from it."

Now all these texts teach most distinctly that Nature preserves a fixed and unchangeable order and that God in all ages known and unknown has been the same; further, that the laws of Nature are so perfect that nothing can be added thereto nor taken therefrom; and, lastly, that miracles only appear as something new because of man's ignorance.

Such is the express teaching of Scripture. Nowhere does Scripture assert that anything happens which contradicts, or cannot follow from the laws of Nature; and therefore we should not attribute to it such a doctrine....

The conclusion, then, that is most plainly put before us is, that miracles were natural occurrences, and must therefore be so explained as to appear neither new (in the words of Solomon) nor contrary to Nature, but, as far as possible, in complete agreement with ordinary events. This can easily be done by any one, now that I have set forth the rules drawn from Scripture. Nevertheless, though I maintain that Scripture teaches this doctrine, I do not assert that it teaches it as a truth necessary to salvation, but only that the prophets were in agreement with ourselves on the point; therefore everyone is free to think on the subject as he likes, according as he thinks it best for himself, and most likely to conduce to the worship of God and to single-hearted religion.

FOOTNOTES:

[10] From the *Tr. Th.-P.*, ch. vi, same title.

[11] N.B. I do not mean here by "Nature," merely matter and its modifications, but infinite other things besides matter.

CHAPTER VIII
OF THE DIVINE NATURE

Definitions

I. By cause of itself, I understand that, whose essence involves existence; or that, whose nature cannot be conceived unless existing.

II. That thing is called finite in its own kind (*in suo genere*) which can be limited by another thing of the same nature. For example, a body is called finite, because we always conceive another which is greater. So a thought is limited by another thought; but a body is not limited by a thought, nor a thought by a body.

III. By substance, I understand that which is in itself and is conceived through itself; in other words, that, the conception of which does not need the conception of another thing from which it must be formed.

IV. By attribute, I understand that which the intellect perceives of substance, as constituting its essence.

V. By mode, I understand the affections of substance, or that which is in another thing through which also it is conceived.

VI. By God, I understand Being absolutely infinite, that is to say, substance consisting of infinite attributes, each one of which expresses eternal and infinite essence.

Explanation.—I say absolutely infinite but not infinite in its own kind (*in suo genere*); for of whatever is infinite only in its own kind (*in suo genere*), we can deny infinite attributes; but to the essence of that which is absolutely infinite pertains whatever expresses essence and involves no negation.

VII. That thing is called free which exists from the necessity of its own nature alone, and is determined to action by itself alone. That thing, on the other hand, is called necessary, or rather compelled, which by another is determined to existence and action in a fixed and prescribed manner.

VIII. By eternity, I understand existence itself, so far as it is conceived necessarily to follow from the definition alone of the eternal thing.

Explanation.—For such existence, like the essence of the thing, is conceived as an eternal truth. It cannot therefore be explained by duration of time, even if the duration be conceived without beginning or end.

Axioms

I. Everything which is, is either in itself or in another.

II. That which cannot be conceived through another must be conceived through itself.

III. From a given determinate cause an effect necessarily follows; and, on the other hand, if no determinate cause be given, it is impossible that an effect can follow.

IV. The knowledge (cognitio) of an effect depends upon and involves the knowledge of the cause.

V. Those things which have nothing mutually in common with one another cannot through one another be mutually understood, that is to say, the conception of the one does not involve the conception of the other.

VI. A true idea must agree with that of which it is the idea (*cum suo ideato*).

VII. The essence of that thing which can be conceived as not existing does not involve existence.

The Essence of God

God, or substance consisting of infinite attributes, each one of which expresses eternal and infinite essence, necessarily exists.

[This can be proved in the following manner]:

For the existence or non-existence of everything there must be a reason or cause. For example, if a triangle exists, there must be a reason or cause why it exists; and if it does not exist, there must be a reason or cause which hinders its existence or which negates it. But this reason or cause must either be contained in the nature of the thing or lie outside it. For example, the nature of the thing itself shows the reason why a square circle does not exist, the reason being that

113

a square circle involves a contradiction. And the reason, on the other hand, why substance exists follows from its nature alone, which involves existence. But the reason why a circle or triangle exists or does not exist is not drawn from their nature, but from the order of corporeal nature generally; for from that it must follow either that a triangle necessarily exists, or that it is impossible for it to exist. But this is self-evident. Therefore it follows that if there be no cause nor reason which hinders a thing from existing, it exists necessarily. If therefore there be no reason nor cause which hinders God from existing, or which negates His existence, we must conclude absolutely that He necessarily exists. But if there be such a reason or cause, it must be either in the nature itself of God or must lie outside it, that is to say, in another substance of another nature. For if the reason lay in a substance of the same nature, the existence of God would be by this very fact admitted. But substance possessing another nature could have nothing in common with God, and therefore could not give Him existence nor negate it. Since, therefore, the reason or cause which could negate the divine existence cannot be outside the divine nature, it will necessarily, supposing that the divine nature does not exist, be in His nature itself, which would therefore involve a contradiction. But to affirm this of the Being absolutely infinite and consummately perfect is absurd. Therefore neither in God nor outside God is there any cause or reason which can negate His existence, and therefore God necessarily exists....

The Corporeality of God

There are those who imagine God to be like a man, composed of body and soul and subject to passions; but it is clear enough from what has already been demonstrated how far off men who believe this are from the true knowledge of God. But these I dismiss, for all men who have in any way looked into the divine nature deny that God is corporeal. That He cannot be so they conclusively prove by showing that by "body" we understand a certain quantity possessing length, breadth, and depth, limited by some fixed form; and that to attribute these to God, a being absolutely infinite, is the greatest absurdity. But yet at the same time, from other arguments by which they endeavor to confirm their proof, they clearly show that they remove altogether from the divine nature substance itself corporeal or extended, affirming that it was created by God. By what divine power, however, it could have been created they are altogether ignorant, so that it is clear they do not understand what they themselves say....

But I will refute my adversaries' arguments, which, taken altogether, come to this. First, that corporeal substance, in so far as it is substance, consists, as they suppose, of parts, and therefore they deny that it can be infinite, and consequently that it can pertain to God. This they illustrate by many examples, one or two of which I will adduce. If corporeal substance, they say, be infinite, let us conceive it to be divided into two parts; each part, therefore, will be either finite or infinite. If each part be finite, then the infinite is composed of two finite parts, which is absurd. If each part be infinite, there is then an infinite twice as great as another infinite, which is also absurd. Again, if infinite quantity be measured by equal parts of a foot each, it must contain an infinite number of such parts, and similarly if it be measured by equal parts of an inch each; and therefore one infinite number will be twelve times greater than another infinite number. Lastly, if from one point of any infinite quantity it be imagined that two lines, AB, AC, which at first are at a certain and determinate distance from one another, be infinitely extended, it is plain that the distance between B and C will be continually increased, and at length from being determinate will be indeterminable. Since therefore these absurdities follow, as they think, from supposing quantity to be infinite, they conclude that corporeal substance must be finite, and consequently cannot pertain to the essence of God. A second argument is assumed from the absolute perfection of God. For God, they say, since He is a being absolutely perfect, cannot suffer; but corporeal substance, since it is divisible, can suffer: it follows, therefore, that it does not pertain to God's essence.

These are the arguments which I find in authors, by which they endeavor to show that corporeal substance is unworthy of the divine nature, and cannot pertain to it.... If any one will rightly consider the matter, he will see that all these absurdities (supposing that they are all absurdities, a point which I will now take for granted), from which these authors attempt to draw the conclusion that substance extended is finite, do not by any means follow from the supposition that quantity is infinite, but from the supposition that infinite quantity is measurable, and that it is made up of finite parts. Therefore, from the absurdities to which this leads nothing can be concluded, excepting that infinite quantity is not measurable, and that it cannot be composed of finite parts. But this is what we [maintain].

... The shaft therefore which is aimed at us turns against those who cast it. If, therefore, from these absurdities any one should attempt to conclude that substance extended must be finite, he would, forsooth, be in the position of the man who supposes a circle to have the properties of a square, and then concludes that it has no center, such that all the lines drawn from it to the circumference are equal. For corporeal substance, which cannot be conceived except as infinite, one and indivisible, is conceived by those against whom I argue to be composed of finite parts, and to be multiplex and divisible, in order that they may prove it finite. Just in the same way others, after they have imagined a line to consist of points, know how to discover many arguments, by which they show that a line cannot be divided *ad infinitum*; and indeed it is not less absurd to suppose that corporeal substance is composed of bodies or parts than to suppose that a body is composed of surfaces, surfaces of lines, and that lines, finally, are composed of points. Everyone who knows that clear reason is infallible ought to admit this, and especially those who deny that a vacuum can exist. For if corporeal substance could be so divided that its parts could be really distinct, why could not one part be annihilated, the rest remaining, as before, connected with one another? And why must all be so fitted together that there can be no vacuum? For of things which are really distinct the one from the other, one can be and remain in its own position without the other. Since therefore it is supposed that there is no vacuum in Nature (about which I will speak at another time), but that all the parts must be united, so that no vacuum can exist, it follows that they cannot be really separated; that is to say, that corporeal substance, in so far as it is substance, cannot be divided.

If, nevertheless, any one should now ask why there is a natural tendency to consider quantity as capable of division, I reply that quantity is conceived by us in two ways: either abstractly or superficially; that is to say, as we imagine it, or else as substance, in which way it is conceived by the intellect alone. If, therefore, we regard quantity (as we do very often and easily) as it exists in the imagination, we find it to be finite, divisible, and composed of parts; but if we regard it as it exists in the intellect, and conceive it in so far as it is substance, which is very difficult, then, as we have already sufficiently demonstrated, we find it to be infinite, one, and indivisible.

This will be plain enough to all who know how to distinguish between the imagination and the intellect, and more especially if we remember that matter is everywhere the same, and that, except in so far as we regard it as affected in different ways, parts are not distinguished in it; that is to say, they are distinguished with regard to mode, but not with regard to reality. For example, we conceive water as being divided, in so far as it is water, and that its parts are separated from one another; but in so far as it is corporeal substance we cannot thus conceive it, for as such it is neither separated nor divided. Moreover, water, in so far as it is water, is originated and destroyed; but in so far as it is substance, it is neither originated nor destroyed.

By this reasoning I think that I have also answered the second argument, since that too is based upon the assumption that matter, considered as substance, is divisible and composed of parts. And even if what I have urged were not true, I do not know why matter should be unworthy of the divine nature, since outside God no substance can exist from which the divine nature could suffer. All things, I say, are in God, and everything which takes place by the laws alone of the infinite nature of God, and follows (as I shall presently show) from the necessity of His essence. Therefore in no way whatever can it be asserted that God suffers from anything, or that substance extended, even if it be supposed divisible, is unworthy of the divine nature, provided only it be allowed that it is eternal and infinite.... Whatever is, is in God, and nothing can either be or be conceived without God.

The Properties of God

I

From the necessity of the divine nature infinite numbers of things in infinite ways (that is to say, all things which can be conceived by the infinite intellect) must follow.

This proposition must be plain to everyone who considers that from the given definition of anything a number of properties necessarily following from it (that is to say, following from the essence of the thing itself) are inferred by the intellect, and just in proportion as the definition of the thing expresses a greater reality, that is to say, just in proportion as the essence of the thing defined involves a greater reality, will more properties be inferred. But the divine nature possesses absolutely infinite attributes (Def. 6), each one of which expresses infinite essence in its own kind (*in suo genere*), and therefore, from the necessity of the divine nature, infinite numbers of things in infinite ways (that is to say, all things which can be conceived by the infinite intellect) must necessarily follow. Hence it follows that God is the efficient cause of all things which can fall under the infinite intellect. It follows, secondly, that God is cause through Himself, and not through that which is contingent (*per accidens*). It follows, thirdly, that God is absolutely the first cause.

II

We have just shown that from the necessity, or (which is the same thing) from the laws only of the divine nature, infinite numbers of things absolutely follow: and we have demonstrated that nothing can be, nor can be conceived, without

God, but that all things are in God. Therefore, outside Himself, there can be nothing by which He may be determined or compelled to act; and therefore He acts from the laws of His own nature only, and is compelled by no one.

Hence it follows, firstly, that there is no cause, either external to God or within Him, which can excite Him to act except the perfection of His own nature. It follows, secondly, that God alone is a free cause; for God alone exists from the necessity alone of His own nature and acts from the necessity alone of His own nature. Therefore He alone is a free cause.

There are some who think that God is a free cause because He can, as they think, bring about that those things which we have said follow from His nature—that is to say, those things which are in His power—should not be, or should not be produced by Him. But this is simply saying that God could bring about that it should not follow from the nature of a triangle that its three angles should be equal to two right angles, or that from a given cause an effect should not follow, which is absurd. But I shall show farther on, without the help of this proposition, that neither intellect nor will pertain to the nature of God.

I know indeed that there are many who think themselves able to demonstrate that intellect of the highest order and freedom of will both pertain to the nature of God, for they say that they know nothing more perfect which they can attribute to Him than that which is the chief perfection in ourselves. But although they conceive God as actually possessing the highest intellect, they nevertheless do not believe that He can bring about that all those things should exist which are actually in His intellect, for they think that by such a supposition they would destroy His power. If He had created, they say, all things which are in His intellect, He could have created nothing more, and this, they believe, does not accord with God's omnipotence; so then they prefer to consider God as indifferent to all things, and creating nothing except that which He has decreed to create by a certain absolute will. But I think that I have shown with sufficient clearness that from the supreme power of God, or from His infinite nature, infinite things in infinite ways, that is to say, all things, have necessarily flowed, or continually follow by the same necessity, in the same way as it follows from the nature of a triangle, from eternity and to eternity, that its three angles are equal to two right angles. The omnipotence of God has therefore been actual from eternity, and in the same actuality will remain to eternity. In this way the omnipotence of God, in my opinion, is far more firmly established.

My adversaries, indeed (if I may be permitted to speak plainly), seem to deny the omnipotence of God, inasmuch as they are forced to admit that He has in His mind an infinite number of things which might be created, but which, nevertheless, He will never be able to create, for if He were to create all things which He has in His mind, He would, according to them, exhaust His omnipotence and make Himself imperfect. Therefore, in order to make a perfect God, they are compelled to make Him incapable of doing all those things to which His power extends, and anything more absurd than this, or more opposed to God's omnipotence, I do not think can be imagined.

Moreover—to say a word, too, here about the intellect and will which we commonly attribute to God—if intellect and will pertain to His eternal essence, these attributes cannot be understood in the sense in which men generally use them, for the intellect and will which could constitute His essence would have to differ entirely from our intellect and will, and could resemble ours in nothing except in name. There could be no further likeness than that between the celestial constellation of the Dog and the animal which barks. This I will demonstrate as follows: If intellect pertains to the divine nature, it cannot, like our intellect, follow the things which are its object (as many suppose), nor can it be simultaneous in its nature with them, since God is prior to all things in causality; but, on the contrary, the truth and formal essence of things is what it is, because as such it exists objectively in God's intellect. Therefore the intellect of God, in so far as it is conceived to constitute His essence, is in truth the cause of things, both of their essence and of their existence,—a truth which seems to have been understood by those who have maintained that God's intellect, will, and power are one and the same thing.

Since, therefore, God's intellect is the sole cause of things, both of their essence and of their existence (as we have already shown), it must necessarily differ from them with regard both to its essence and existence; for an effect differs from its cause precisely in that which it has from its cause. For example, one man is the cause of the existence but not of the essence of another, for the essence is an eternal truth; and therefore with regard to essence the two men may exactly resemble one another, but with regard to existence they must differ. Consequently if the existence of one should perish, that of the other will not therefore perish; but if the essence of one could be destroyed and become false, the essence of the other would be likewise destroyed. Therefore a thing which is the cause both of the essence and of the existence of any effect must differ from that effect both with regard to its essence and with regard to its existence. But the intellect of God is the cause both of the essence and existence of our intellect; therefore the intellect of God, so far as it is conceived to constitute the divine essence, differs from our intellect both with regard to its essence and its existence, nor can it coincide with our intellect in anything except the name, which is what we essayed to prove. The same demonstration may be applied to the will, as any one may easily see for himself.

III

All things which are, are in God and must be conceived through Him and therefore He is the cause of the things which are in Himself. Moreover, outside God there can be no substance, that is to say (Def. 3), outside Him nothing can exist which is in itself. God, therefore, is the imminent, but not the transitive cause of all things.

The Necessity of All Things

In nature there is nothing contingent, but all things are determined from the necessity of the divine nature to exist and act in a certain manner.... That which has not been thus determined by God cannot determine itself to action. A thing which has been determined by God to any action cannot render itself indeterminate.

... All things have necessarily followed from the given nature of God and from the necessity of His nature have been determined to existence and action in a certain manner. If therefore things could have been of another nature, or could have been determined in another manner to action, so that the order of nature would have been different, the nature of God might then be different to that which it now is, and hence that different nature would necessarily exist, and there might consequently be two or more Gods, which is absurd. Therefore things could be produced by God in no other manner and in no other order than that in which they have been produced.

Since I have thus shown, with greater clearness, than that of noonday light, that in things there is absolutely nothing by virtue of which they can be called contingent, I wish now to explain in a few words what is to be understood by *contingent*, but, firstly, what is to be understood by *necessary* and *impossible*.

A thing is called necessary either in reference to its essence or its cause. For the existence of a thing necessarily follows either from the essence and definition of the thing itself, or from a given efficient cause. In the same way a thing is said to be impossible either because the essence of the thing itself or its definition involves a contradiction, or because no external cause exists determinate to the production of such a thing. But a thing cannot be called contingent unless with reference to a deficiency in our knowledge. For if we do not know that the essence of a thing involves a contradiction, or if we actually know that it involves no contradiction, and nevertheless we can affirm nothing with certainty about its existence because the order of causes is concealed from us, that thing can never appear to us either as necessary or impossible, and therefore we call it either contingent or possible.

From what has gone before it clearly follows that things have been produced by God in the highest degree of perfection, since they have necessarily followed from the existence of a most perfect nature. Nor does this doctrine accuse God of any imperfection, but, on the contrary, His perfection has compelled us to affirm it. Indeed, from its contrary would clearly follow, as I have shown above, that God is not absolutely perfect, since, if things had been produced in any other fashion, another nature would have had to be assigned to Him, different from that which the consideration of the most perfect Being compels us to assign to Him. I do not doubt that many will reject this opinion as ridiculous, nor will they care to apply themselves to its consideration, and this from no other reason than that they have been in the habit of assigning to God another liberty widely different from that absolute will which (Def. 7) we have taught. On the other hand, I do not doubt, if they were willing to study the matter and properly to consider the series of our demonstrations, that they would altogether reject this liberty which they now assign to God, not only as of no value, but as a great obstacle to knowledge. Neither is there any need that I should here repeat those things which are said [above][12].

But for the sake of those who differ from me, I will here show that although it be granted that will pertains to God's essence, it follows nevertheless from His perfection that things could be created in no other mode or order by Him. This it will be easy to show if we first consider that which my opponents themselves admit, that it depends upon the decree and will of God alone that each thing should be what it is, for otherwise God would not be the cause of all things. It is also admitted that all God's decrees were decreed by God Himself from all eternity, for otherwise imperfection and inconstancy would be proved against Him. But since in eternity there is no *when* nor *before* nor *after*, it follows from the perfection of God alone that He neither can decree nor could ever have decreed anything else than that which He has decreed; that is to say, God has not existed before His decrees, and can never exist without them. But it is said that although it be supposed that God had made the nature of things different from that which it is, or that from eternity He had decreed something else about Nature and her order, it would not thence follow that any imperfection exists in God. But if this be said, it must at the same time be allowed that God can change His decrees. For if God had decreed something about Nature and her order other than that which He has decreed—that is to say, if He had willed and conceived something else about Nature—He would necessarily have had an intellect and a will different from those which He now has. And if it be allowed to assign to God another intellect and another will without any change of His essence and of His perfection, what is the reason why He cannot now change His decrees about creation and nevertheless remain equally perfect? For His intellect and will regarding created things and their order remain the same in relationship to His essence and perfection in whatever manner His intellect and will are conceived.

Moreover, all the philosophers whom I have seen admit that there is no such thing as an intellect existing potentially in God, but only an intellect existing actually. But since His intellect and His will are not distinguishable from His essence, as all admit, it follows from this also that if God had had another intellect actually and another will, His essence would have been necessarily different, and hence, as I showed at the beginning, if things had been produced by God in a manner different from that in which they now exist, God's intellect and will, that is to say, His essence (as has been granted), must have been different, which is absurd.

Since, therefore, things could have been produced by God in no other manner or order, this being a truth which follows from His absolute perfection, there is no sound reasoning which can persuade us to believe that God was unwilling to create all things which are in His intellect with the same perfection as that in which they exist in His intellect. But we shall be told that there is no perfection nor imperfection in things, but that that which is in them by reason of which they are perfect or imperfect and are said to be good or evil depends upon the will of God alone, and therefore if God had willed He could have effected that that which is now perfection should have been the extreme of imperfection, and *vice versa*. But what else would this be than openly to affirm that God, who necessarily understands what He wills, is able by His will to understand things in a manner different from that in which He understands them, which, as I have just shown, is a great absurdity? I can therefore turn the argument on my opponents in this way. All things depend upon the power of God. In order that things may be differently constituted, it would be necessary that God's will should be differently constituted; but God's will cannot be other than it is as we have lately most clearly deduced from His perfection. Things therefore cannot be differently constituted.

I confess that this opinion, which subjects all things to a certain indifferent God's will, and affirms that all things depend upon God's good pleasure, is at a less distance from the truth than the opinion of those who affirm that God does everything for the sake of the Good. For these seem to place something outside of God which is independent of Him, to which He looks while He is at work as to a model, or at which He aims as if at a certain mark. This is indeed nothing else than to subject God to fate, the most absurd thing which can be affirmed of Him whom we have shown to be the first and only free cause of the essence of all things as well as of their existence. Therefore it is not worth while that I should waste time in refuting this absurdity.

Before I go any farther, I wish here to explain or rather to recall to recollection, what we mean by *natura naturans* and what by *natura naturata*. For, from what has gone before, I think it is plain that by *natura naturans* we are to understand that which is in itself and is conceived through itself, or those attributes of substance which express eternal and infinite essence, that is to say, God in so far as He is considered as a free cause. But by *natura naturata* I understand everything which follows from the necessity of the nature of God, or of any one of God's attributes, that is to say, all the modes of God's attributes in so far as they are considered as things which are in God, and which without God can neither be nor can be conceived.

... Individual things are nothing but affections or modes of God's attributes, expressing those attributes in a certain and determinate manner.

General Conclusions

I have now explained the nature of God and its properties. I have shown that He necessarily exists; that He is one God; that from the necessity alone of His own nature He is and acts; that He is, and in what way He is, the free cause of all things; that all things are in Him, and so depend upon Him that without Him they can neither be nor can be conceived; and, finally, that all things have been predetermined by Him, not indeed from freedom of will or from absolute good pleasure, but from His absolute nature or infinite power.

Moreover, wherever an opportunity was afforded, I have endeavored to remove prejudices which might hinder the perception of the truth of what I have demonstrated; but because not a few still remain which have been and are now sufficient to prove a very great hindrance to the comprehension of the connection of things in the manner in which I have explained it, I have thought it worth while to call them up to be examined by reason. But all these prejudices which I here undertake to point out depend upon this solely: that it is commonly supposed that all things in Nature, like men, work to some end; and indeed it is thought to be certain that God Himself directs all things to some sure end, for it is said that God has made all things for man, and man that he may worship God.

This, therefore, I will first investigate by inquiring, firstly, why so many rest in this prejudice, and why all are so naturally inclined to embrace it? I shall then show its falsity, and, finally, the manner in which there have arisen from it prejudices concerning *good* and *evil*, *merit* and *sin*, *praise* and *blame*, *order* and *disorder*, *beauty* and *deformity*, and so forth. This, however, is not the place to deduce these things from the nature of the human mind. It will be sufficient if I here take as an axiom that which no one ought to dispute, namely, that man is born ignorant of the causes of things, and that he has a desire, of which he is conscious, to seek that which is profitable to him. From this it follows, firstly, that he thinks himself free because he is conscious of his wishes and appetites, whilst at the same time he is ignorant of the causes by which he is led to wish and desire, not dreaming what they are; and, secondly, it follows that man does everything for an end, namely, for that which is profitable to him, which is what he seeks. Hence it happens that he attempts to discover merely the final causes of that which has happened; and when he has heard them he is satisfied, because there is no longer any cause for further uncertainty. But if he cannot hear from another what these final causes are, nothing remains but to turn to himself and reflect upon the ends which usually determine him to the like actions, and thus by his own mind he necessarily judges that of another.

Moreover, since he discovers, both within and without himself a multitude of means which contribute not a little to the attainment of what is profitable to himself—for example, the eyes, which are useful for seeing, the teeth for mastication, plants and animals for nourishment, the sun for giving light, the sea for feeding fish, etc.—it comes to pass that all natural objects are considered as means for obtaining what is profitable. These too being evidently discovered and not created by man, hence he has a cause for believing that some other person exists, who has prepared them for man's use. For having considered them as means it was impossible to believe that they had created themselves, and so he was obliged to infer from the means which he was in the habit of providing for himself that some ruler or rulers of Nature exist, endowed with human liberty, who have taken care of all things for him, and have made all things for his use. Since he never heard anything about the mind of these rulers, he was compelled to judge of it from his own, and hence he affirmed that the gods direct everything for his advantage, in order that he may be bound to them and hold them in the highest honor. This is the reason why each man has devised for himself, out of his own brain, a different mode of worshiping God, so that God might love him above others, and direct all Nature to the service of his blind cupidity and insatiable avarice.

Thus has this prejudice been turned into a superstition and has driven deep roots into the mind—a prejudice which was the reason why everyone has so eagerly tried to discover and explain the final causes of things. The attempt, however, to show that Nature does nothing in vain (that is to say, nothing which is not profitable to man), seems to end in showing that Nature, the gods, and man are alike mad.

Do but see, I pray, to what all this has led. Amidst so much in Nature that is beneficial, not a few things must have been observed which are injurious, such as storms, earthquakes, diseases, and it was affirmed that these things happened either because the gods were angry because of wrongs which had been inflicted on them by man, or because of sins committed in the method of worshiping them; and although experience daily contradicted this, and showed by an infinity of examples that both the beneficial and the injurious were indiscriminately bestowed on the pious and the impious, the inveterate prejudices on this point have not therefore been abandoned. For it was much easier for a man to place these things aside with others of the use of which he was ignorant, and thus retain his present and inborn state of ignorance, than to destroy the whole superstructure and think out a new one. Hence it was looked upon as indisputable that the judgments of the gods far surpass our comprehension; and this opinion alone would have been sufficient to keep the human race in darkness to all eternity, if mathematics, which does not deal with ends, but with the essences and properties of forms, had not placed before us another rule of truth. In addition to mathematics, other causes also might be assigned, which it is superfluous here to enumerate, tending to make men reflect upon these universal prejudices, and leading them to a true knowledge of things.

I have thus sufficiently explained what I promised in the first place to explain. There will now be no need of many words to show that Nature has set no end before herself, and that all final causes are nothing but human fictions. For I believe that this is sufficiently evident both from the foundations and causes of this prejudice, as well as from all those propositions in which I have shown

125

that all things are begotten by a certain eternal necessity of Nature and in absolute perfection. Thus much, nevertheless, I will add, that this doctrine concerning an end altogether overturns nature. For that which is in truth the cause it considers as the effect, and *vice versa*. Again, that which is first in Nature it puts last; and, finally, that which is supreme and most perfect it makes the most imperfect. For, passing by the first two assertions as self-evident, it is plain that that effect is the most perfect which is immediately produced by God, and in proportion as intermediate causes are necessary for the production of a thing is it imperfect. But if things which are immediately produced by God were made in order that He might obtain the end He had in view, then the last things for the sake of which the first exist, must be the most perfect of all.

Again, this doctrine does away with God's perfection. For if God works to obtain an end, He necessarily seeks something of which he stands in need. And although theologians and metaphysicians distinguish between the end of want and the end of assimilation (*finem indigentiæ et finem assimilationis*), they confess that God has done all things for His own sake, and not for the sake of the things to be created, because before the creation they can assign nothing excepting God for the sake of which God could do anything; and therefore they are necessarily compelled to admit that God stood in need of and desired those things for which He determined to prepare means. This is self-evident. Nor is it here to be overlooked that the adherents of this doctrine, who have found a pleasure in displaying their ingenuity in assigning the ends of things, have introduced a new species of argument, not the *reductio ad impossible*, but the *reductio ad ignorantiam*, to prove their position, which shows that it had no other method of defense left.

For, by way of example, if a stone had fallen from some roof on somebody's head and killed him, they will demonstrate in this manner that the stone has fallen in order to kill the man. For if it did not fall for that purpose by the will of God, how could so many circumstances concur through chance (and a number often simultaneously do concur)? You will answer, perhaps, that the event happened because the wind blew and the man was passing that way. But, they will urge, why did the wind blow at that time, and why did the man pass that way precisely at the same moment? If you again reply that the wind rose then because the sea on the preceding day began to be stormy, the weather hitherto having been calm, and that the man had been invited by a friend, they will urge again—because there is no end of questioning—But why was the sea agitated? why was the man invited at that time? And so they will not cease from asking the causes of causes, until at last you fly to the will of God, the refuge for ignorance.

So, also, when they behold the structure of the human body, they are amazed; and because they are ignorant of the causes of such art, they conclude that the body was made not by mechanical but by a supernatural or divine art, and has been formed in such a way so that the one part may not injure the other. Hence it happens that the man who endeavors to find out the true causes of miracles, and who desires as a wise man to understand Nature, and not to gape at it like a fool, is generally considered and proclaimed to be a heretic and impious by those whom the vulgar worship as the interpreters both of Nature and the gods. For these know that if ignorance be removed, amazed stupidity, the sole ground on which they rely in arguing or in defending their authority, is taken away also. But these things I leave and pass on to that which I determined to do in the third place.

After man has persuaded himself that all things which exist are made for him, he must in everything adjudge that to be of the greatest importance which is most useful to him, and he must esteem that to be of surpassing worth by which he is most beneficially affected. In this way he is compelled to form those notions by which he explains Nature; such, for instance, as *good*, *evil*, *order*, *confusion*, *heat*, *cold*, *beauty*, and *deformity*, etc.; and because he supposes himself to be free, notions like those of *praise* and *blame*, *sin* and *merit*, have arisen. These latter I shall hereafter explain when I have treated of human nature; the former I will here briefly unfold.

It is to be observed that man has given the name *good* to everything which leads to health and the worship of God; on the contrary, everything which does not lead thereto he calls *evil*. But because those who do not understand Nature affirm nothing about things themselves, but only imagine them, and take the imagination to be understanding, they therefore, ignorant of things and their nature, firmly believe an *order* to be in things; for when things are so placed that if they are represented to us through the senses, we can easily imagine them, and consequently easily remember them, we call them well arranged; but if they are not placed so that we can imagine and remember them, we call them badly arranged or *confused*. Moreover, since those things are more especially pleasing to us which we can easily imagine, men therefore prefer order to confusion, as if order were something in Nature apart from our own imagination; and they say that God has created everything in order, and in this manner they ignorantly attribute imagination to God, unless they mean perhaps that God, out of consideration for the human imagination, has disposed things in the manner in which they can most easily be imagined. No hesitation either seems to be caused by the fact that an infinite number of things are discovered which far surpass our imagination, and very many which confound it through its weakness. But enough of this.

The other notions which I have mentioned are nothing but modes in which the imagination is affected in different ways, and nevertheless they are regarded by the ignorant as being specially attributes of things, because, as we have remarked, men consider all things as made for themselves, and call the nature of a thing good, evil, sound, putrid, or corrupt, just as they are affected by it. For example, if the motion by which the nerves are affected by means of objects represented to the eye conduces to well-being, the objects by which it is caused are called *beautiful*; while those exciting a contrary motion are called *deformed*. Those things, too, which stimulate the senses through the nostrils are called sweet-smelling or stinking; those which act through the taste are called sweet or bitter, full-flavored or insipid; those which act through the touch, hard or soft, heavy or light; those, lastly, which act through the ears are said to make a noise, sound, or harmony, the last having caused men to lose their senses to such a degree that they have believed that God even is delighted with it. Indeed, philosophers may be found who have persuaded themselves that the celestial motions beget a harmony.

All these things sufficiently show that everyone judges things by the constitution of his brain, or rather accepts the affections of his imagination in the place of things.[13] It is not, therefore, to be wondered at, as we may observe in passing, that all those controversies which we see have arisen amongst men, so that at last skepticism has been the result. For although human bodies agree in many things, they differ in more, and therefore that which to one person is good will appear to another evil, that which to one is well arranged to another is confused, that which pleases one will displease another, and so on in other cases which I pass by both because we cannot notice them at length here, and because they are within the experience of everyone. For everyone has heard the expressions: So many heads, so many ways of thinking; Everyone is satisfied with his own way of thinking; Differences of brains are not less common than differences of taste;—all which maxims show that men decide upon matters according to the constitution of their brains, and imagine rather than understand things.

If men understood things, they would, as mathematics prove, at least be all alike convinced if they were not all alike attracted. We see, therefore, that all those methods by which the common people are in the habit of explaining Nature are only different sorts of imaginations, and do not reveal the nature of anything in itself, but only the constitution of the imagination; and because they have names as if they were entities existing apart from the imagination, I call them entities not of the reason but of the imagination. All argument therefore, urged against us based upon such notions can be easily refuted.

Many people, for instance, are accustomed to argue thus:—If all things have followed from the necessity of the most perfect nature of God, how is it that so many imperfections have arisen in Nature—corruption, for instance, of things till they stink; deformity, exciting disgust; confusion, evil, crime, etc.? But, as I have just observed, all this is easily answered. For the perfection of things is to be judged by their nature and power alone; nor are they more or less perfect because they delight or offend the human senses, or because they are beneficial or prejudicial to human nature. But to those who ask why God has not created all men in such a manner that they might be controlled by the dictates of reason alone, I give but this answer: Because to Him material was not wanting for the creation of everything, from the highest down to the very lowest grade of perfection; or, to speak more properly, because the laws of His nature were so ample that they sufficed for the production of everything which can be conceived by an infinite intellect, as I have demonstrated.

These are the prejudices which I undertook to notice here. If any others of a similar character remain, they can easily be rectified with a little thought by any one.

FOOTNOTES:

[12] Pp. 132-135.

[13] Beauty, my dear Sir, is not so much a quality of the object beheld, as an effect in him who beholds it. If our sight were longer or shorter, or, if our constitution were different, what now appears beautiful to us would seem misshapen and what we now think misshapen we should regard as beautiful. The most beautiful hand seen through the microscope will appear horrible. Some things are beautiful at a distance, but ugly near; thus things regarded in themselves, and in relation to God, are neither ugly nor beautiful. Therefore, he who says that God has created the world so that it might be beautiful is bound to adopt one of the two alternatives: either that God created the world for the sake of men's pleasure and eyesight, or else that He created men's pleasure and eyesight for the sake of the world. *From a letter to Hugo Boxel* (1674).

SECOND PART

ON MAN

The more things the mind knows, the better it understands its own powers and the order of Nature. The better it understands its own powers, so much the more easily can it direct itself and propose rules to itself. The better, also, it understands the order of Nature, the more easily can it restrain itself from what is useless.

SPINOZA.

CHAPTER IX

THE NATURE AND ORIGIN OF THE HUMAN MIND

Introductory

I pass on now to explain those things which must necessarily follow from the essence of God or the Being eternal and infinite; not indeed to explain all these things, for we have demonstrated that an infinitude of things must follow in an infinite number of ways,—but to consider those things only which may conduct us, as it were, by the hand to a knowledge of the human mind and its highest happiness.

Definitions

I. By body, I understand a mode which expresses in a certain and determinate manner the essence of God in so far as He is considered as the thing extended.

II. I say that to the essence of anything pertains that, which being given, the thing itself is necessarily posited, and being taken away, the thing is necessarily taken; or, in other words, that, without which the thing can neither be nor be conceived, and which in its turn cannot be nor be conceived without the thing.

III. By idea, I understand a conception of the mind which the mind forms because it is a thinking thing.

Explanation.—I use the word conception rather than perception because the name perception seems to indicate that the mind is passive in its relation to the object. But the word conception seems to express the action of the mind.

IV. By adequate idea, I understand an idea which, in so far as it is considered in itself, without reference to the object, has all the properties or internal signs (*denominationes intrinsecas*) of a true idea.

Explanation.—I say internal, so as to exclude that which is external, the agreement, namely, of the idea with its object.

V. Duration is the indefinite continuation of existence.

Explanation.—I call it indefinite because it cannot be determined by the nature itself of the existing thing nor by the efficient cause, which necessarily posits the existence of the thing but does not take it away.

VI. By reality and perfection I understand the same thing.

VII. By individual things I understand things which are finite and which have a determinate existence; and if a number of individuals so unite in one action that they are all simultaneously the cause of one effect, I consider them all, so far, as one individual thing.

Axioms

I. The essence of man does not involve necessary existence; that is to say, the existence as well as the non-existence of this or that man may or may not follow from the order of Nature.

II. Man thinks.

III. Modes of thought, such as love, desire, or the emotions of the mind, by whatever name they may be called, do not exist, unless in the same individual the idea exist of a thing loved, desired, etc. But the idea may exist although no other mode of thinking exist.

IV. We perceive that a certain body is affected in many ways.

V. No individual things are felt or perceived by us excepting bodies and modes of thought.

The Mind of God

Individual thoughts, or this and that thought, are modes which express the nature of God in a certain and determinate manner. God therefore possesses an attribute, the conception of which is involved in all individual thoughts, and through which they are conceived. Thought, therefore, is one of the infinite attributes of God which expresses the eternal and infinite essence of God or, in other words, God is a thinking thing.

This proposition is plain from the fact that we can conceive an infinite thinking Being. For the more things a thinking being can think, the more reality or perfection we conceive it to possess, and therefore the being which can think an infinitude of things in infinite ways is necessarily infinite by his power of thinking. Since, therefore, we can conceive an infinite Being by attending to thought alone, thought is necessarily one of the infinite attributes of God.[14]

God can think an infinitude of things in infinite ways, or (which is the same thing) can form an idea of His essence and of all the things which necessarily follow from it. But everything which is in the power of God is necessary. Therefore in God there necessarily exists the idea of His essence, and of all things which necessarily follow from His essence.

The infinite intellect comprehends nothing but the attributes of God and His modes. But God is one. Therefore the idea of God, from which infinite numbers of things follow in infinite ways, can be one only.

The common people understand by God's power His free will and right over all existing things, which are therefore commonly looked upon as contingent; for they say that God has the power of destroying everything and reducing it to nothing. They very frequently, too, compare God's power with the power of kings. That there is any similarity between the two we have disproved. We have shown that God does everything with that necessity with which He understands Himself; that is to say, as it follows from the necessity of the divine nature that God understands Himself (a truth admitted by all), so by the same necessity it follows that God does an infinitude of things in infinite ways. Moreover, we have shown that the power of God is nothing but the active essence of God, and therefore it is as impossible for us to conceive that God does not act as that He does not exist. If it pleased me to go farther, I could show besides that the power which the common people ascribe to God is not only a human power (which shows that they look upon God as a man, or as being like a man), but that it also involves weakness. But I do not care to talk so much upon the same subject. Again and again I ask the reader to consider and reconsider what is said upon this subject [above].[15] For it is not possible for any one properly to understand the things which I wish to prove unless he takes great care not to confound the power of God with the human power and right of kings.

The Order and Dependence of Ideas in God

The formal Being of ideas is a mode of thought (as is self-evident); that is to say, a mode which expresses in a certain manner the nature of God in so far as He is a thinking thing. It is a mode, therefore, that involves the conception of no other attribute of God, and consequently is the effect of no other attribute except that of thought; therefore the formal Being of ideas recognizes God for its cause in so far only as He is considered as a thinking thing, and not in so far as He is manifested by any other attribute; that is to say, the ideas both of God's attributes and of individual things do not recognize as their efficient cause the objects of the ideas or the things which are perceived, but God Himself in so far as He is a thinking thing.[16]

God's power of thinking is equal to His actual power of acting; that is to say, whatever follows *formally* from the infinite nature of God, follows from the idea of God (idea Dei), in the same order and in the same connection *objectively* in God.

The order and connection of ideas is the same as the order and connection of things.

Before we go any farther, we must here recall to our memory what we have already demonstrated, that everything which can be perceived by the infinite intellect as constituting the essence of substance pertains entirely to the one sole substance only, and consequently that substance thinking and substance extended are one and the same substance, which is now comprehended under this attribute and now under that. Thus, also, a mode of extension and the idea of that mode are one and the same thing expressed in two different ways—a truth which some of the Hebrews appear to have seen as if through a cloud, since they say that God, the intellect of God, and the things which are the objects of that intellect are one and the same thing. For example, the circle existing in nature and the idea that is in God of an existing circle are one and the same thing, which is manifested through different attributes; and, therefore, whether we think of Nature under the attribute of extension, or under the attribute of thought, or under any other attribute whatever, we shall discover one and the same order, or one and the same connection of causes; that is to say, in every case the same sequence of things. Nor have I had any other reason for saying that God is the cause of the idea, for example, of the circle in so far only as He is a thinking thing, and of the circle itself in so far as He is an extended thing, but this, that the formal Being of the idea of a circle can only be perceived through another mode of thought, as its proximate cause, and this again must be perceived through another, and so on *ad infinitum*. So that when things are considered as modes of thought, we must explain the order of the whole of Nature or the connection of causes by the attribute of thought alone, and when things are considered as modes of extension, the order of the whole of Nature must be explained through the attribute of extension alone, and so with other attributes. Therefore God is in truth the cause of things as they are in themselves in so far as He consists of infinite attributes, nor for the present can I explain the matter more clearly.

The Origin of the Human Mind

The human mind is a part of the infinite intellect of God, and therefore, when we say that the human mind perceives this or that thing, we say nothing else than that God has this or that idea; not indeed in so far as He is infinite, but in so far as He is manifested through the nature of the human mind, or in so far as He forms the essence of the human mind; and when we say that God has this or that idea, not merely in so far as He forms the nature of the human mind, but in so far as He has at the same time with the human mind the idea also of another thing, then we say that the human mind perceives the thing partially or inadequately.

... When you ask me my opinion on the question[17] raised concerning our knowledge of the means, whereby each part of Nature agrees with its whole, and the manner in which it is associated with the remaining parts, I presume you are asking for the reasons which induce us to believe that each part of Nature agrees with its whole, and is associated with the remaining parts. For as to the means whereby the parts are really associated, and each part agrees with its whole, I told you in my former letter that I am in ignorance. To answer such a question we should have to know the whole of Nature and its several parts. I will therefore endeavor to show the reason which led me to make the statement; but I will promise that I do not attribute to Nature either beauty or deformity, order or confusion. Only in relation to our imagination can things be called beautiful or deformed, ordered or confused.

By the association of parts, then, I merely mean that the laws or nature of one part adapt themselves to the laws or nature of another part, so as to cause the least possible inconsistency. As to the whole and the parts, I mean that a given number of things are parts of a whole, in so far as the nature of each of them is adapted to the nature of the rest so that they all, as far as possible, agree together. On the other hand, in so far as they do not agree, each of them forms, in our minds, a separate idea, and is to that extent considered as a whole, not as a part. For instance, when the parts of lymph, chyle, etc., combine, according to the proportion of the figure and size of each, so as to evidently unite, and form one fluid, the chyle, lymph, etc., considered under this aspect, are part of the blood; but, in so far as we consider the particles of lymph as differing in figure and size from the particles of chyle, we shall consider each of the two as a whole, not as a part.

Let us imagine, with your permission, a little worm, living in the blood, able to distinguish by sight the particles of blood, lymph, etc., and to reflect on the manner in which each particle, on meeting with another particle, either is repulsed, or communicates a portion of its own motion. This little worm would live in the blood in the same way as we live in a part of the universe, and would consider each particle of blood, not as a part, but as a whole. He would be unable to determine how all the parts are modified by the general nature of blood, and are compelled by it to adapt themselves so as to stand in a fixed relation to one another. For if we imagine that there are no causes external to the blood, which could communicate fresh movements to it, nor any space beyond the blood, nor any bodies whereto the particles of blood could communicate their motion, it is certain that the blood would always remain in the same state, and its particles would undergo no modifications, save those which may be conceived as arising from the relations of motion existing between the lymph, the chyle, etc. The blood would then always have to be considered as a whole, not as a part. But as there exist, as a matter of fact, very many causes which modify, in a given manner, the nature of blood, and are, in turn, modified thereby, it follows that other motions and other relations arise in the blood, springing not from the mutual relations of its parts only, but from the mutual relations between the blood as a whole and external causes. Thus the blood comes to be regarded as a part, not as a whole. So much for the whole and the part.

All natural bodies can and ought to be considered in the same way as we have here considered the blood, for all bodies are surrounded by others, and are mutually determined to exist and operate in a fixed and definite proportion, while the relations between motion and rest in the sum total of them, that is, in the whole universe, remain unchanged. Hence it follows that each body, in so far as it exists as modified in a particular manner, must be considered as a part of the whole universe, as agreeing with the whole, and associated with the remaining parts. As the nature of the universe is not limited, like the nature of blood, but is absolutely infinite, its parts are by this nature of infinite power infinitely modified, and compelled to undergo infinite variations....

You see, therefore, how and why I think that the human body is a part of Nature. As regards the human mind, I believe that it also is a part of Nature; for I maintain that there exists in Nature an infinite power of thinking, which, in so far as it is infinite, contains subjectively the whole of Nature, and its thoughts proceed in the same manner as Nature—that is, in the sphere of ideas. Further, I take the human mind to be identical with this said power, not in so far as it is infinite, and perceives the whole of Nature, but in so far as it is finite, and perceives only the human body. In this manner, I maintain that the human mind is part of an infinite understanding.

The Nature of the Human Mind

The essence of man is formed by certain modes of the attributes of God, that is to say, modes of thought, the idea of all of them being prior by nature to the modes of thought themselves; and if this idea exists, other modes (which also have an idea in nature prior to them) must exist in the same individual likewise. Therefore an idea is the first thing which forms the Being of the human mind. But it is not the idea of a non-existent thing, for then the idea itself could not be said to exist. It will therefore be the idea of something actually existing. Neither will it be the idea of an infinite thing, for an infinite thing must always necessarily exist, and this is absurd. Therefore the first thing which forms the actual Being of the human mind is the idea of an individual thing actually existing.

The knowledge of everything which happens in the object of any idea necessarily exists in God, in so far as He is considered as modified by the idea of that object; that is to say, in so far as He forms the mind of any being. The knowledge, therefore, necessarily exists in God of everything which happens in the object of the idea constituting the human mind; that is to say, it exists in Him in so far as He forms the nature of the human mind; or, whatever happens in the object of the idea constituting the human mind must be perceived by the human mind; in other words, an idea of that thing will necessarily exist in the human mind. That is to say, if the object of the idea constituting the human mind be a body, nothing can happen in that body which is not perceived by the mind.

If the body were not the object of the human mind, the ideas of the modifications of the body would not be in God, in so far as He has formed our mind, but would be in Him in so far as He has formed the mind of another thing; that is to say, the ideas of the modifications of the body would not be in our mind. But we have ideas of the modifications of a body; therefore the object of the idea constituting the human mind is a body, and that, too, actually existing. Again, if there were also any other object of the mind besides a body, since nothing exists from which some effect does not follow, the idea of some effort produced by this object would necessarily exist in our mind. But there is no such idea. Therefore the object of the idea constituting the human mind is a body, or a certain mode of extension actually existing, and nothing else.

Hence it follows that man is composed of mind and body, and that the human body exists as we perceive it.

Hence we see not only that the human mind is united to the body, but also what is to be understood by the union of the mind and body. But no one can understand it adequately or distinctly without knowing adequately beforehand the nature of our body; for those things which we have proved hitherto are altogether general, nor do they refer more to man than to other individuals, all of which are animate, although in different degrees. For of everything there necessarily exists in God an idea of which He is the cause, in the same way as the idea of the human body exists in Him; and therefore everything that we have said of the idea of the human body is necessarily true of the idea of any other thing. We cannot, however, deny that ideas, like objects themselves, differ from one another, and that one is more excellent and contains more reality than another, just as the object of one idea is more excellent and contains more reality than another. Therefore, in order to determine the differences between the human mind and other things and its superiority over them, we must first know, as we have said, the nature of its object, that is to say, the nature of the human body. I am not able to explain it here, nor is such an explanation necessary for what I wish to demonstrate.

This much, nevertheless, I will say generally, that in proportion as one body is better adapted than another to do or suffer many things, in the same proportion will the mind at the same time be better adapted to perceive many things, and the more the actions of a body depend upon itself alone, and the less other bodies co-operate with it in action, the better adapted will the mind be for distinctly understanding. We can thus determine the superiority of one mind to another; we can also see the reason why we have only a very confused knowledge of our body, together with many other things which I shall deduce in what follows.

The Complexity of the Human Mind

The idea which constitutes the formal Being of the human mind is the idea of a body which is composed of a number of individuals composite to a high degree. But an idea of each individual composing the body must necessarily exist in God; therefore the idea of the human body is composed of these several ideas of the component parts. The idea which constitutes the formal Being of the human mind is not simple, but is composed of a number of ideas.

All ways in which anybody is affected follow at the same time from the nature of the affected body, and from the nature of the affecting body; therefore the idea of these modifications necessarily involves the nature of each body, and therefore the idea of each way in which the human body is affected by an external body involves the nature of the human body and of the external body.

Hence it follows, in the first place, that the human mind perceives the nature of many bodies together with that of its own body.

It follows, secondly, that the ideas we have of external bodies indicate the constitution of our own body rather than the nature of external bodies.

Imagination

If the human body be affected in a way which involves the nature of any external body, the human mind will contemplate that external body as actually existing or as present, until the human body be affected by a mode which excludes the existence or presence of the external body.

When external bodies so determine the fluid parts of the human body that they often strike upon the softer parts, the fluid parts change the plane of the soft parts, and thence it happens that the fluid parts are reflected from the new planes in a direction different from that in which they used to be reflected, and that also afterwards when they strike against these new planes by their own spontaneous motion, they are reflected in the same way as when they were impelled towards those planes by external bodies. Consequently those fluid bodies produce a modification in the human body while they keep up this reflex motion similar to that produced by the presence of an external body. The mind, therefore, will think as before, that is to say, it will again contemplate the external body as present. This will happen as often as the fluid parts of the human body strike against those planes by their own spontaneous motion. Therefore, although the external bodies by which the human body was once affected do not exist the mind will perceive them as if they were present so often as this action is repeated in the body.

We see, therefore, how it is possible for us to contemplate things which do not exist as if they were actually present. This may indeed be produced by other causes, but I am satisfied with having here shown one cause through which I could explain it, just as if I had explained it through the true cause. I do not think, however, that I am far from the truth, since no postulate which I have assumed contains anything which is not confirmed by an experience that we cannot mistrust, after we have proved the existence of the human body as we perceive it.

We clearly see, moreover, what is the difference between the idea, for example, of Peter, which constitutes the essence of the mind itself of Peter, and the idea of Peter himself which is in another man; for example, in Paul. For the former directly manifests the essence of the body of Peter himself, nor does it involve existence unless so long as Peter exists; the latter, on the other hand, indicates rather the constitution of the body of Paul than the nature of Peter; and therefore so long as Paul's body exists with that constitution, so long will Paul's mind contemplate Peter as present, although he does not exist. But in order that we may retain the customary phraseology, we will give to those modifications of the human body, the ideas of which represent to us external bodies as if they were present, the name of *images of things*, although they do not actually reproduce the forms of the things. When the mind contemplates bodies in this way, we will say that it imagines. Here I wish it to be observed, in order that I may begin to show what *error* is, that these imaginations of the mind, regarded by themselves, contain no error, and that the mind is not in error because it imagines, but only in so far as it is considered as wanting in an idea which excludes the existence of those things which it imagines as present. For if the mind, when it imagines non-existent things to be present, could at the same time know that those things did not really exist, it would think its power of imagination to be a virtue of its nature and not a defect, especially if this faculty of imagining depended upon its own nature alone, that is to say, if this faculty of the mind were free.

Association of Ideas and Memory

If the human body has at any time been simultaneously affected by two or more bodies, whenever the mind afterwards imagines one of them, it will also remember the others.

We clearly understand by this what memory is. It is nothing else than a certain concatenation of ideas, involving the nature of things which are outside the human body, a concatenation which corresponds in the mind to the order and concatenation of the modifications of the human body. I say, firstly, that it is a concatenation of those ideas only which involve the nature of things which are outside the human body, and not of those ideas which explain the nature of those things, for there are in truth ideas of the modifications of the human body, which involve its nature as well as the nature of external bodies. I say, in the second place, that this concatenation takes place according to the order and concatenation of the modifications of the human body, that I may distinguish it from the concatenation of ideas which takes place according to the order of the intellect, and enables the mind to perceive things through their first causes, and is the same in all men.

Hence we can clearly understand how it is that the mind from the thought of one thing at once turns to the thought of another thing which is not in any way like the first. For example, from the thought of the word *pomum* a Roman immediately turned to the thought of the fruit, which has no resemblance to the articulate sound *pomum*, nor anything in common with it, excepting this, that the body of that man was often affected by the thing and the sound; that is to say, he often heard the word *pomum* when he saw the fruit. In this manner each person will turn from one thought to another according to the manner in which the habit of each has arranged the images of things in the body. The soldier, for instance, if he sees the footsteps of a horse in the sand, will immediately turn from the thought of a horse to the thought of a horseman, and so to the thought of war. The countryman, on the other hand, from the thought of a horse will turn to the thought of his plow, his field, etc.; and thus each person will turn from one thought to this or that thought, according to the manner in which he has been accustomed to connect and bind together the images of things in his mind.

FOOTNOTES:

[14] [Similarly, it can be demonstrated that] extension is an attribute of God, or God is an extended thing.

[15] Chapter Eight.

[16] The formal Being of things which are not modes of thought does not follow from the divine nature because of His prior knowledge of these things, but, just as ideas follow from the attribute of thought, in the same manner and with the same necessity the objects of ideas follow and are concluded from their attributes.

[17] From a letter to Henry Oldenburg (1665).

CHAPTER X

THE NATURE AND EXTENT OF HUMAN KNOWLEDGE

Of Truth

All the ideas which are in God always agree with those things of which they are the ideas. Therefore, all ideas, in so far as they are related to God, are true.

A true idea[18] (for we possess a true idea) is something different from its correlate (*ideatum*); thus a circle is different from the idea of a circle. The idea of a circle is not something having a circumference and a center, as a circle has; nor is the idea of a body that body itself. Now, as it is something different from its correlate, it is capable of being understood through itself; in other words, the idea, in so far as its actual essence (*essentia formalis*) is concerned, may be the subject of another subjective essence. And, again, this second subjective essence will, regarded in itself, be something real and capable of being understood; and so on indefinitely. For instance, the man Peter is something real; the true idea of Peter is the reality of Peter represented subjectively, and is in itself something real, and quite distinct from the actual Peter. Now, as this true idea of Peter is in itself something real, and has its own individual existence, it will also be capable of being understood—that is, of being the subject of another idea which will contain by representation all that the idea of Peter contains actually. And, again, this idea of the idea of Peter has its own individuality, which may become the subject of yet another idea; and so on indefinitely. This everyone may make trial of for himself, by reflecting that he knows what Peter is, and also knows that he knows, and further knows that he knows that he knows, etc. Hence, it is plain that, in order to understand the actual Peter, it is not necessary first to understand the idea of Peter, and still less the idea of the idea of Peter. This is the same as saying that in order to know, there is no need to know that we know, much less to know that we know that we know. This is no more necessary than to know the nature of a circle before knowing the nature of a triangle. But with these ideas the contrary is the case; for in order to know that I know, I must first know. Hence it is clear that certainty is nothing else than the subjective essence of a thing: in other words, the mode in which we perceive an actual reality is certainty. Further, it is also evident that for the certitude of truth no further sign is necessary beyond the possession of a true idea; for, as I have shown, it is not necessary to know that we know that we know....

He who has a true idea knows at the same time that he has a true idea, nor can he doubt the truth of the thing. For no one who has a true idea is ignorant that a true idea involves the highest certitude; to have a true idea signifying just this, to know a thing perfectly or as well as possible. No one, in fact, can doubt this, unless he supposes an idea to be something dumb, like a picture on a tablet, instead of being a mode of thought, that is to say, intelligence itself. Moreover, I ask who can know that he understands a thing unless he first of all understands that thing? that is to say, who can know that he is certain of anything unless he is first of all certain of that thing? Then, again, what can be clearer or more certain than a true idea as the standard of truth? Just as light reveals both itself and the darkness, so truth is the standard of itself and of the false.

Of Falsity

There is nothing positive in ideas which can constitute a form of falsity. But falsity cannot consist in absolute privation (for we say that minds and not bodies err and are mistaken); nor can it consist in absolute ignorance, for to be ignorant and to be in error are different. Falsehood, therefore, consists in the privation of knowledge which is involved by inadequate knowledge of things or by inadequate and confused ideas. For instance, men are deceived because they think themselves free, and the sole reason for thinking so is that they are conscious of their own actions, and ignorant of the causes by which those actions are determined. Their idea of liberty therefore is this—that they know no cause for their own actions; for as to saying that their actions depend upon their will, these are words to which no idea is attached. What the will is, and in what manner it moves the body, everyone is ignorant, for those who pretend otherwise, and devise seats and dwelling-places of the soul, usually excite our laughter or disgust. Just in the same manner, when we look at the sun, we imagine its distance from us to be about 200 feet; the error not consisting solely in the imagination, but arising from our not knowing what the true distance is when we imagine, and what are the causes of our imagination. For although we may afterwards know that the sun is more than 600 diameters of the earth distant from us, we still imagine it near us, since we imagine it to be so near, not because we are ignorant of its true distance, but because a modification of our body involves the essence of the sun, in so far as our body itself is affected by it.

The Origin and Nature of Confused Ideas

The ideas of the modifications of the human body involve the nature both of external bodies and of the human body itself and must involve the nature not only of the human body, but of its parts, for the modifications are ways in which the parts of the human body, and consequently the whole body, are affected. But an adequate knowledge of external bodies and of the parts composing the human body does not exist in God in so far as He is considered as affected by the human mind, but in so far as He is affected by other ideas. These ideas of modifications, therefore, in so far as they are related to the human mind alone, are like conclusions without premises, that is to say, as is self-evident, they are confused ideas.

The idea which forms the nature of the mind is demonstrated in the same way not to be clear and distinct when considered in itself. So also with the idea of the human mind, and the ideas of the ideas of the modifications of the human body, in so far as they are related to the mind alone, as everyone may easily see.

All ideas are in God and in so far as they are related to God are true and adequate. No ideas, therefore, are inadequate or confused unless in so far as they are related to the individual mind of some person. All ideas, therefore, both adequate and inadequate, follow by the same necessity.

The Origin and Nature of Adequate Ideas

Let there be something, A, which is common to all bodies, and which is equally in the part of each body and in the whole. I say that A can only be adequately conceived. For the idea of A will necessarily be adequate in God, both in so far as He has the idea of the human body and in so far as He has the idea of its modifications, which involve the nature of the human body, and partly also the nature of external bodies; that is to say, this idea will necessarily be adequate in God in so far as He constitutes the human mind, or in so far as He has ideas which are in the human mind. The mind, therefore, necessarily perceives A adequately, both in so far as it perceives itself or its own or any external body; nor can A be conceived in any other manner.

Hence it follows that some ideas or notions exist which are common to all men, for all bodies agree in some things, which must be adequately, that is to say, clearly and distinctly, perceived by all.

Hence it follows also that the more things the body has in common with other bodies, the more things will the mind be adapted to perceive.

Those ideas are also adequate which follow in the mind from ideas which are adequate in it. For when we say that an idea follows in the human mind from ideas which are adequate in it, we do but say that in the divine intellect itself an idea exists of which God is the cause, not in so far as He is infinite, nor in so far as He is affected by the ideas of a multitude of individual things, but in so far only as He constitutes the essence of the human mind.

I have thus explained the origin of those notions which are called common, and which are the foundations of our reasoning; but of some axioms or notions other causes exist which it would be advantageous to explain by our method, for we should thus be able to distinguish those notions which are more useful than others, and those which are scarcely of any use; those which are common; those which are clear and distinct only to those persons who do not suffer from prejudice; and, finally, those which are ill-founded. Moreover, it would be manifest whence these notions which are called *second*, and consequently the axioms founded upon them, have taken their origin, and other things, too, would be explained which I have thought about at different times. Since, however, I have set apart this subject for another treatise, and because I do not wish to create disgust with excessive prolixity, I have determined to pass by these matters here.

But not to omit anything which is necessary for us to know, I will briefly give the causes from which terms called *Transcendental*, such as *Being, Thing, Something*, have taken their origin. These terms have arisen because the human body, inasmuch as it is limited, can form distinctly in itself a certain number only of images at once. If this number be exceeded, the images will become confused; and if the number of images which the body is able to form distinctly be greatly exceeded, they will all run one into another. Since this is so, it is clear that in proportion to the number of images which can be formed at the same time in the body will be the number of bodies which the human mind can imagine at the same time. If the images in the body, therefore, are all confused, the mind will confusedly imagine all the bodies without distinguishing the one from the other, and will include them all, as it were, under one attribute, that of being or thing.

The same confusion may also be caused by lack of uniform force in the images and from other analogous causes, which there is no need to discuss here, the consideration of one cause being sufficient for the purpose we have in view. For it all comes to this, that these terms signify ideas in the highest degree confused. It is in this way that those notions have arisen which are called *Universal*, such as, *Man, Horse, Dog*, etc.; that is to say, so many images of men, for instance, are formed in the human body at once, that they exceed the power of the imagination, not entirely, but to such a degree that the mind has no power to imagine the determinate number of men and the small differences of each, such as color and size, etc. It will therefore distinctly imagine that only in which all of them agree in so far as the body is affected by them, for by that the body was chiefly affected, that is to say, by each individual, and this it will express by the name *man*, covering thereby an infinite number of individuals; to imagine a determinate number of individuals being out of its power.

But we must observe that these notions are not formed by all persons in the same way, but that they vary in each case according to the thing by which the body is more frequently affected, and which the mind more easily imagines or recollects. For example, those who have more frequently looked with admiration upon the stature of men, by the name *man* will understand an animal of erect stature, while those who have been in the habit of fixing their thoughts on something else, will form another common image of men, describing man, for instance, as an animal capable of laughter, a biped without feathers, a rational animal, and so on; each person forming universal images of things according to the temperament of his own body. It is not therefore to be wondered at that so many controversies have arisen amongst those philosophers who have endeavored to explain natural objects by the images of things alone.

The Three Kinds of Knowledge

From what has been already said, it clearly appears that we perceive many things and form universal ideas:

1. From individual things, represented by the senses to us in a mutilated and confused manner, and without order to the intellect. These perceptions I have therefore been in the habit of calling knowledge from vague experience.

2. From signs; as, for example, when we hear or read certain words, we recollect things and form certain ideas of them similar to them, through which ideas we imagine things. These two ways of looking at things I shall hereafter call knowledge of the first kind, opinion or imagination.

3. From our possessing common notions and adequate ideas of the properties of things. This I shall call reason and knowledge of the second kind.

Besides these two kinds of knowledge, there is a third, as I shall hereafter show, which we shall call intuitive science. This kind of knowing advances from an adequate idea of the formal essence of certain attributes of God to the adequate knowledge of the essence of things. All this I will explain by one example. Let there be three numbers given through which it is required to discover a fourth which shall be to the third as the second is to the first. A merchant does not hesitate to multiply the second and third together and divide the product by the first, either because he has not yet forgotten the things which he heard without any demonstration from his school-master, or because he has seen the truth of the rule with the more simple numbers, or because from the 19th Prop. in the 7th book of Euclid he understands the common property of all proportionals.

But with the simplest numbers there is no need of all this. If the numbers 1, 2, 3, for instance, be given, everyone can see that the fourth proportional is 6 much more clearly than by any demonstration, because from the ratio in which we see by one intuition that the first stands to the second we conclude the fourth.

To knowledge of the first kind we have said that all those ideas belong which are inadequate and confused, and, therefore, this knowledge alone is the cause of falsity. Moreover, to knowledge of the second and third kind we have said that those ideas belong which are adequate, and therefore this knowledge is necessarily true.

It is the knowledge of the second and third, and not that of the first kind, which teaches us to distinguish the true from the false. For he who knows how to distinguish between the true and the false must have an adequate idea of the true and the false, that is to say, he must know the true and the false by the second or third kind of knowledge.

Reason and Imagination

It is in the nature of reason to perceive things truly, that is to say, as they are in themselves, that is to say, not as contingent but as necessary.

Hence it follows that it is through the imagination alone that we look upon things as contingent both with reference to the past and the future.

How this happens I will explain in a few words. We have shown above that unless causes occur preventing the present existence of things, the mind always imagines them present before it, even if they do not exist. Again, we have shown that if the human body has once been simultaneously affected by two external bodies, whenever the mind afterwards imagines one it will imme-diately remember the other; that is to say, it will look upon both as present before it, unless causes occur which prevent the present existence of the things. No one doubts, too, that we imagine time because we imagine some bodies to move with a velocity less, or greater than, or equal to that of others.

Let us therefore suppose a boy who yesterday, for the first time, in the morning saw Peter, at midday Paul, in the evening Simeon, and to-day in the morning again sees Peter. It is plain that as soon as he sees the morning light he will imagine the sun passing through the same part of the sky as on the day preced-ing; that is to say, he will imagine the whole day, and at the same time Peter will be connected in his imagination with the morning, Paul with midday, and Simeon with the evening. In the morning, therefore, the existence of Paul and Simeon will be imagined in relation to future time, while in the evening, if the boy should see Simeon, he will refer Peter and Paul to the past, since they will be connected with the past in his imagination. This process will be constant in proportion to the regularity with which he sees Peter, Paul, and Simeon in this order. If it should by some means happen that on some other evening, in the place of Simeon, he should see James, on the following morning he will con-nect in his imagination with the evening at one time Simeon and at another James, but not both together. For he is supposed to have seen one and then the other in the evening, but not both together. His imagination will therefore fluc-tuate, and he will connect with a future evening first one and then the other; that is to say, he will consider neither as certain, but both as a contingency in the future.

This fluctuation of the imagination will take place in the same way if the im-agination is dealing with things which we contemplate in the same way with reference to past or present time, and consequently we imagine things related to time past, present, or future as contingent.

Sub Specie Æternitatis

It is of the nature of reason to consider things as necessary and not as contin-gent. This necessity of things it perceives truly, that is to say, as it is in itself. But this necessity of things is the necessity itself of the eternal nature of God. Therefore it is of the nature of reason to consider things under this form of eternity. Moreover, the foundations of reason are notions which explain those things which are common to all, and these things explain the essence of no individual thing, and must therefore be conceived without any relation to time, but under a certain form of eternity.

The Limits of Human Knowledge

I

The parts composing the human body pertain to the essence of the body itself only in so far as they communicate their motions to one another by some certain method, and not in so far as they can be considered as individuals without relation to the human body. For the parts of the human body are individuals, composite to a high degree, parts of which can be separated from the human body and communicate their motions to other bodies in another way, although the nature and form of the human body itself is closely preserved. Therefore the idea or knowledge of each part will be in God in so far as He is considered as affected by another idea of an individual thing, which individual thing is prior to the part itself in the order of Nature. The same thing may be said of each part of the individual itself composing the human body, and therefore the knowledge of each part composing the human body exists in God in so far as He is affected by a number of ideas of things, and not in so far as He has the idea of the human body only; that is to say, the idea which constitutes the nature of the human mind; and therefore the human mind does not involve an adequate knowledge of the parts composing the human body.

We have shown that the idea of a modification of the human body involves the nature of an external body so far as the external body determines the human body in some certain manner. But in so far as the external body is an individual which is not related to the human body, its idea or knowledge is in God, in so far as He is considered as affected by the idea of another thing, which idea is prior by nature to the external body itself. Therefore the adequate knowledge of an external body is not in God in so far as He has the idea of the modification of the human body, or, in other words, the idea of the modification of the human body does not involve an adequate knowledge of an external body.

When the human mind through the ideas of the modifications of its body contemplates external bodies, we say that it then imagines, nor can the mind in any other way imagine external bodies as actually existing. Therefore in so far as the mind imagines external bodies it does not possess an adequate knowledge of them.

II

The idea of a modification of the human body does not involve an adequate knowledge of the body itself, or, in other words, does not adequately express its nature, that is to say, it does not correspond adequately with the nature of the human mind, and therefore the idea of this idea does not adequately express the nature of the human mind, nor involve an adequate knowledge of it.

From this it is evident that the human mind, when it perceives things in the common order of Nature, has no adequate knowledge of itself nor of its own body, nor of external bodies, but only a confused and mutilated knowledge; for the mind does not know itself unless in so far as it perceives the ideas of the modifications of the body. Moreover, it does not perceive its body unless through those same ideas of the modifications by means of which alone it perceives external bodies. Therefore in so far as it possesses these ideas it possesses an adequate knowledge neither of itself, nor of its body, nor of external bodies, but merely a mutilated and confused knowledge.

I say expressly that the mind has no adequate knowledge of itself, nor of its body, nor of external bodies, but only a confused knowledge, as often as it perceives things in the common order of Nature, that is to say, as often as it is determined to the contemplation of this or that *externally*—namely, by a chance coincidence, and not as often as it is determined *internally*—for the reason that it contemplates several things at once, and is determined to understand in what they differ, agree, or oppose one another; for whenever it is internally disposed in this or in any other way, it then contemplates things clearly and distinctly.

III

The duration of our body does not depend upon its essence, nor upon the absolute nature of God, but the body is determined to existence and action by causes which also are determined by others to existence and action in a certain and determinate manner, whilst these, again, are determined by others, and so on *ad infinitum*. The duration, therefore, of our body depends upon the common order of Nature and the constitution of things. But an adequate knowledge of the way in which things are constituted, exists in God in so far as He possesses the ideas of all things, and not in so far as He possesses only the idea of the human body. Therefore the knowledge of the duration of our body is altogether inadequate in God, in so far as He is only considered as constituting the nature of the human mind, that is to say, this knowledge in our mind is altogether inadequate.

Each individual thing, like the human body, must be determined to existence and action by another individual thing in a certain and determinate manner, and this again by another, and so on *ad infinitum*. But we have demonstrated in the preceding proposition, from this common property of individual things, that we have but a very inadequate knowledge of the duration of our own body; therefore the same conclusion is to be drawn about the duration of individual things, that is to say, that we can have but a very inadequate knowledge of it.

Hence it follows that all individual things are contingent and corruptible, for we can have no adequate knowledge concerning their duration and this is what is to be understood by us as their contingency and capability of corruption; for there is no other contingency but this.

The Mind's Knowledge of God

The idea of an individual thing actually existing necessarily involves both the essence and existence of the thing itself. But individual things cannot be conceived without God, and since God is their cause in so far as He is considered under that attribute of which they are modes, their ideas must necessarily involve the conception of that attribute, or, in other words, must involve the eternal and infinite essence of God.

By existence is to be understood here not duration, that is, existence considered in the abstract, as if it were a certain kind of quantity, but I speak of the nature itself of the existence which is assigned to individual things, because from the eternal necessity of the nature of God infinite numbers of things follow in infinite ways. I repeat, that I speak of the existence itself of individual things in so far as they are in God. For although each individual thing is determined by another individual thing to existence in a certain way, the force nevertheless by which each thing perseveres in its existence follows from the eternal necessity of the nature of God.

The demonstration of the preceding proposition is universal, and whether a thing be considered as a part or as a whole, its idea, whether it be of a part or whole, will involve the eternal and infinite essence of God. Therefore that which gives a knowledge of the eternal and infinite essence of God is common to all, and is equally in the part and in the whole. This knowledge therefore will be adequate.

The human mind possesses ideas by which it perceives itself and its own body, together with external bodies, as actually existing. Therefore it possesses an adequate knowledge of the eternal and infinite essence of God.

Hence we see that the infinite essence and the eternity of God are known to all; and since all things are in God and are conceived through Him, it follows that we can deduce from this knowledge many things which we can know adequately, and that we can thus form that third sort of knowledge. The reason why we do not possess a knowledge of God as distinct as that which we have of common notions is, that we cannot imagine God as we can bodies; and because we have attached the name God to the images of things which we are in the habit of seeing, an error we can hardly avoid, inasmuch as we are continually affected by external bodies.

Many errors, of a truth, consist merely in the application of the wrong names to things. For if a man says that the lines which are drawn from the center of the circle to the circumference are not equal, he understands by the circle, at all events for the time, something else than mathematicians understand by it. So when men make errors in calculation, the numbers which are in their minds are not those which are upon the paper. As far as their mind is concerned there is no error, although it seems as if there were, because we think that the numbers in their minds are those which are upon the paper. If we did not think so, we should not believe them to be in error. For example, when I lately heard a man complaining that his court had flown into one of his neighbor's fowls, I understood what he meant, and therefore did not imagine him to be in error. This is the source from which so many controversies arise—that men either do not properly explain their own thoughts, or do not properly interpret those of other people; for, in truth, when they most contradict one another, they either think the same things or something different, so that those things which they suppose to be errors and absurdities in another person are not so.

FOOTNOTES:

[18] From the *Improvement of the Understanding*, §§ 33-35.

CHAPTER XI

DETERMINISM AND MORALS

The Mind Is Necessarily Determined

The mind is a certain and determinate mode of thought, and therefore it cannot be the free cause of its own actions, or have an absolute faculty of willing or not willing, but must be determined to this or that volition by a cause which is also determined by another cause, and this again by another, and so on *ad infinitum.*

In the same manner it is demonstrated that in the mind there exists no absolute faculty of understanding, desiring, loving, etc. These and the like faculties, therefore, are either altogether fictitious, or else are nothing but metaphysical or universal entities, which we are in the habit of forming from individual cases. The intellect and will, therefore, are related to this or that idea or volition as rockiness is related to this or that rock, or as man is related to Peter or Paul. The reason why men imagine themselves to be free we have already explained.

Faculty Psychology Fallacious

Before, however, I advance any further, I must observe that by the will I understand a faculty of affirming or denying, but not a desire; a faculty, I say, by which the mind affirms or denies that which is true or false, and not a desire by which the mind seeks a thing or turns away from it. But now that we have demonstrated that these faculties are universal notions which are not distinguishable from the individual notions from which they are formed, we must now inquire whether the volitions themselves are anything more than the ideas of things. We must inquire, I say, whether in the mind there exists any other affirmation or negation than that which the idea involves in so far as it is an idea. For this purpose see the following, so that thought may not fall into pictures. For by ideas I do not understand the images which are formed at the back of the eye, or, if you please, in the middle of the brain, but rather the conceptions of thought.

In the mind there exists no absolute faculty of willing or not willing. Only individual volitions exist, that is to say, this and that affirmation and this and that negation. Let us conceive, therefore, any individual volition, that is, any mode of thought, by which the mind affirms that the three angles of a triangle are equal to two right angles. This affirmation involves the conception or idea of the triangle, that is to say, without it the affirmation cannot be conceived. For to say that *A* must involve the conception *B*, is the same as saying that *A* cannot be conceived without *B*. Moreover, without the idea of the triangle this affirmation cannot be, and it can therefore neither be nor be conceived without that idea. But this idea of the triangle must involve this same affirmation that its three angles are equal to two right angles. Therefore also, *vice versa*, this idea of the triangle without this affirmation can neither be nor be conceived. Therefore this affirmation pertains to the essence of the idea of the triangle, nor is it anything else besides this. Whatever too we have said of this volition (since it has been taken arbitrarily) applies to all other volitions, that is to say, they are nothing but ideas.

The will and the intellect are nothing but the individual volitions and ideas themselves. But the individual volition and idea are one and the same. Therefore the will and the intellect are one and the same.

False Doctrines about Error Exposed

I have thus removed what is commonly thought to be the cause of error. It has been proved above that falsity consists solely in the privation which mutilated and confused ideas involve. A false idea, therefore, in so far as it is false, does not involve certitude. Consequently, when we say that a man assents to what is false and does not doubt it, we do not say that he is certain, but merely that he does not doubt, that is to say, that he assents to what is false, because there are no causes sufficient to make his imagination waver. Although, therefore, a man may be supposed to adhere to what is false, we shall never on that account say that he is certain. For by certitude we understand something positive, and not the privation of doubt; but by the privation of certitude we understand falsity.

If the preceding proposition, however, is to be more clearly comprehended, a word or two must be added; it yet remains also that I should answer the objections which may be brought against our doctrine, and finally, in order to remove all scruples, I have thought it worth while to indicate some of its advantages. I say some, as the principal advantages will be better understood later.

I begin, therefore, with the first, and I warn my readers carefully to distinguish between an idea or conception of the mind and the images of things formed by our imagination. Secondly, it is necessary that we should distinguish between ideas and the words by which things are signified. For it is because these three things, images, words, and ideas, are by many people either altogether confounded or not distinguished with sufficient accuracy and care that such ignorance exists about this doctrine of the will, so necessary to be known both for the purposes of speculation and for the wise government of life. Those who think that ideas consist of images, which are formed in us by meeting with external bodies, persuade themselves that those ideas of things of which we can form no similar image are not ideas, but mere fancies constructed by the free power of the will. They look upon ideas, therefore, as dumb pictures on a tablet, and being prepossessed with this prejudice, they do not see that an idea, in so far as it is an idea, involves affirmation or negation. Again, those who confound words with the idea, or with the affirmation itself which the idea involves, think that they can will contrary to their perception, because they affirm or deny something in words alone contrary to their perception. It will be easy for us, however, to divest ourselves of these prejudices if we attend to the nature of thought, which in no way involves the conception of extension, and by doing this we clearly see that an idea, since it is a mode of thought, is not an image of anything, nor does it consist of words. For the essence of words and images is formed of bodily motions alone, which involve in no way whatever the conception of thought.

Let thus much suffice under this head. I pass on now to the objections to which I have already alluded.

Freedom of the Will

The first is, that it is supposed to be certain that the will extends itself more widely than the intellect, and is therefore different from it. The reason why men suppose that the will extends itself more widely than the intellect is because they say they have discovered that they do not need a larger faculty of assent—that is to say, of affirmation—and denial than that which they now have for the purpose of assenting to an infinite number of other things which we do not perceive, but that they do need a greater faculty for understanding them. The will, therefore, is distinguished from the intellect, the latter being finite, the former infinite. The second objection which can be made is that there is nothing which experience seems to teach more clearly than the possibility of suspending our judgment, so as not to assent to the things we perceive; and we are strengthened in this opinion because no one is said to be deceived in so far as he perceives a thing, but only in so far as he assents to it or dissents from it. For example, a man who imagines a winged horse does not therefore admit the existence of a winged horse; that is to say, he is not necessarily deceived, unless he grants at the same time that a winged horse exists. Experience, therefore, seems to show nothing more plainly than that the will or faculty of assent is free, and different from the faculty of the intellect.

Thirdly, it may be objected that one affirmation does not seem to contain more reality than another; that is to say, it does not appear that we need a greater power for affirming a thing to be true which is true than for affirming a thing to be true which is false. Nevertheless, we observe that one idea contains more reality or perfection than another, for as some objects are nobler than others, in the same proportion are their ideas more perfect. It appears indisputable, therefore, that there is a difference between the will and the intellect.

Fourthly, it may be objected that if a man does not act from freedom of the will, what would he do if he were in a state of equilibrium, like the ass of Buridanus? Would he not perish from hunger and thirst? and if this be granted, do we not seem to conceive him as a statue of a man or as an ass? If I deny that he would thus perish, he will consequently determine himself and possess the power of going where he likes and doing what he likes.

There may be other objections besides these, but as I am not bound to discuss what everyone may dream, I shall therefore make it my business to answer as briefly as possible those only which I have mentioned.

In reply to the first objection, I grant that the will extends itself more widely than the intellect, if by the intellect we understand only clear and distinct ideas; but I deny that the will extends itself more widely than the perceptions or the faculty of conception; nor, indeed, do I see why the faculty of will should be said to be infinite any more than the faculty of feeling; for as by the same faculty of will we can affirm an infinite number of things (one after the other, for we cannot affirm an infinite number of things at once), so also by the same faculty of feeling we can feel or perceive (one after another) an infinite number of bodies. If it be said that there are an infinite number of things which we cannot perceive, I reply that such things as these we can reach by no thought, and consequently by no faculty of will. But it is said that if God wished us to perceive those things, it would be necessary for Him to give us a larger faculty of perception, but not a larger faculty of will than He has already given us, which is the same thing as saying that if God wished us to understand an infinite number of other beings, it would be necessary for Him to give us a greater intellect, but not a more universal idea of being (in order to embrace that infinite number of beings), than He has given us. For we have shown that the will is a Universal, or the idea by which we explain all individual volitions, that is to say, that which is common to them all. It is not to be wondered at, therefore, that those who believe this common or universal idea of all the volitions to be a faculty should say that it extends itself infinitely beyond the limits of the intellect. For the universal is predicated of one or of many, or of an infinite number of individuals.

The second objection I answer by denying that we have free power of suspending judgment. For when we say that a person suspends judgment, we only say in other words that he sees that he does not perceive the thing adequately. The suspension of the judgment, therefore, is in truth a perception and not free will.

In order that this may be clearly understood, let us take the case of a boy who imagines a horse and perceives nothing else. Since this imagination involves the existence of the horse, and the boy does not perceive anything which negates its existence, he will necessarily contemplate it as present, nor will he be able to doubt its existence although he may not be certain of it. This is a thing which we daily experience in dreams, nor do I believe that there is any one who thinks that he has the free power during dreams of suspending his judgment upon those things which he dreams, and of causing himself not to dream those things which he dreams that he sees; and yet in dreams it nevertheless happens that we suspend our judgment, for we dream that we dream.

I grant, it is true, that no man is deceived in so far as he perceives; that is to say, I grant that mental images considered in themselves involve no error; but I deny that a man in so far as he perceives affirms nothing. For what else is it to perceive a winged horse than to affirm of the horse that it has wings? For if the mind perceived nothing else but this winged horse, it would regard it as present, nor would it have any reason for doubting its existence, nor any power of refusing assent to it, unless the image of the winged horse be joined to an idea which negates its existence, or the mind perceives that the idea of the winged horse which it has is inadequate. In either of the two latter cases it will necessarily deny or doubt the existence of the horse.

With regard to the third objection, what has been said will perhaps be a sufficient answer—namely, that the will is something universal, which is predicated of all ideas, and that it signifies that only which is common to them all, that is to say, affirmation. Its adequate essence, therefore, in so far as it is thus considered in the abstract, must be in every idea, and in this sense only must it be the same in all; but not in so far as it is considered as constituting the essence of an idea, for so far, the individual affirmations differ just as the ideas differ. For example, the affirmation which the idea of a circle involves differs from that which the idea of a triangle involves, just as the idea of a circle differs from the idea of a triangle. Again, I absolutely deny that we need a power of thinking in order to affirm that to be true which is true, equal to that which we need in order to affirm that to be true which is false. For these two affirmations, if we look to the mind, are related to one another as being and non-being, for there is nothing positive in ideas which constitutes a form of falsity.

Here therefore particularly is it to be observed how easily we are deceived when we confuse universals with individuals, and the entities of reason and abstractions with realities.

With regard to the fourth objection, I say that I entirely grant that if a man were placed in such a state of equilibrium he would perish of hunger and thirst, supposing he perceived nothing but hunger and thirst, and the food and drink which were equidistant from him. If you ask me whether such a man would not be thought an ass rather than a man, I reply that I do not know; nor do I know what ought to be thought of a man who hangs himself, or of children, fools, and madmen.

The Independence of Mind and Body

All modes of thought have God for a cause in so far as He is a thinking thing, and not in so far as He is manifested by any other attribute. That which determines the mind to thought, therefore, is a mode of thought and not of extension, that is to say, it is not the body. Again, the motion and rest of the body must be derived from some other body, which has also been determined to motion or rest by another, and, absolutely, whatever arises in the body must arise from God, in so far as He is considered as affected by some mode of extension, and not in so far as He is considered as affected by any mode of thought, that is to say, whatever arises in the body cannot arise from the mind, which is a mode of thought. Therefore, the body cannot determine the mind to thought, neither can the mind determine the body to motion nor rest, nor to anything else, if there be anything else.

This proposition will be better understood from what has been said, that is to say, that the mind and the body are one and the same thing, conceived at one time under the attribute of thought, and at another under that of extension. For this reason, the order or concatenation of things is one, whether nature be conceived under this or under that attribute, and consequently the order of the actions and passions of our body is coincident in Nature with the order of the actions and passions of the mind.

Although these things are so, and no ground for doubting remains, I scarcely believe, nevertheless, that, without a proof derived from experience, men will be induced calmly to weigh what has been said, so firmly are they persuaded that, solely at the bidding of the mind, the body moves or rests, and does a number of things which depend upon the will of the mind alone, and upon the power of thought. For what the body can do no one has hitherto determined, that is to say, experience has taught no one hitherto what the body, without being determined by the mind, can do and what it cannot do from the laws of Nature alone, in so far as Nature is considered merely as corporeal. For no one as yet has understood the structure of the body so accurately as to be able to explain all its functions, not to mention the fact that many things are observed in brutes which far surpass human sagacity, and that sleep-walkers in their sleep do very many things which they dare not do when awake; all this show- ing that the body itself can do many things from the laws of its own nature alone at which the mind belonging to that body is amazed.

Again, nobody knows by what means or by what method the mind moves the body, nor how many degrees of motion it can communicate to the body, nor with what speed it can move the body. So that it follows that when men say that this or that action of the body springs from the mind which has com- manded over the body, they do not know what they say, and they do nothing but confess with pretentious words that they know nothing about the cause of the action, and see nothing in it to wonder at.

But they will say, that whether they know or do not know by what means the mind moves the body, it is nevertheless in their experience that if the mind were not fit for thinking the body would be inert. They say, again, it is in their experience that the mind alone has power both to speak and be silent, and to do many other things which they therefore think to be dependent on a decree of the mind.

But with regard to the first assertion, I ask them if experience does not also teach that if the body be sluggish the mind at the same time is not fit for think- ing? When the body is asleep, the mind slumbers with it, and has not the power to think, as it has when the body is awake. Again, I believe that all have dis- covered that the mind is not always equally fitted for thinking about the same subject, but in proportion to the fitness of the body for this or that image to be excited in it will the mind be better fitted to contemplate this or that object. But my opponents will say, that from the laws of Nature alone, in so far as it is considered to be corporeal merely, it cannot be that the causes of architecture, painting, and things of this sort, which are the results of human art alone, could be deduced, and that the human body, unless it were determined and guided by the mind, would not be able to build a temple. I have already shown, however, that they do not know what the body can do, nor what can be deduced from the consideration of its nature alone, and that they find that many things are done merely by the laws of Nature which they would never have believed to be possible without the direction of the mind, as, for example, those things which sleep-walkers do in their sleep, and at which they themselves are astonished when they wake. I adduce also here the structure itself of the human body, which so greatly surpasses in workmanship all those things which are constructed by human art, not to mention what I have already proved, that an infinitude of things follows from Nature under whatever attribute it may be considered.

With regard to the second point, I should say that human affairs would be much more happily conducted if it were equally in the power of men to be silent and to speak. But experience shows over and over again that there is nothing which men have less power over than the tongue, and that there is nothing which they are less able to do than to govern their appetites, so that many persons believe that we do those things only with freedom which we seek indifferently; as the desire for such things can easily be lessened by the recollection of another thing which we frequently call to mind; it being impossible, on the other hand, to do those things with freedom which we seek with such ardor that the recollection of another thing is unable to mitigate it.

But if, however, we had not found out that we do many things which we afterwards repent, and that when agitated by conflicting emotions we see that which is better and follow that which is worse, nothing would hinder us from believing that we do everything with freedom. Thus the infant believes that it is by free will that it seeks the breast; the angry boy believes that by free will he wishes vengeance; the timid man thinks it is with free will he seeks flight; the drunkard believes that by a free command of his mind he speaks the things which when sober he wishes he had left unsaid. Thus the madman, the chatterer, the boy, and others of the same kind, all believe that they speak by a free command of the mind, whilst, in truth, they have no power to restrain the impulse which they have to speak, so that experience itself, no less than reason, clearly teaches that men believe themselves to be free simply because they are conscious of their own actions, knowing nothing of the causes by which they are determined. It[19] teaches, too, that the decrees of the mind are nothing but the appetites themselves, which differ, therefore, according to the different temper of the body. For every man determines all things from his emotion; those who are agitated by contrary emotions do not know what they want, whilst those who are agitated by no emotion are easily driven hither and thither.

All this plainly shows that the decree of the mind, the appetite, and determination of the body are coincident in Nature, or rather that they are one and the same thing, which, when it is considered under the attribute of thought and manifested by that, is called a decree, and when it is considered under the attribute of extension and is deduced from the laws of motion and rest, is called a determination.

This, however, will be better understood as we go on, for there is another thing which I wish to be observed here—that we cannot by a mental decree do a thing unless we recollect it. We cannot speak a word, for instance, unless we recollect it. But it is not in the free power of the mind either to recollect a thing or to forget it. It is believed, therefore, that the power of the mind extends only thus far—that from a mental decree we can speak or be silent about a thing only when we recollect it. But when we dream that we speak, we believe that we do so from a free decree of the mind; and yet we do not speak, or, if we do, it is the result of a spontaneous motion of the body. We dream, again, that we are concealing things, and that we do this by virtue of a decree of the mind like that by which, when awake, we are silent about things we know. We dream, again, that from a decree of the mind, we do some things which we should not dare to do when awake. And I should like to know, therefore, whether there are two kinds of decrees in the mind—one belonging to dreams and the other free. If this be too great nonsense, we must necessarily grant that this decree of the mind, which is believed to be free, is not distinguishable from the imagination or memory, and is nothing but the affirmation which the idea necessarily involves in so far as it is an idea. These decrees of the mind, therefore, arise in the mind by the same necessity as the ideas of things actually existing. Consequently, those who believe that they speak, or are silent, or do anything else from a free decree of the mind, dream with their eyes open.

The Moral Values of Determinism

I

It remains for me now to show what service to our own lives a knowledge of this doctrine is. This we shall easily understand from the remarks which follow. Notice—

1. It is of service in so far as it teaches us that we do everything by the will of God alone, and that we are partakers of the divine nature in proportion as our actions become more and more perfect and we more and more understand God. This doctrine, therefore, besides giving repose in every way to the soul, has also this advantage, that it teaches us in what our highest happiness or blessedness consists, namely, in the knowledge of God alone, by which we are drawn to do those things only which love and piety persuade. Hence we clearly see how greatly those stray from the true estimation of virtue who expect to be distinguished by God with the highest rewards for virtue and the noblest actions as if for the completest servitude, just as if virtue itself and the service of God were not happiness itself and the highest liberty.

2. It is of service to us in so far as it teaches us how we ought to behave with regard to the things of fortune, or those which are not in our power, that is to say, which do not follow from our own nature; for it teaches us with equal mind to wait for and bear each form of fortune, because we know that all things follow from the eternal decree of God, according to that same necessity by which it follows from the essence of a triangle that its three angles are equal to two right angles.

3. This doctrine contributes to the welfare of our social existence, since it teaches us to hate no one, to despise no one, to mock no one, to be angry with no one, and to envy no one. It teaches everyone, moreover, to be content with his own, and to be helpful to his neighbor, not from any womanish pity, from partiality, or superstition, but by the guidance of reason alone, according to the demand of time and circumstance, as I shall show.

4. This doctrine contributes not a little to the advantage of common society, in so far as it teaches us by what means citizens are to be governed and led; not in order that they may be slaves, but that they may freely do those things which are best.

II

At[21] last I see, what it was that you begged me not to publish. However, as it forms the chief foundation of everything in the treatise[22] which I intend to bring out, I should like briefly to explain here, in what sense I assert that a fatal necessity presides over all things and actions.

God I in no wise subject to fate: I conceive that all things follow with inevitable necessity from the nature of God, in the same way as everyone conceives that it follows from God's nature that God understands Himself. This latter consequence all admit to follow necessarily from the divine nature, yet no one conceives that God is under the compulsion of any fate, but that He understands Himself quite freely, though necessarily.

Further, this inevitable necessity in things does away neither with divine nor human laws. The principles of morality, whether they receive from God Himself the form of laws or institutions, or whether they do not, are still divine and salutary; whether we receive the good, which flows from virtue and the divine love, as from God in the capacity of a judge, or as from the necessity of the divine nature, it will in either case be equally desirable; on the other hand, the evils following from wicked actions and passions are not less to be feared because they are necessary consequences.[23] Lastly, in our actions, whether they be necessary or contingent, we are led by hope and fear.

Men are only without excuse before God, because they are in God's power, as clay is in the hands of the potter, who from the same lump makes vessels, some to honor, some to dishonor.... [24] When I said in my former letter that we are inexcusable, because we are in the power of God, like clay in the hands of the potter, I meant to be understood in the sense that no one can bring a complaint against God for having given him a weak nature, or infirm spirit. A circle might as well complain to God for not being endowed with the properties of a sphere, or a child who is tortured, say, with stone, for not being given a healthy body, as a man of feeble spirit, because God has denied to him fortitude, and the true knowledge and love of the Deity, or because he is endowed with so weak a nature that he cannot check or moderate his desires. For the nature of each thing is only competent to do that which follows necessarily from its given cause.

That every man cannot be brave, and that we can no more command for ourselves a healthy body than a healthy mind, nobody can deny, without giving the lie to experience, as well as to reason. "But," you urge, "if men sin by nature, they are excusable"; but you do not state the conclusion you draw, whether that God cannot be angry with them, or that they are worthy of blessedness—that is, of the knowledge and love of God. If you say the former, I fully admit that God cannot be angry, and that all things are done in accordance with His will; but I deny that all men ought, therefore, to be blessed—men may be excusable, and nevertheless, be without blessedness and afflicted in many ways.[25] A horse is excusable for being a horse and not a man; but, nevertheless, he must needs be a horse and not a man. He who goes mad from the bite of a dog is excusable, yet he is rightly suffocated. Lastly, he who cannot govern his desires, and keep them in check with the fear of the laws, though his weakness may be excusable, yet he cannot enjoy with contentment, the knowledge and love of God, but necessarily perishes.

FOOTNOTES:

[19] ... I say that a thing is free, which exists and acts solely by the necessity of its own nature. Thus also God understands Himself and all things freely, because it follows solely from the necessity of His nature that He should understand all things. You see I do not place freedom in free decision, but in free necessity. However, let us descend to created things, which are all determined by external causes to exist and operate in a given determinate manner. In order that this may be clearly understood, let us conceive a very simple thing. For instance, a stone receives from the impulsion of an external cause a certain quantity of motion, by virtue of which it continues to move after the impulsion given by the external cause has ceased. The permanence of the stone's motion is constrained, not necessary because it must be defined by the impulsion of an external cause. What is true of the stone is true of an individual, however complicated its nature, or varied its functions, inasmuch as every individual thing is necessarily determined by some external cause to exist and operate in a fixed and determinate manner.

Further conceive, I beg, that a stone, while continuing in motion, should be capable of thinking and knowing, that it is endeavoring, as far as it can, to continue to move. Such a stone, being conscious merely of its own endeavor and not at all indifferent, would believe itself to be completely free, and would think that it continued in motion solely because of its own wish. This is that human freedom, which all boast that they possess, and which consists solely in the fact, that men are conscious of their own desire, but are ignorant of the causes whereby that desire has been determined.[20] ...

[20] *From a letter to G. H. Schaller* (1674).

[21] *From a letter to Henry Oldenburg* (Dec., 1675).

[22] The *Ethics.*—ED.

[23] I received on Saturday last your very short letter dated 15th Nov. In it you merely indicated the points in the theological treatise which have given pain to readers, whereas I had hoped to learn from it what were the opinions which militated against the practice of religious virtue.... I make this chief distinction between religion and superstition; the latter is founded on ignorance, the former on knowledge. This, I take it, is the reason why Christians are distin-

guished from the rest of the world, not by faith, nor by charity, nor by the other fruits of the Holy Spirit, but solely by their opinions, inasmuch as they defend their cause, like everyone else, by miracles, that is, by ignorance, which is the source of all malice. Thus they turn a faith, which may be true, into superstition. *From a letter to Henry Oldenburg* (Dec., 1675).

[24] *From a letter to Henry Oldenburg* (Feb. 7, 1676).

[25] A mouse no less than an angel, and sorrow no less than joy depend on God; yet a mouse is not a kind of angel, neither is sorrow a kind of joy. *From a letter to Wm. Blyenbergh* (March 13, 1665).

CHAPTER XII

THE ORIGIN AND NATURE OF THE EMOTIONS

Introductory

Most persons who have written about the emotions and man's conduct of life seem to discuss, not the natural things which follow the common laws of Nature, but things which are outside her. They seem indeed to consider man in Nature as a kingdom within a kingdom. For they believe that man disturbs rather than follows her order; that he has an absolute power over his own actions; and that he is altogether self-determined. They then proceed to attribute the cause of human weakness and changeableness, not to the common power of Nature, but to some vice of human nature, which they therefore bewail, laugh at, mock, or, as is more generally the case, detest; whilst he who knows how to revile most eloquently or subtly the weakness of the mind is looked upon as divine.

It is true that very eminent men have not been wanting, to whose labor and industry we confess ourselves much indebted, who have written many excellent things about the right conduct of life, and who have given to mortals counsels full of prudence. But no one so far as I know has determined the nature and strength of the emotions, and what the mind is able to do towards controlling them. I remember, indeed, that the celebrated Descartes, although he believed that the mind is absolute master over its own actions, tried nevertheless to explain by their first causes human emotions, and at the same time to show the way by which the mind could obtain absolute power over them. But in my opinion he has shown nothing but the acuteness of his great intellect, as I shall make evident in the proper place, for I wish to return to those who prefer to detest and scoff at human affects and actions than understand them.

To such as these it will doubtless seem a marvelous thing for me to endeavor to treat by a geometrical method the vices and follies of men, and to desire by a sure method to demonstrate those things which these people cry out against as being opposed to reason, or as being vanities, absurdities, and monstrosities. The following is my reason for so doing. Nothing happens in Nature which can be attributed to any vice of Nature, for she is always the same and everywhere one. Her virtue is the same, and her power of acting; that is to say, her laws and rules, according to which all things are and are changed from form to form, are everywhere and always the same; so that there must also be one and the same method of understanding the nature of all things whatsoever, that is to say, by the universal laws and rules of Nature. The emotions, therefore, of hatred, anger, envy, considered in themselves, follow from the same necessity and virtue of Nature as other individual things; they have therefore certain causes through which they are to be understood, and certain properties which are just as worthy of being known as the properties of any other thing in the contemplation alone of which we delight. I shall, therefore, pursue the same method in considering the nature and strength of the emotions and the power of the mind over them which I pursued in our previous discussion of God and the mind, and I shall consider human actions and appetites just as if I were considering lines, planes or bodies.

Definitions

I.—I call that an adequate cause whose effect can be clearly and distinctly perceived by means of the cause. I call that an inadequate or partial cause whose effect cannot be understood by means of the cause alone.

II.—I say that we act when anything is done, either within us or without us, of which we are the adequate cause, that is to say (by the preceding Definition), when from our nature anything follows, either within us or without us, which by that nature alone can be clearly and distinctly understood. On the other hand, I say that we suffer when anything is done within us, or when anything follows from our nature, of which we are not the cause excepting partially.

III.—By emotion I understand the modifications of the body, by which the power of acting of the body itself is increased, diminished, helped, or hindered, together with the ideas of these modifications.

If, therefore, we can be the adequate cause of any of these modifications, I understand the emotion to be an action, otherwise it is a passion.

Postulates

1.—The human body can be affected in many ways by which its power of acting is increased or diminished, and also in other ways which make its power of acting neither greater nor less.

2.—The human body is capable of suffering many changes, and, nevertheless, can retain the impressions or traces of objects, and consequently the same images of things.

The Two States of Mind: Active and Passive

In every human mind some ideas are adequate, and others mutilated and confused. But the ideas which in any mind are adequate are adequate in God in so far as He forms the essence of that mind, while those again which are inadequate in the mind are also adequate in God, not in so far as He contains the essence of that mind only, but in so far as He contains the ideas of other things at the same time in Himself. Again, from any given idea some effect must necessarily follow, of which God is the adequate cause, not in so far as He is infinite, but in so far as He is considered as affected with the given idea. But of that effect of which God is the cause, in so far as He is affected by an idea which is adequate in any mind, that same mind is the adequate cause. Our mind, therefore, in so far as it has adequate ideas, necessarily at times acts. Again, if there be anything which necessarily follows from an idea which is adequate in God, not in so far as He contains within Himself the mind of one man only, but also, together with this, the ideas[26] of other things, then the mind of that man is not the adequate cause of that thing, but is only its partial cause, and therefore, in so far as the mind has inadequate ideas, it necessarily at times suffers.

The Basic Endeavor of All Things

Individual things are modes by which the attributes of God are expressed in a certain and determinate manner; that is to say, they are things which express in a certain and determinate manner the power of God, by which He is and acts. A thing, too, has nothing in itself through which it can be destroyed, or which can negate its existence,[27] but, on the contrary, it is opposed to everything which could negate its existence. Therefore, in so far as it can and is in itself, it endeavors to persevere in its own being.

The Three Primary Emotions

I

Desire

The essence of the mind is composed of adequate and inadequate ideas (as we have shown), and therefore both in so far as it has the former and in so far as it has the latter, it endeavors to persevere in its being, and endeavors to persevere in it for an indefinite time. But since the mind, through the ideas of the modifications of the body, is necessarily conscious of itself, it is therefore conscious of its effort.

This effort, when it is related to the mind alone, is called *will*, but when it is related at the same time both to the mind and the body, is called *appetite*, which is therefore nothing but the very essence of man, from the nature of which necessarily follow those things which promote his preservation, and thus he is determined to do those things. Hence there is no difference between appetite and desire, unless in this particular, that desire is generally related to men in so far as they are conscious of their appetites, and it may therefore be defined as appetite of which we are conscious. From what has been said it is plain, therefore, that we neither strive for, wish, seek, nor desire anything because we think it to be good, but, on the contrary, we adjudge a thing to be good because we strive for, wish, seek, or desire it.

II

Joy and Sorrow

If anything increases, diminishes, helps, or limits our body's power of action, the idea of that thing increases, diminishes, helps, or limits our mind's power of thought.

We thus see that the mind can suffer great changes, and can pass now to a greater and now to a lesser perfection; these passions explaining to us the emotions of joy and sorrow. By *joy*, therefore, in what follows, I shall understand the passion by which the mind passes to a greater perfection; by *sorrow*, on the other hand, the passion by which it passes to a less perfection. The emotion of joy, related at the same time both to the mind and the body, I call *pleasurable excitement* (*titillatio*) or *cheerfulness*; that of sorrow I call *pain* or *melancholy*. It is, however, to be observed that pleasurable excitement and pain are related to a man when one of his parts is affected more than the others; cheerfulness and melancholy, on the other hand, when all parts are equally affected. What the nature of desire is I have explained; and besides these three—joy, sorrow, and desire—I know of no other primary emotion, the others springing from these.

Definitions of the Principal Emotions

I.—*Desire* is the essence itself of man in so far as it is conceived as determined to any action by any one of his modifications.

Explanation.—We have said above, that desire is appetite which is self-conscious, and that appetite is the essence itself of man in so far as it is determined to such acts as contribute to his preservation. But I have taken care to remark that in truth I cannot recognize any difference between human appetite and desire. For whether a man be conscious of his appetite or not, it remains one and the same appetite, and so, lest I might appear to be guilty of tautology, I have not explained desire by appetite, but have tried to give such a definition of desire as would include all the efforts of human nature to which we give the name of appetite, desire, will, or impulse. For I might have said that desire is the essence itself of man in so far as it is considered as determined to any action; but from this definition it would not follow that the mind could be conscious of its desire or appetite, and therefore, in order that I might include the cause of this consciousness, it was necessary to add the words, *in so far as it is conceived as determined to any action by any one of his modifications*. For by a modification of the human essence we understand any constitution of that essence, whether it be innate, whether it be conceived through the attribute of thought alone or of extension alone, or whether it be related to both. By the word "desire," therefore, I understand all the efforts, impulses, appetites, and volitions of a man, which vary according to his changing disposition, and not unfrequently are so opposed to one another that he is drawn hither and thither, and knows not whither he ought to turn.

II. *Joy* is man's passage from a less to a greater perfection.

III. *Sorrow* is man's passage from a greater to a less perfection.

Explanation.—I say passage, for joy is not perfection itself. If a man were born with the perfection to which he passes, he would possess it without the emotion of joy; a truth which will appear the more clearly from the emotion of sorrow, which is the opposite to joy. For that sorrow consists in the passage to a less perfection, but not in the less perfection itself, no one can deny, since in so far as a man shares any perfection he cannot be sad. Nor can we say that sorrow consists in the privation of a greater perfection for privation is nothing. But the emotion of sorrow is a reality, and it therefore must be the reality of the passage to a lesser perfection, or the reality by which man's power of acting is diminished or limited. As for the definitions of cheerfulness, pleasurable excitement, melancholy, and grief, I pass these by, because they are related rather to the body than to the mind, and are merely different kinds of joy or of sorrow.

IV. *Astonishment* is the imagination of an object in which the mind remains fixed because this particular imagination has no connection with others.

Explanation.—That which causes the mind from the contemplation of one thing immediately to pass to the thought of another is that the images of these things are connected one with the other, and are so arranged that the one follows the other; a process which cannot be conceived when the image of the thing is new, for the mind will be held in the contemplation of the same object until other causes determine it to think of other things. The imagination, therefore, considered in itself, of a new object is of the same character as other imaginations; and for this reason I do not class astonishment among the emotions, nor do I see any reason why I should do it, since this abstraction of the mind arises from no positive cause by which it is abstracted from other things, but merely from the absence of any cause by which from the contemplation of one thing the mind is determined to think other things. I acknowledge, therefore, only three primitive or primary emotions, those of joy, sorrow, and desire; and the only reason which has induced me to speak of astonishment is, that it has been the custom to give other names to certain emotions derived from the three primitives whenever these emotions are related to objects at which we are astonished. This same reason also induces me to add the definition of contempt.

V. *Contempt* is the imagination of an object which so little touches the mind that the mind is moved by the presence of the object to imagine those qualities which are not in it rather than those which are in it.

The definitions of veneration and scorn I pass by here, because they give a name, so far as I know, to none of the emotions.

VI. *Love* is joy with the accompanying idea of an external cause.

Explanation.—This definition explains with sufficient clearness the essence of love; that which is given by some authors, who define love to be the will of the lover to unite himself to the beloved object, expresses not the essence of love but one of its properties. In as much as these authors have not seen with sufficient clearness what is the essence of love, they could not have a distinct conception of its properties, and consequently their definition has by everybody been thought very obscure. I must observe, however, when I say that it is a property in a lover to will a union with the beloved object, that I do not understand by will a consent or deliberation or a free decree of the mind (for that this is a fiction we have demonstrated above), nor even a desire of the lover to unite himself with the beloved object when it is absent, nor a desire to continue in its presence when it is present, for love can be conceived without either one or the other of these desires; but by will I understand the satisfaction that the beloved object produces in the lover by its presence, by virtue of which the joy of the lover is strengthened, or at any rate supported.

VII. *Hatred* is sorrow with the accompanying idea of an external cause.

Explanation.—What is to be observed here will easily be seen from what has been said in the explanation of the preceding definition.

VIII. *Inclination* (*propensio*) is a joy with the accompanying idea of some object as being accidentally the cause of joy.

IX. *Aversion* is sorrow with the accompanying idea of some object which is accidentally the cause of the sorrow.

X. *Devotion* is love towards an object which astonishes us.

Explanation.—Astonishment arises from the novelty of the object. If, therefore, it should happen that we often imagine the object at which we are astonished, we shall cease to be astonished at it, and hence we see that the emotion of devotion easily degenerates into simple love.

XI. *Derision* is joy arising from the imagination that something we despise is present in an object we hate.

Explanation.—In so far as we despise a thing we hate do we deny its existence, and so far do we rejoice. But inasmuch as we suppose that a man hates what he ridicules, it follows that this joy is not solid.

XII. *Hope* is a joy not constant, arising from the idea of something future or past, about the issue of which we sometimes doubt.

XIII. *Fear* is a sorrow not constant, arising from the idea of something future or past, about the issue of which we sometimes doubt.

Explanation.—From these definitions it follows that there is no hope without fear nor fear without hope, for the person who wavers in hope and doubts concerning the issue of anything is supposed to imagine something which may exclude its existence, and so far, therefore, to be sad, and consequently while he wavers in hope, to fear lest his wishes should not be accomplished. So also the person who fears, that is to say, who doubts whether what he hates will not come to pass, imagines something which excludes the existence of what he hates, and therefore is rejoiced, and consequently so far hopes that it will not happen.

XIV. *Confidence* is joy arising from the idea of a past or future object from which cause for doubting is removed.

XV. *Despair* is sorrow arising from the idea of a past or future object from which cause for doubting is removed.

Explanation.—Confidence, therefore, springs from hope and despair from fear, whenever the reason for doubting the issue is taken away; a case which occurs either because we imagine a thing past or future to be present and contemplate it as present, or because we imagine other things which exclude the existence of those which made us to doubt.

For although we can never be sure about the issue of individual objects, it may nevertheless happen that we do not doubt it. For elsewhere we have shown that it is one thing not to doubt and another to possess certitude, and so it may happen that from the image of an object either past or future we are affected with the same emotion of joy or sorrow as that by which we should be affected from the image of an object present.

XVI. *Gladness* (*gaudium*) is a joy with the accompanying idea of something past, which, unhoped for, has happened.

XVII. *Remorse* is sorrow with the accompanying idea of something past, which, unhoped for, has happened.

XVIII. *Commiseration* is sorrow with the accompanying idea of evil which has happened to someone whom we imagine like ourselves.

Explanation.—Between commiseration and compassion there seems to be no difference, excepting perhaps that commiseration refers rather to an individual emotion and compassion to it as a habit.

XIX. *Favor* is love towards those who have benefited others.

XX. *Indignation* is hatred towards those who have injured others.

Explanation.—I am aware that these names in common bear a different meaning. But my object is not to explain the meaning of words but the nature of things, and to indicate them by words whose customary meaning shall not be altogether opposed to the meaning which I desire to bestow upon them. I consider it sufficient to have said this once for all.

XXI. *Over-estimation* consists in thinking too highly of another person in consequence of our love for him.

XXII. *Contempt* consists in thinking too little of another person in consequence of our hatred for him.

Explanation.—Over-estimation and contempt are therefore respectively effects or properties of love or hatred, and so over-estimation may be defined as love in so far as it affects a man so that he thinks too much of the beloved object; and, on the contrary, contempt may be defined as hatred in so far as it affects a man so that he thinks too little of the object he hates.

XXIII. *Envy* is hatred in so far as it affects a man so that he is sad at the good fortune of another person and is glad when any evil happens to him.

Explanation.—To envy is generally opposed compassion (*misericordia*), which may therefore be defined as follows, notwithstanding the usual signification of the word:—

XXIV. *Compassion* is love in so far as it affects a man so that he is glad at the prosperity of another person and is sad when any evil happens to him.

I pass now to consider other emotions which are attended by the idea of something within us as the cause.

XXV. *Self-satisfaction* is the joy which is produced by contemplating ourselves and our own power of action.

XXVI. *Humility* is the sorrow which is produced by contemplating our impotence or helplessness.

Self-satisfaction is opposed to humility in so far as we understand by the former the joy which arises from contemplating our power of action, but in so far as we understand by it joy attended with the idea of something done, which we believe has been done by a free decree of our mind, it is opposed to repentance, which we may thus define:—

XXVII. *Repentance* is sorrow accompanied with the idea of something done which we believe has been done by a free decree of our mind.

It is not to be wondered at that sorrow should always follow all those actions which are from *custom* called wicked, and that joy should follow those which are called good. But that this is chiefly the effect of education will be evident from what we have before said. Parents, by reprobating what are called bad actions, and frequently blaming their children whenever they commit them, while they persuade them to what are called good actions, and praise their children when they perform them, have caused the emotions of sorrow to connect themselves with the former, and those of joy with the latter. Experience proves this, for custom and religion are not the same everywhere; but, on the contrary, things which are sacred to some are profane to others, and what are honorable with some are disgraceful with others. Education alone, therefore, will determine whether a man will repent of any deed or boast of it.

XXVIII. *Pride* is thinking too much of ourselves, through self-love.

Explanation.—Pride differs, therefore, from over-estimation, inasmuch as the latter is related to an external object, but pride to the man himself who thinks of himself too highly. As over-estimation, therefore, is an effect or property of love, so pride is an effect or property of self-love, and it may therefore be defined as love of ourselves or self-satisfaction, in so far as it affects us so that we think too highly of ourselves.

To this emotion a contrary does not exist, for no one, through hatred of himself, thinks too little of himself; indeed, we may say that no one thinks too little of himself, in so far as he imagines himself unable to do this or that thing. For whatever he imagines that he cannot do, that thing he necessarily imagines, and by his imagination is so disposed that he is actually incapable of doing what he imagines he cannot do. So long, therefore, as he imagines himself unable to do this or that thing, so long is he not determined to do it, and consequently so long it is impossible for him to do it. If, however, we pay attention to what depends upon opinion alone, we shall be able to conceive it possible for a man to think too little of himself, for it may happen that while he sorrowfully contemplates his own weakness he will imagine himself despised by everybody, although nothing could be further from their thoughts than to despise him. A man may also think too little of himself if in the present he denies something of himself in relation to a future time of which he is not sure; for example, when he denies that he can conceive of nothing with certitude, and that he can desire and do nothing which is not wicked and base. We may also say that a man thinks too little of himself when we see that, from an excess of fear or shame, he does not dare to do what others who are his equals dare to do. This emotion, to which I will give the name of despondency, may therefore be opposed to pride; for as self-satisfaction springs from pride, so despondency springs from humility, and it may therefore be defined thus:

XXIX. *Despondency* is thinking too little of ourselves through sorrow.

Explanation.—We are, nevertheless, often in the habit of opposing humility to pride, but only when we attend to their effects rather than to their nature. For we are accustomed to call a man proud who boasts too much, who talks about nothing but his own virtues and other people's vices, who wishes to be preferred to everybody else, and who marches along with that stateliness and pomp which belong to others whose position is far above his. On the other hand, we call a man humble who often blushes, who confesses his own faults and talks about the virtues of others, who yields to everyone, who walks with bended head, and who neglects to adorn himself. These emotions, humility and despondency, are very rare, for human nature, considered in itself, struggles against them as much as it can, and hence those who have the most credit for being abject and humble are generally the most ambitious and envious.

XXX. Self-exaltation is joy with the accompanying idea of some action we have done, which we imagine people praise.

XXXI. *Shame* is sorrow, with the accompanying idea of some action which we imagine people blame.

Explanation.—A difference, however, is here to be observed between shame and modesty. Shame is sorrow which follows a deed of which we are ashamed. Modesty is the dread or fear of shame, which keeps a man from committing any disgraceful act. To modesty is usually opposed impudence, which indeed is not an emotion, as I shall show in the proper place; but the names of emotions, as I have already said, are matters rather of custom than indications of the nature of the emotions. I have thus discharged the task which I set myself of explaining the emotions of joy and sorrow. I will advance now to those which I ascribe to desire.

XXXII. *Regret* is the desire or longing to possess something, the emotion being strengthened by the memory of the object itself, and at the same time being restrained by the memory of other things which exclude the existence of the desired object.

Explanation.—Whenever we recollect a thing, as we have often said, we are thereby necessarily disposed to contemplate it with the same emotion as if it were present before us. But this disposition or effort, while we are awake, is generally restrained by the images of things which exclude the existence of the thing which we recollect. Whenever, therefore, we recollect a thing which affects us with any kind of joy, we thereby endeavor to contemplate it with the same emotion of joy as if it were present,—an attempt which is, however, immediately restrained by the memory of that which excludes the existence of the thing. Regret, therefore, is really a sorrow which is opposed to the joy which arises from the absence of what we hate. But because the name *regret* seems to connect this emotion with desire, I therefore ascribe it to desire.

XXXIII. *Emulation* is the desire which is begotten in us of a thing because we imagine that other persons have the same desire.

Explanation.—He who seeks flight because others seek it, he who fears because he sees others fear, or even he who withdraws his hand and moves his body as if his hand were burning because he sees that another person has burnt his hand, such as these, I say, although they may indeed imitate the emotion of another, are not said to emulate it; not because we have recognized one cause for emulation and another for imitation, but because it has been the custom to call that man only emulous who imitates what we think noble, useful, or pleasant.

XXXIV. *Thankfulness* or *gratitude* is the desire or endeavor of love with which we strive to do good to others who, from a similar emotion of love, have done good to us.

XXXV. *Benevolence* is the desire to do good to those whom we pity.

XXXVI. *Anger* is the desire by which we are impelled, through hatred, to injure those whom we hate.

XXXVII. *Vengeance* is the desire which, springing from mutual hatred, urges us to injure those who, from a similar emotion, have injured us.

XXXVIII. *Cruelty* or *ferocity* is the desire by which a man is impelled to injure any one whom we love or pity.

Explanation.—To cruelty is opposed mercy, which is not a passion, but a power of the mind by which a man restrains anger and vengeance.

XXXIX. *Fear* is the desire of avoiding the greater of two dreaded evils by the less.

XL. *Audacity* is the desire by which we are impelled to do something which is accompanied with a danger which our equals fear to meet.

XLI. A person is said to be *pusillanimous* whose desire is restrained by the fear of a danger which his equals dare to meet.

Explanation.—Pusillanimity, therefore, is nothing but the dread of some evil which most persons do not usually fear, and therefore I do not ascribe it to the emotions of desire. I wished, notwithstanding, to explain it here, because in so far as we attend to desire, pusillanimity is the true opposite of the emotion of audacity.

XLII. *Consternation* is affirmed of the man whose desire of avoiding evil is restrained by astonishment at the evil which he fears.

Explanation.—Consternation is therefore a kind of pusillanimity. But because consternation springs from a double fear, it may be more aptly defined as that dread which holds a man stupefied or vacillating, so that he cannot remove an evil. I say *stupefied*, in so far as we understand his desire of removing the evil to be restrained by his astonishment. I say also *vacillating*, in so far as we conceive the same desire to be restrained by the fear of another evil which equally tortures him, so that he does not know which of the two evils to avoid.

XLIII. *Courtesy* or *moderation* is the desire of doing those things which please men and omitting those which displease them.

XLIV. *Ambition* is the immoderate desire of glory.

Explanation.—Ambition is a desire which increases and strengthens all the emotions, and that is the reason why it can hardly be kept under control. For so long as a man is possessed by any desire, he is necessarily at the same time possessed by this. *Every noble man,* says Cicero, *is led by glory, and even the philosophers who write books about despising glory place their names on the title-page.*

XLV. *Luxuriousness* is the immoderate desire or love of good living.

XLVI. *Drunkenness* is the immoderate desire and love of drinking.

XLVII. *Avarice* is the immoderate desire and love of riches.

XLVIII. *Lust* is the immoderate desire and love of sexual intercourse.

Explanation.—This desire of sexual intercourse is usually called lust, whether it be held within bounds or not. I may add that the five last-mentioned emotions have no contraries, for moderation is a kind of ambition, and I have already observed that temperance, sobriety, and chastity show a power and not a passion of the mind. Even supposing that an avaricious, ambitious, or timid man refrains from an excess of eating, drinking, or sexual intercourse, avarice, ambition, and fear are not therefore the opposites of voluptuousness, drunkenness, or lust. For the avaricious man generally desires to swallow as much meat and drink as he can, provided only it belong to another person. The ambitious man, too, if he hopes he can keep it a secret, will restrain himself in nothing, and if he lives amongst drunkards and libertines, will be more inclined to their vices just because he is ambitious. The timid man, too, does what he does not will; and although, in order to avoid death, he may throw his riches into the sea, he remains avaricious; nor does the lascivious man cease to be lascivious because he is sorry that he cannot gratify his desire. Absolutely, therefore, these emotions have reference not so much to the acts themselves of eating and drinking as to the appetite and love itself. Consequently nothing can be opposed to these emotions but nobility of soul and strength of mind, as we shall see afterwards.

The definitions of jealousy and the other vacillations of the mind I pass over in silence, both because they are compounded of the emotions which we have already defined, and also because many of them have no names,—a fact which shows that, for the purposes of life, it is sufficient to know these combinations generally. Moreover, it follows from the definitions of the emotions which we have explained that, they all arise from desire, joy, or sorrow, or rather that there are none but these three, which pass under names varying as their relations and external signs vary. If, therefore, we attend to these primitive emotions and to what has been said above about the nature of the mind, we shall be able here to define the emotions in so far as they are related to the mind alone.

General definition of the emotions.—Emotion, which is called *animi pathema*, is a confused idea by which the mind affirms of its body, or any part of it, a greater or less power of existence than before; and this increase of power being given, the mind itself is determined to one particular thought rather than to another.

Explanation.—I say, in the first place, that an emotion or passion of the mind *is a confused idea.* For we have shown that the mind suffers only in so far as it has inadequate or confused ideas. I say again, *by which the mind affirms of its body, or any part of it, a greater or less power of existence than before.* For all ideas which we possess of bodies indicate the actual constitution of our body rather than the nature of the external body; but this idea, which constitutes the form of an emotion, must indicate or express the constitution of the body, or of some part of it; which constitution the body or any part of it possesses from the fact that its power of action or force of existence is increased or diminished, helped or limited. But it is to be observed, that when I say *a greater or less power of existence than before*, I do not mean that the mind compares the present with the past constitution of the body, but that the idea which constitutes the form of emotion affirms something of the body which actually involves more or less reality than before. Moreover, since the essence of the mind consists in its affirmation of the actual existence of its body, and since we understand by perfection the essence itself of the thing, it follows that the mind passes to a greater or less perfection when it is able to affirm of its body, or some part of it, something which involves a greater or less reality than before. When, therefore, I have said that the mind's power of thought is increased or diminished, I have wished to be understood as meaning nothing else than that the mind has formed an idea of its body, or some part of its body, which expresses more or less reality than it had hitherto affirmed of the body. For the value of ideas and the actual power of thought are measured by the value of the object. Finally, I added, *which being given, the mind itself is determined to one particular thought rather than to another*, that I might also express the nature of desire in addition to that of joy and sorrow, which is explained by the first part of the definition.

I have now, I think, explained the principal emotions and vacillations of the mind which are compounded of the three primary emotions, desire, joy, and sorrow, and have set them forth through their first causes. From what has been said it is plain that we are disturbed by external causes in a number of ways, and that, like the waves of the sea agitated by contrary winds, we fluctuate in our ignorance of our future and destiny. I have said, however, that I have only explained the principal mental complications, and not all which may exist. For by the same method which we have pursued above it would be easy to show that love unites itself to repentance, scorn, shame, etc.; but I think it has already been made clear to all that the emotions can be combined in so many ways, and that so many variations can arise, that no limits can be assigned to their number. It is sufficient for my purpose to have enumerated only those which are of consequence; the rest, of which I have taken no notice, being more curious than important.

There is one constantly recurring characteristic of love which I have yet to notice, and that is, that while we are enjoying the thing which we desired, the body acquires from that fruition a new disposition by which it is otherwise determined, and the images of other things are excited in it, and the mind begins to imagine and to desire other things. For example, when we imagine anything which usually delights our taste, we desire to enjoy it by eating it. But whilst we enjoy it the stomach becomes full, and the constitution of the body becomes altered. If, therefore, the body being now otherwise disposed, the image of the food, in consequence of its being present, and therefore also the effort or desire to eat it, become more intense, then this new disposition of the body will oppose this effort or desire, and consequently the presence of the food which we desired will become hateful to us, and this hatefulness is what we call loathing or disgust.

As for the external modifications of the body which are observed in the emotions, such as trembling, paleness, sobbing, laughter, and the like, I have neglected to notice them, because they belong to the body alone without any relationship to the mind.

FOOTNOTES:

[26] Hence it follows that the mind is subject to passions in proportion to the number of inadequate ideas which it has, and that it acts in proportion to the number of adequate ideas which it has.

[27] This proposition is self-evident, for the definition of any given thing affirms and does not deny the existence of the thing; that is to say, it posits the essence of the thing and does not negate it. So long, therefore, as we attend only to the thing itself, and not to external causes, we shall discover nothing in it which can destroy it.

CHAPTER XIII

THE PSYCHOLOGY OF THE EMOTIONS

The Association of the Emotions

If the human body has at any time been simultaneously affected by two bodies, whenever the mind afterwards imagines one of them, it will immediately remember the other. But the imaginations of the mind indicate rather the modifications of our body than the nature of external bodies, and therefore if the body, and consequently the mind, has been at any time, simultaneously affected by two emotions, whenever it is afterwards affected by one of them, it will also be affected by the other.

Let the mind be supposed to be affected at the same time by two emotions, its power of action not being increased or diminished by one, while it is increased or diminished by the other. From the preceding proposition it is plain that when the mind is afterwards affected by the first emotion through its true cause, which (by hypothesis) of itself neither increases nor diminishes the mind's power of thinking, it will at the same time be affected by the other emotion, which does increase or diminish that power, that is to say, it will be affected with joy or sorrow; and thus the thing itself will be the cause of joy or of sorrow, not of itself, but accidentally. In the same way it can easily be shown that the same thing may accidentally be the cause of desire.

The fact that we have contemplated a thing with an emotion of joy or sorrow, of which it is not the efficient cause, is a sufficient reason for being able to love or hate it.

We now understand why we love or hate certain things from no cause which is known to us, but merely from sympathy or antipathy, as they say. To this class, too, are to be referred those objects which affect us with joy or sorrow solely because they are somewhat like objects which usually affect us with those emotions. I know indeed that the writers who first introduced the words "Sympathy" and "Antipathy" desired thereby to signify certain hidden qualities of things, but nevertheless I believe that we shall be permitted to understand by those names qualities which are plain and well known.

Anything may be accidentally the cause either of hope or fear. Things which are accidentally the causes either of hope or fear are called good or evil omens. In so far as the omens are the cause of hope and fear are they the cause of joy or of sorrow, and consequently so far do we love them or hate them, and endeavor to use them as means to obtain those things for which we hope, or to remove them as obstacles or causes of fear. Our natural constitution, too, is such that we easily believe the things we hope for, and believe with difficulty those we fear, and we think too much of the former and too little of the latter. Thus have superstitions arisen, by which men are everywhere disquieted. I do not consider it worthwhile to go any further, and to explain here all those vacillations of mind which arise from hope and fear, since it follows from the definition alone of these emotions that hope cannot exist without fear, nor fear without hope.

If we imagine a certain thing to possess something which resembles an object which usually affects the mind with joy or sorrow, although the quality in which the thing resembles the object is not the efficient cause of these emotions, we shall nevertheless, by virtue of the resemblance alone, love or hate the thing.

If we have been affected with joy or sorrow by anyone who belongs to a class or nation different from our own, and if our joy or sorrow is accompanied with the idea of this person as its cause, under the common name of his class or nation, we shall not love or hate him merely, but the whole of the class or nation to which he belongs.

The Imitation and Reciprocation of the Emotions

I

The images of things are modifications of the human body, and the ideas of these modifications represent to us external bodies as if they were present, that is to say, these ideas involve both the nature of our own body and at the same time the present nature of the external body. If, therefore, the nature of the external body be like that of our body, then the idea of the external body which we imagine will involve a modification of our body like that of the external body. Therefore, if we imagine anyone who is like ourselves to be affected by a modification, this imagination will express a modification of our body like that modification, and therefore we shall be modified with a similar modification ourselves, because we imagine something like us to be modified with the same. If, on the other hand, we hate a thing which is like ourselves, we shall so

186

far be modified by a modification contrary and not similar to that with which it is modified.

If we imagine that a person enjoys a thing, that will be a sufficient reason for making us love the thing and desiring to enjoy it. If we imagine that a person enjoys a thing which only one can possess, we do all we can to prevent his possessing it. His enjoyment of the thing is an obstacle to our joy, and we endeavor to bring into existence everything which we imagine conduces to joy, and to remove or destroy everything opposed to it, or which we imagine conduces to sorrow.

We see, therefore, that the nature of man is generally constituted so as to pity those who are in adversity and envy those who are in prosperity, and he envies with a hatred which is the greater in proportion as he loves what he imagines another possesses. We see also that from the same property of human nature from which it follows that men pity one another it also follows that they are envious and ambitious. If we will consult experience, we shall find that she teaches the same doctrine, especially if we consider the first years of our life. For we find that children, because their body is, as it were, continually in equilibrium, laugh and cry merely because they see others do the same; whatever else they see others do they immediately wish to imitate; everything which they think is pleasing to other people they want. And the reason is, as we have said, that the images of things are the modifications themselves of the human body, or the ways in which it is modified by external causes and disposed to this or that action.

II

If we imagine that we are hated by another without having given him any cause for it, we shall hate him in return. If we imagine that we have given just cause for the hatred, we shall then be affected with shame. This, however, rarely happens; we endeavor to affirm everything, both concerning ourselves and concerning the beloved object which we imagine will affect us or the object with joy, and, on the contrary, we endeavor to deny everything that will affect either it or ourselves with sorrow.

This reciprocity of hatred may also arise from the fact that hatred is followed by an attempt to bring evil upon him who is hated. If, therefore, we imagine that we are hated by any one else, we shall imagine him as the cause of some evil or sorrow, and thus we shall be affected with sorrow or apprehension accompanied with the idea of the person who hates us as a cause; that is to say, we shall hate him in return, as we have said above.

If we imagine that the person we love is affected with hatred towards us, we shall be agitated at the same time both with love and hatred. For in so far as we imagine that we are hated are we determined to hate him in return. But (by hypothesis) we love him notwithstanding, and therefore we shall be agitated both by love and hatred.

If we imagine that an evil has been brought upon us through the hatred of some person towards whom we have hitherto been moved by no emotion, we shall immediately endeavor to return that evil upon him.

If we imagine that any one like ourselves is affected with hatred towards an object like ourselves which we love, we shall hate him. If we imagine that we are beloved by a person without having given any cause for the love we shall love him in return.

If we imagine that we have given just cause for love, we shall pride ourselves upon it. This frequently occurs, and we have said that the contrary takes place when we believe that we are hated by another person. This reciprocal love, and consequently this attempt to do good to the person who loves us, and who endeavors to do good to us, is called *thankfulness* or *gratitude*, and from this we can see how much readier men are to revenge themselves than to return a benefit.

If we imagine that we are loved by a person we hate, we shall at the same time be agitated both by love and hatred. If the hatred prevail, we shall endeavor to bring evil upon the person by whom we are loved. This emotion is called Cruelty, especially if it is believed that the person who loves has not given any ordinary reason for hatred.

The "Herd Instinct"

If we imagine men to love or hate a thing, we shall therefore love or hate it; that is to say, we shall therefore rejoice or be sad at the presence of the thing, and therefore we shall endeavor to do everything which we imagine men[28] will look upon with joy, and, on the contrary, we shall be averse to doing anything to which we imagine men are averse.

He who imagines that he affects others with joy or sorrow will necessarily be affected with joy or sorrow. But since man is conscious of himself by means of the emotions by which he is determined to act; therefore if a person has done anything which he imagines will affect others with joy, he also will be affected with joy, accompanied with an idea of himself as its cause; that is to say, he will look upon himself with joy. If, on the other hand, he has done anything which he imagines will affect others with sorrow, he will look upon himself with sorrow.

If we imagine that a person loves, desires, or hates a thing which we ourselves love, desire, or hate, we shall on that account love, desire, or hate the thing more steadily. If, on the other hand, we imagine that he is averse to the thing we love or loves the thing to which we are averse, we shall then suffer vacillation of mind.

It follows from this proposition that everyone endeavors as much as possible to make others love what he loves, and to hate what he hates. Hence the poet says:

Speremus pariter, pariter metuamus amantes;Ferreus est, si quis, quod sinit alter, amat.

This effort to make everyone approve what we love or hate is in truth ambition, and so we see that each person by nature desires that other persons should live according to his way of thinking; but if everyone does this, then all are a hindrance to one another, and if everyone wishes to be praised or beloved by the rest, then they all hate one another.

The Varieties of Emotion

Joy and sorrow, and consequently the emotions which are compounded of these or derived from them, are passions. But we necessarily suffer in so far as we have inadequate ideas, and only in so far as we have them; that is to say, we necessarily suffer only in so far as we imagine, or in so far as we are affected by a modification which involves the nature of our body and that of an external body. The nature, therefore, of each passion must necessarily be explained in such a manner, that the nature of the object by which we are affected is expressed. The joy, for example, which springs from an object A involves the nature of that object A, and the joy which springs from B involves the nature of that object B, and therefore these two emotions of joy are of a different nature, because they arise from causes of a different nature. In like manner the emotion of sorrow which arises from one object is of a different kind from that which arises from another cause, and the same thing is to be understood of love, hatred, hope, fear, vacillation of mind, etc.; so that there are necessarily just as many kinds of joy, sorrow, love, hatred, etc., as there are kinds of objects by which we are affected. But desire is the essence itself or nature of a person in so far as this nature is conceived from its given constitution as determined towards any action, and therefore as a person is affected by external causes with this or that kind of joy, sorrow, love, hatred, etc., that is to say, as his nature is constituted in this or that way, so must his desire vary and the nature of one desire differ from that of another, just as the emotions from which each desire arises differ. There are as many kinds of desires, therefore, as there are kinds of joy, sorrow, love, etc., and, consequently (as we have just shown), as there are kinds of objects by which we are affected.

All emotions are related to desire, joy, or sorrow, as the definitions show which we have given of those emotions. But desire is the very nature or essence of a person and therefore the desire of one person differs from the desire of another as much as the nature or essence of the one differs from that of the other. Again, joy and sorrow are passions by which the power of a person or his effort to persevere in his own being is increased or diminished, helped, or limited. But by the effort to persevere in his own being, in so far as it is related at the same time to the mind and the body, we understand appetite and desire, and therefore joy and sorrow are desire or appetite in so far as the latter is increased, diminished, helped, or limited by external causes; that is to say they are the nature itself of each person.

The joy or sorrow of one person therefore differs from the joy or sorrow of another as much as the nature or essence of one person differs from that of the other, and consequently the emotion of one person differs from the corresponding emotion of another.

Hence it follows that the emotions of animals which are called irrational (for after we have learned the origin of the mind we can in no way doubt that brutes feel) differ from human emotions as much as the nature of a brute differs from that of a man. Both the man and the horse, for example, are swayed by the lust to propagate, but the horse is swayed by equine lust and the man by that which is human. The lusts and appetites of insects, fishes, and birds must vary in the same way; and so, although each individual lives contented with its own nature and delights in it, nevertheless the life with which it is contented and its joy are nothing but the idea or soul of that individual, and so the joy of one differs in character from the joy of the other as much as the essence of the one differs from the essence of the other. Finally, it follows from the preceding proposition that the joy by which the drunkard is enslaved is altogether different from the joy which is the portion of the philosopher,—a thing I wished just to hint in passing.

The Inconstancy of the Emotions

The human body is affected by external bodies in a number of ways. Two men, therefore, may be affected in different ways at the same time, and therefore they can be affected by one and the same object in different ways. Again the human body may be affected now in this and now in that way, and consequently it may be affected by one and the same object in different ways at different times.

We thus see that it is possible for one man to love a thing and for another man to hate it; for this man to fear what this man does not fear, and for the same man to love what before he hated, and to dare to do what before he feared. Again, since each judges according to his own emotion what is good and what is evil, what is better and what is worse, it follows that men may change in their judgment as they do in their emotions, and hence it comes to pass that when we compare men, we distinguish them solely by the difference in their emotions, calling some brave, others timid, and others by other names.

For example, I shall call a man *brave* who despises an evil which I usually fear, and if, besides this, I consider the fact that his desire of doing evil to a person whom he hates or doing good to one whom he loves is not restrained by that fear of evil by which I am usually restrained, I call him *audacious*. On the other hand, the man who fears an evil which I usually despise will appear *timid*, and if, besides this, I consider that his desire is restrained by the fear of an evil which has no power to restrain me, I call him *pusillanimous*; and in this way everybody will pass judgment.

Finally, from this nature of man and the inconstancy of his judgment, in consequence of which he often judges things from mere emotion, and the things which he believes contribute to his joy or his sorrow, and which, therefore, he endeavors to bring to pass or remove, are often only imaginary—to say nothing about the uncertainty of things—it is easy to see that a man may often be himself the cause of his sorrow or his joy, or of being affected with sorrow or joy accompanied with the idea of himself as its cause, so that we can easily understand what repentance and what self-approval are.

Love and hatred towards any object, for example, towards Peter, are destroyed if the joy and the sorrow which they respectively involve be joined to the idea of another cause; and they are respectively diminished in proportion as we imagine that Peter has not been their sole cause.

For the same reason, love or hatred towards an object we imagine to be free must be greater than towards an object which is under necessity.

An object which we imagine to be free must be perceived through itself and without others. If, therefore, we imagine it to be the cause of joy or sorrow, we shall for that reason alone love or hate it, and that too with the greatest love or the greatest hatred which can spring from the given emotion. But if we imagine that the object which is the cause of that emotion is necessary, then we shall imagine it as the cause of that emotion, not alone, but together with other causes, and so our love or hatred towards it will be less.

Hence it follows that our hatred or love towards one another is greater than towards other things, because we think we are free.

The Power of Love Over Hate

If we imagine that the person we hate is affected with hatred towards us, a new hatred is thereby produced, the old hatred still remaining (by hypothesis). If, on the other hand, we imagine him to be affected with love towards us, in so far as we imagine it shall we look upon ourselves with joy, and endeavor to please him; that is to say, in so far shall we endeavor not to hate him nor to affect him with sorrow. This effort will be greater or less as the emotion from which it arises is greater or less, and, therefore, should it be greater than that which springs from hatred, and by which we endeavor to affect with sorrow the object we hate, then it will prevail and banish hatred from the mind. Hatred is increased through return of hatred, but may be destroyed by love.

Hatred which is altogether overcome by love passes into love, and the love is therefore greater than if hatred had not preceded it. For if we begin to love a thing which we hated, or upon which we were in the habit of looking with sorrow, we shall rejoice for the very reason that we love, and to this joy which love involves a new joy is added, which springs from the fact that the effort to remove the sorrow which hatred involves, is so much assisted, there being also present before us as the cause of our joy the idea of the person whom we hated.

Notwithstanding the truth of this proposition, no one will try to hate a thing or will wish to be affected with sorrow in order that he may rejoice the more; that is to say, no one will desire to inflict loss on himself in the hope of recovering the loss, or to become ill in the hope of getting well, inasmuch as everyone will always try to preserve his being and to remove sorrow from himself as much as possible. Moreover, if it can be imagined that it is possible for us to desire to hate a person in order that we may love him afterwards the more, we must always desire to continue the hatred. For the love will be the greater as the hatred has been greater, and therefore we shall always desire the hatred to be more and more increased. Upon the same principle we shall desire that our sickness may continue and increase in order that we may afterwards enjoy the greater pleasure when we get well, and therefore we shall always desire sickness, which is absurd.

FOOTNOTES:

[28] Both here and in what follows to whom we are moved by no emotion I understand by the word *men*, men (Sp.).

THIRD PART

ON MAN'S WELL-BEING

All happiness or unhappiness solely depends upon the quality of the object to which we are attached by love. Love for an object eternal and infinite feeds the mind with joy alone, a joy that is free from all sorrow.

SPINOZA.

CHAPTER XIV

OF HUMAN BONDAGE

Introductory

The impotence of man to govern or restrain the emotions I call bondage, for a man who is under their control is not his own master, but is mastered by fortune, in whose power he is, so that he is often forced to follow the worse, although he sees the better before him. I propose in this part to demonstrate why this is, and also to show what of good and evil the emotions possess.

But before I begin I should like to say a few words about perfection and imperfection, and about good and evil. If a man has proposed to do a thing and has accomplished it, he calls it perfect, and not only he, but everyone else who has really known or has believed that he has known the mind and intention of the author of that work will call it perfect too. For example, having seen some work (which I suppose to be as yet not finished), if we know that the intention of the author of that work is to build a house, we shall call the house imperfect; while, on the other hand, we shall call it perfect as soon as we see the work has been brought to the end which the author had determined for it. But if we see any work such as we have never seen before, and if we do not know the mind of the workman, we shall then not be able to say whether the work is perfect or imperfect.

This seems to have been the first signification of these words; but afterwards men began to form universal ideas, to think out for themselves types of houses, buildings, castles, and to prefer some types of things to others; and so it happened that each person called a thing perfect which seemed to agree with the universal idea which he had formed of that thing, and, on the other hand, he called a thing imperfect which seemed to agree less with his typal conception, although, according to the intention of the workman, it had been entirely completed. This appears to be the only reason why the words *perfect* and *imperfect* are commonly applied to natural objects which are not made with human hands; for men are in the habit of forming, both of natural as well as of artificial objects, universal ideas which they regard as types of things, and which they think Nature has in view, setting them before herself as types too; it being the common opinion that she does nothing except for the sake of some end.

When, therefore, men see something done by Nature which does not altogether answer to that typal conception which they have of the thing, they think that Nature herself has failed or committed an error, and that she has left the thing imperfect.

Thus we see that the custom of applying the words *perfect* and *imperfect* to natural objects has arisen rather from prejudice than from true knowledge of them. For we have shown that Nature does nothing for the sake of an end, for that eternal and infinite Being whom we call God or Nature acts by the same necessity by which He exists; for we have shown that He acts by the same necessity of nature as that by which He exists. The reason or cause, therefore, why God or Nature acts and the reason why He exists are one and the same. Since, therefore, He exists for no end, He acts for no end; and since He has no principle or end of existence, He has no principle or end of action. A final cause, as it is called, is nothing, therefore, but human desire, in so far as this is considered as the principle or primary cause of anything. For example, when we say that the having a house to live in was the final cause of this or that house, we merely mean that a man, because he imagined the advantages of a domestic life, desired to build a house. Therefore, having a house to live in, in so far as it is considered as a final cause, is merely this particular desire, which is really an efficient cause, and is considered as primary, because men are usually ignorant of the causes of their desires; for, as I have often said, we are conscious of our actions and desires, but ignorant of the causes by which we are determined to desire anything. As for the vulgar opinion that Nature sometimes fails or commits an error, or produces imperfect things, I class it amongst those fictions mentioned above.[29]

Perfection, therefore, and imperfection are really only modes of thought; that is to say, notions which we are in the habit of forming from the comparison with one another of individuals of the same species or genus, and this is the reason why I have said that by reality and perfection I understand the same thing; for we are in the habit of referring all individuals in Nature to one genus, which is called the most general; that is to say, to the notion of being, which embraces absolutely all the individual objects in Nature. In so far, therefore, as we refer the individual objects in Nature to this genus, and compare them one with another, and discover that some possess more being or reality than others, in so far do we call some more perfect than others; and in so far as we assign to the latter anything which, like limitation, termination, impotence, etc., involves negation, shall we call them imperfect, because they do not affect our minds so strongly as those we call perfect, but not because anything which really belongs to them is wanting, or because Nature has committed an error. For nothing belongs to the nature of anything excepting that which follows from the necessity of the nature of the efficient cause, and whatever follows from the necessity of the nature of the efficient cause necessarily happens.

With regard to good and evil, these terms indicate nothing positive in things considered in themselves, nor are they anything else than modes of thought, or notions which we form from the comparison of one thing with another. For one and the same thing may at the same time be both good and evil or indifferent. Music, for example, is good to a melancholy person, bad to one mourning, while to a deaf man it is neither good nor bad. But although things are so, we must retain these words. For since we desire to form for ourselves an idea of man upon which we may look as a model of human nature, it will be of service to us to retain these expressions in the sense I have mentioned.

By *good*, therefore, I understand in the following pages everything which we are certain is a means by which we may approach nearer and nearer to the model of human nature we set before us. By *evil*, on the contrary, I understand everything which we are certain hinders us from reaching that model. Again, I shall call men more or less perfect or imperfect in so far as they approach more or less nearly to this same model. For it is to be carefully observed, that when I say that an individual passes from a less to a greater perfection and *vice versa*, I do not understand that from one essence or form he is changed into another (for a horse, for instance, would be as much destroyed if it were changed into a man as if it were changed into an insect), but rather we conceive that his power of action, in so far as it is understood by his own nature, is increased or diminished. Finally, by perfection generally, I understand, as I have said, reality; that is to say, the essence of any object in so far as it exists and acts in a certain manner, no regard being paid to its duration. For no individual thing can be said to be more perfect because for a longer time it has persevered in existence; inasmuch as the duration of things cannot be determined by their essence, the essence of things involving no fixed or determined period of existence; any object, whether it be more or less perfect, always being able to persevere in existence with the same force as that with which it commenced existence. All things, therefore, are equal in this respect.

Definitions

I.—By good, I understand that which we certainly know is useful to us.

II. By evil, on the contrary, I understand that which we certainly know hinders us from possessing anything that is good.

With regard to these two definitions, see the close of the preceding.

III. I call individual things contingent in so far as we discover nothing, whilst we attend to their essence alone, which necessarily posits their existence or which necessarily excludes it.

IV. I call these individual things possible, in so far as we are ignorant, whilst we attend to the cause from which they must be produced, whether these causes are determined to the production of these things.

V. By contrary emotions, I understand in the following pages those which, although they may be of the same kind, draw a man in different directions; such as voluptuousness and avarice, which are both a species of love, and are not contrary to one another by nature, but only by accident.

VI. I here call a thing past or future in so far as we have been or shall be affected by it; for example, in so far as we have seen a thing or are about to see it, in so far as it has strengthened us or will strengthen us, has injured or will injure us. For in so far as we thus imagine it do we affirm its existence; that is to say, the body is affected by no mode which excludes the existence of the thing, and therefore the body is affected by the image of the thing in the same way as if the thing itself were present. But because it generally happens that those who possess much experience hesitate when they think of a thing as past or future, and doubt greatly concerning its issue, therefore the emotions which spring from such images of things are not so constant, but are generally disturbed by the images of other things, until men become more sure of the issue.

However, it is to be observed that it is the same with time as it is with place; for as beyond a certain limit we can form no distinct imagination of distance—that is to say, as we usually imagine all objects to be equally distant from us, and as if they were on the same plane, if their distance from us exceeds 200 feet, or if their distance from the position we occupy is greater than we can distinctly imagine—so we imagine all objects to be equally distant from the present time, and refer them as if to one moment, if the period to which their existence belongs is separated from the present by a longer interval than we can usually imagine distinctly.

VII. By end for the sake of which we do anything, I understand appetite.

VIII. By virtue and power, I understand the same thing; that is to say, virtue, in so far as it is related to man, is the essence itself or nature of the man in so far as it has the power of effecting certain things which can be understood through the laws of its nature alone.

Axiom

There is no individual thing in Nature which is not surpassed in strength and power by some other thing; but any individual thing being given, another and a stronger is also given, by which the former can be destroyed.

Man's Place in Nature

The power by which individual things and, consequently, man preserve their being is the actual power of God or Nature, not in so far as it is infinite, but in so far as it can be manifested by the actual essence of man. The power therefore of man, in so far as it is manifested by his actual essence is part of the infinite power of God or Nature, that is to say, part of His essence. Again, if it were possible that man could suffer no changes but those which can be understood through his nature alone, it would follow that he could not perish, but that he would exist forever necessarily; and this necessary existence must result from a cause whose power is either finite or infinite, that is to say, either from the power of man alone, which would be able to place at a distance from himself all other changes which could take their origin from external causes, or it must result from the infinite power of Nature by which all individual things would be so directed that man could suffer no changes but those tending to his preservation.

But the first case is absurd. The force by which man perseveres in existence is limited, and infinitely surpassed by the power of external causes. This is evident from the Axiom. Therefore if it were possible for a man to suffer no changes but those which could be understood through his own nature alone, and consequently (as we have shown) that he should always necessarily exist, this must follow from the infinite power of God; and therefore from the necessity of the divine nature, in so far as it is considered as affected by the idea of any one man, the whole order of Nature, in so far as it is conceived under the attributes of thought and extension, would have to be deduced. From this it would follow that man would be infinite, which (by the first part of this demonstration) is an absurdity. It is impossible, therefore, that a man can suffer no changes but those of which he is the adequate cause.

Hence it follows that a man is necessarily always subject to passions, and that he follows and obeys the common order of Nature, accommodating himself to it as far as the nature of things requires. The force and increase of any passion and its perseverance in existence are not limited by the power by which we endeavor to persevere in existence, but by the power of an external cause compared with our own power.

The Nature of Good and Evil

We call a thing good which contributes to the preservation of our being, and we call a thing evil if it is an obstacle to the preservation of our being; that is to say, a thing is called by us good or evil as it increases or diminishes, helps or restrains, our power of action. In so far, therefore, as we perceive that any object affects us with joy or sorrow do we call it good or evil, and therefore the knowledge of good or evil is nothing but an idea of joy or sorrow which necessarily follows from the emotion itself of joy or sorrow. But this idea is united to the emotion in the same way as the mind is united to the body, or, in other words, this idea is not actually distinguished from the emotion itself; that is to say, it is not actually distinguished from the idea of the modification of the body, unless in conception alone. This knowledge, therefore, of good and evil is nothing but the emotion itself of joy and sorrow in so far as we are conscious of it.

The Control of the Emotions

An emotion, in so far as it is related to the mind, is an idea by which the mind affirms a greater or less power of existence for its body than the body possessed before. Whenever, therefore, the mind is agitated by any emotion, the body is at the same time affected with a modification by which its power of action is increased or diminished. Again, this modification of the body receives from its own cause a power to persevere in its own being, a power, therefore, which cannot be restrained nor removed unless by a bodily cause affecting the body with a modification contrary to the first, and stronger than it. Thus the mind is affected by the idea of a modification stronger than the former and contrary to it; that is to say, it will be affected with an emotion stronger than the former and contrary to it, and this stronger emotion will exclude the existence of the other or remove it. Thus an emotion cannot be restrained nor removed unless by an opposed and stronger emotion.

An emotion, in so far as it is related to the mind, cannot be restrained nor removed unless by the idea of a bodily modification opposed to that which we suffer and stronger than it. For the emotion which we suffer cannot be restrained nor removed unless by an opposed and stronger emotion; that is to say, it cannot be removed unless by the idea of a bodily modification stronger than that which affects us, and opposed to it.

The force and increase of any passion and its perseverance in existence are limited by the power of an external cause compared with our own power and therefore the other actions or power of a man may be so far surpassed by force of some passion or emotion, that the emotion may obstinately cling to him.

An emotion is an idea by which the mind affirms a greater or less power of existence for the body than it possessed before, and therefore this idea has nothing positive which can be removed by the presence of the truth, and consequently the true knowledge of good and evil, in so far as it is true, can restrain no emotion. But in so far as it is an emotion will it restrain any other emotion, provided that the latter be the weaker of the two.

From the true knowledge of good and evil, in so far as this is an emotion, necessarily arises desire, which is greater in proportion as the emotion from which it springs is greater. But this desire (by hypothesis), because it springs from our understanding, something truly follows therefore in us in so far as we act, and therefore must be understood through our essence alone, and consequently its strength and increase must be limited by human power alone. But the desires which spring from the emotions by which we are agitated are greater as the emotions themselves are greater, and therefore their strength and increase must be limited by the power of external causes, a power which, if it be compared with our own, indefinitely surpasses it. The desires, therefore, which take their origin from such emotions as these may be much stronger than that which takes its origin from a true knowledge of good and evil, and the former may be able to restrain and extinguish the latter.

Desire is the very essence of man, that is to say, the effort by which a man strives to persevere in his being. The desire, therefore, which springs from joy, by that very emotion of joy is assisted or increased, while that which springs from sorrow, by that very emotion of sorrow is lessened or restrained, and so the force of the desire which springs from joy must be limited by human power, together with the power of an external cause, while that which springs from sorrow must be limited by human power alone. The latter is, therefore, weaker than the former.

How the Strength of the Emotions Varies

I

The imagination is an idea by which the mind contemplates an object as present, an idea which nevertheless indicates the constitution of the human body rather than the nature of the external object. Imagination, therefore, is an emotion in so far as it indicates the constitution of the body. But the imagination increases in intensity in proportion as we imagine nothing which excludes the present existence of the external object. If, therefore, we imagine the cause of an emotion to be actually present with us, that emotion will be intenser or stronger than if we imagined the cause not to be present.

When I said that we are affected by the image of an object in the future or the past with the same emotion with which we should be affected if the object we imagined were actually present, I was careful to warn the reader that this was true in so far only as we attend to the image alone of the object itself, for the image is of the same nature whether we have imagined the object or not; but I have not denied that the image becomes weaker when we contemplate as present other objects which exclude the present existence of the future object.

The image of a past or future object, that is to say, of an object which we contemplate in relation to the past or future to the exclusion of the present, other things being equal, is weaker than the image of a present object, and consequently the emotion towards a future or past object, other things being equal, is weaker then than the emotion towards a present object.

The desire which springs from a knowledge of good and evil can be easily extinguished or restrained, in so far as this knowledge is connected with the future, by the desire of things which in the present are sweet.

II

In so far as we imagine any object to be necessary do we affirm its existence, and, on the other hand, we deny its existence in so far as we imagine it to be not necessary and therefore the emotion towards an object which we imagine as necessary, other things being equal, is stronger than that towards an object that is possible, contingent, or not necessary.

In so far as we imagine an object as contingent, we are not affected by the image of any other object which posits the existence of the first, but, on the contrary (by hypothesis), we imagine some things which exclude its present existence. But in so far as we imagine any object in the future to be possible do we imagine some things which posit its existence, that is to say, things which foster hope or fear, and therefore the emotion towards an object which we know does not exist in the present, and which we imagine as possible, other things being equal, is stronger than the emotion towards a contingent object.

The emotion towards an object which we imagine to exist in the present is stronger than if we imagined it as future, and is much stronger if we imagine the future to be at a great distance from the present time. The emotion, therefore, towards an object which we imagine will not exist for a long time is so much feebler than if we imagined it as present, and nevertheless is stronger than if we imagined it as contingent; and therefore the emotion towards a contingent object is much feebler than if we imagined the object to be present to us.

In so far as we imagine an object as contingent, we are affected with no image of any other object which posits the existence of the first. On the contrary, we imagine (by hypothesis) certain things which exclude its present existence. But in so far as we imagine it in relationship to past time are we supposed to imagine something which brings it back to the memory or which excites its image and therefore so far causes us to contemplate it as present. Therefore, the emotion towards a contingent object which we know does not exist in the present, other things being equal, will be weaker than the emotion towards a past object.

In these propositions I consider that I have explained why men are more strongly influenced by an opinion than by true reason, and why the true knowledge of good and evil causes disturbance in the mind, and often gives way to every kind of lust, whence the saying of the poet, "*Video meliora proboque, deteriora sequor.*" The same thought appears to have been in the mind of the Preacher when he said, "*He that increaseth knowledge increaseth sorrow.*" I say these things not because I would be understood to conclude, therefore, that it is better to be ignorant than to be wise, or that the wise man in governing his passions is nothing better than the fool, but I say them because it is necessary for us to know both the strength and weakness of our nature, so that we may determine what reason can do and what it cannot do in governing our emotions.

FOOTNOTES:

[29] Chapter Eight *ad fin.*

CHAPTER XV

THE FOUNDATIONS OF THE MORAL LIFE

Introductory

I have briefly explained the causes of human impotence and want of stability, and why men do not obey the dictates of reason. It remains for me now to show what it is which reason prescribes to us, which emotions agree with the rules of human reason, and which, on the contrary, are opposed to these rules. Before, however, I begin to demonstrate these things by our full method, I should like briefly to set forth here these dictates of reason, in order that what I have in my mind about them may be easily comprehended by all.

Since reason demands nothing which is opposed to Nature, it demands, therefore, that every person should love himself, should seek his own profit—what is truly profitable to him—should desire everything that really leads man to greater perfection, and absolutely that everyone should endeavor, as far as in him lies, to preserve his own being. This is all true as necessarily as that the whole is greater than its part. Again, since virtue means nothing but acting according to the laws of our own nature, and since no one endeavors to preserve his being except in accordance with the laws of his own nature, it follows: *Firstly,* That the foundation of virtue is that endeavor itself to preserve our own being, and that happiness consists in this—that a man can preserve his own being. *Secondly,* It follows that virtue is to be desired for its own sake, nor is there anything more excellent or more useful to us than virtue, for the sake of which virtue ought to be desired. *Thirdly,* It follows that all persons who kill themselves are impotent in mind, and have been thoroughly overcome by external causes opposed to their nature.

Again, we can never free ourselves from the need of something outside us for the preservation of our being, and we can never live in such a manner as to have no intercourse with objects which are outside us. Indeed, so far as the mind is concerned, our intellect would be less perfect if the mind were alone, and understood nothing but itself. There are many things, therefore, outside us which are useful to us, and which, therefore, are to be sought. Of all these, none more excellent can be discovered than those which exactly agree with our nature. If, for example, two individuals of exactly the same nature are joined together, they make up a single individual, doubly stronger than each alone. Nothing, therefore, is more useful to man than man. Men can desire, I say, nothing more excellent for the preservation of their being than that all should so agree at every point that the minds and bodies of all should form, as it were, one mind and one body; that all should together endeavor as much as possible to preserve their being, and that all should together seek the common good of all. From this it follows that men who are governed by reason—that is to say, men who, under the guidance of reason, seek their own profit—desire nothing for themselves which they do not desire for other men, and that, therefore, they are just, faithful, and honorable.

These are those dictates of reason which I purposed briefly to set forth before commencing their demonstration by a fuller method, in order that, if possible, I might win the attention of those who believe that this principle—that everyone is bound to seek his own profit—is the foundation of impiety, and not of virtue and piety.

The Essence of Virtue

I

According to the laws of his own nature each person necessarily desires that which he considers to be good, and avoids that which he considers to be evil.

The more each person strives and is able to seek his own profit, that is to say, to preserve his being, the more virtue does he possess; on the other hand, in so far as each person neglects his own profit, that is to say, neglects to preserve his own being, is he impotent.

No one, therefore, unless defeated by external causes and those which are contrary to his nature, neglects to seek his own profit or preserve his being. No one, I say, refuses food or kills himself from a necessity of his nature, but only when forced by external causes. The compulsion may be exercised in many ways. A man kills himself under compulsion by another when that other turns the right hand, with which the man had by chance laid hold of a sword, and compels him to direct the sword against his own heart; or the command of a tyrant may compel a man, as it did Seneca, to open his own veins, that is to say, he may desire to avoid a greater evil by a less. External and hidden causes also may so dispose his imagination and may so affect his body as to cause it to put on another nature contrary to that which it had at first, and one whose idea cannot exist in the mind; but a very little reflection will show that it is as impossible that a man, from the necessity of his nature, should endeavor not to exist, or to be changed into some other form, as it is that something should be begotten from nothing.

The endeavor after self-preservation is the essence itself of a thing. If, therefore, any virtue could be conceived prior to this of self-preservation, the essence itself of the thing would be conceived as prior to itself, which (as is self-evident) is absurd.

The endeavor after self-preservation is the primary and only foundation of virtue. For prior to this principle no other can be conceived, and without it no virtue can be conceived.

No one endeavors to preserve his own being for the sake of another object. For if a man endeavored to preserve his being for the sake of any other object, this object would then become the primary foundation of virtue (as is self-evident), which is an absurdity.

No one can desire to be happy, to act well and live well, who does not at the same time desire to be, to act, and to live, that is to say, actually to exist.

II

To act absolutely in conformity with virtue is nothing but acting according to the laws of our own proper nature. But only in so far as we understand do we act. Therefore, to act in conformity with virtue is nothing but acting, living, and preserving our being as reason directs, and doing so from the ground of seeking our own profit.[30]

In so far as a man is determined to action because he has inadequate ideas he suffers, that is to say, he does something which through his essence alone cannot be perceived, that is to say, which does not follow from his virtue. But in so far as he is determined to any action because he understands, he acts, that is to say he does something which is perceived through his essence alone, or which adequately follows from his virtue.

The Highest Virtue of Reason

All efforts which we make through reason are nothing but efforts to understand, and the mind, in so far as it uses reason, adjudges nothing as profitable to itself excepting that which conduces to understanding.

The mind, in so far as it reasons, desires nothing but to understand, nor does it adjudge anything to be profitable to itself excepting what conduces to understanding. But the mind possesses no certitude, unless in so far as it possesses adequate ideas, or in so far as it reasons. We do not know, therefore, that anything is certainly good, excepting that which actually conduces to understanding, and, on the other hand, we do not know that anything is evil excepting that which can hinder us from understanding.

The highest thing which the mind can understand is God, that is to say, Being absolutely infinite, and without whom nothing can be nor can be conceived, and therefore that which is chiefly profitable to the mind, or which is the highest good of the mind, is the knowledge of God. Again, the mind acts only in so far as it understands and only in so far can it be absolutely said to act in conformity with virtue. To understand, therefore, is the absolute virtue of the mind. But the highest thing which the mind can understand is God (as we have already demonstrated), and therefore the highest virtue of the mind is to understand or know God.

THE MORAL VALUE OF THE EMOTIONS

I

General Principles

That which so disposes the human body that it can be affected in many ways, or which renders it capable of affecting external bodies in many ways, is profitable to man, and is more profitable in proportion as by its means the body becomes better fitted to be affected in many ways, and to affect other bodies; on the other hand, that thing is injurious which renders the body less fitted to affect or be affected.

Whatever is effective to preserve the proportion of motion and rest which the parts of the human body bear to each other is good, and, on the contrary, that is evil which causes the parts of the human body to have a different proportion of motion and rest to each other.

In what degree these things may injure or profit the mind will be explained below. Here I observe merely that I understand the body to die when its parts are so disposed as to acquire a different proportion of motion and rest to each other. For I dare not deny that the human body, though the circulation of the blood and the other things by means of which it is thought to live be preserved, may, nevertheless, be changed into another nature altogether different from its own. No reason compels me to affirm that the body never dies unless it is changed into a corpse. Experience, indeed, seems to teach the contrary. It happens sometimes that a man undergoes such changes that he cannot very well be said to be the same man, as was the case with a certain Spanish poet of whom I have heard, who was seized with an illness, and although he recovered, remained, nevertheless, so oblivious of his past life that he did not believe the tales and tragedies he had composed were his own, and he might, indeed, have been taken for a grown-up child if he had also forgotten his native tongue. But if this seems incredible, what shall we say of children? The man of mature years believes the nature of children to be so different from his own, that it would be impossible to persuade him he had ever been a child, if he did not conjecture regarding himself from what he sees of others. But in order to avoid giving to the superstitious matter for new questions, I prefer to go no farther in the discussion of these matters.

II

Value of Joy and Sorrow

Joy is an emotion by which the body's power of action is increased or assisted. Sorrow, on the other hand, is an emotion by which the body's power of action is lessened or restrained, and therefore joy is not directly evil, but good; sorrow, on the other hand, is directly evil.

III

The Good Emotions

Cheerfulness is joy, which, in so far as it is related to the body, consists in this, that all the parts of the body are equally affected, that is to say, the body's power of action is increased or assisted, so that all the parts acquire the same proportion of motion and rest to each other. Cheerfulness, therefore, is always good, and can never be excessive. But melancholy is sorrow, which, in so far as it is related to the body consists in this, that the body's power of action is absolutely lessened or restrained, and melancholy, therefore, is always evil.

Pleasurable excitement is joy, which, in so far as it is related to the body, consists in this, that one or some of the parts of the body are affected more than others. The power of this emotion may, therefore, be so great as to overcome the other actions of the body. It may cling obstinately to the body; it may impede the body in such a manner as to render it less capable of being affected in many ways, and therefore may be evil. Again, pain, which, on the contrary, is sorrow, considered in itself alone cannot be good. But because its power and increase is limited by the power of an external cause compared with our own power, we can therefore conceive infinite degrees of strength of this emotion, and infinite kinds of it, and we can therefore conceive it to be such that it can restrain an excess of pleasurable excitement, and so far (by the first part of this proposition) preventing the body from becoming less capable. So far, therefore, will pain be good.

Love is joy with the accompanying idea of an external cause. Pleasurable excitement, therefore with the accompanying idea of an external cause, is love, and therefore love may be excessive. Again, desire is greater as the emotion from which it springs is greater. Inasmuch, therefore, as an emotion may overpower the other actions of a man, so also the desire which springs from this emotion may also overpower the other desires, and may therefore exist in the same excess which we have shown (in the preceding proposition) that pleasurable excitement possesses.

Cheerfulness, which I have affirmed to be good, is more easily imagined than observed; for the emotions by which we are daily agitated are generally related to some part of the body which is affected more than the others, and therefore it is that the emotions exist for the most part in excess, and so hold the mind down to the contemplation of one object alone, that it can think about nothing else; and although men are subject to a number of emotions, and therefore few are found who are always under the control of one and the same emotion, there are not wanting those to whom one and the same emotion obstinately clings. We see men sometimes so affected by one object, that although it is not present, they believe it to be before them; and if this happens to a man who is not asleep, we say that he is delirious or mad. Nor are those believed to be less mad who are inflamed by love, dreaming about nothing but a mistress or harlot day and night, for they excite our laughter. But the avaricious man who thinks of nothing else but gain or money, and the ambitious man who thinks of nothing but glory, inasmuch as they do harm, and are, therefore, thought worthy of hatred, are not believed to be mad. In truth, however, avarice, lust, etc., are a kind of madness, although they are not reckoned amongst diseases.

IV

The Evil Emotions

The man whom we hate we endeavor to destroy, that is to say we endeavor to do something which is evil. Therefore hatred can never be good.[31]

Envy, mockery, contempt, anger, revenge, and the other affects which are related to hatred or arise from it, are evil.

Everything which we desire because we are affected by hatred is base and unjust in the State.

I make a great distinction between mockery (which I have said is bad) and laughter; for laughter and merriment are nothing but joy, and therefore, provided they are not excessive, are in themselves good. Nothing but a gloomy and sad superstition forbids enjoyment. For why is it more seemly to extinguish hunger and thirst than to drive away melancholy? My reasons and my conclusions are these: No God and no human being, except an envious one, is delighted by my impotence or my trouble, or esteems as any virtue in us tears, sighs, fears, and other things of this kind, which are signs of mental impotence; on the contrary, the greater the joy with which we are affected, the greater the perfection to which we pass thereby, that is to say, the more do we necessarily partake of the divine nature. To make use of things, therefore, and to delight in them as much as possible (provided we do not disgust ourselves with them, which is not delighting in them), is the part of a wise man. It is the part of a wise man, I say, to refresh and invigorate himself with moderate and pleasant eating and drinking, with sweet scents and the beauty of green plants, with ornament, with music, with sports, with the theater, and with all things of this kind which one man can enjoy without hurting another. For the human body is composed of a great number of parts of diverse nature, which constantly need new and varied nourishment, in order that the whole of the body may be equally fit for everything which can follow from its nature, and consequently that the mind may be equally fit to understand many things at once. This mode of living best of all agrees both with our principles and with common practice; therefore this mode of living is the best of all, and is to be universally commended. There is no need, therefore, to enter more at length into the subject.

All emotions of hatred are evil and therefore the man who lives according to the guidance of reason will strive as much as possible to keep himself from being agitated by the emotions of hatred and, consequently, will strive to keep others from being subject to the same emotions. But hatred is increased by reciprocal hatred, and, on the other hand, can be extinguished by love, so that hatred passes into love. Therefore he who lives according to the guidance of reason will strive to repay the hatred of another, etc., with love, that is to say, with generosity. He who wishes to avenge injuries by hating in return does indeed live miserably. But he who, on the contrary, strives to drive out hatred by love, fights joyfully and confidently, with equal ease resisting one man or a number of men, and needing scarcely any assistance from fortune. Those whom he conquers yield gladly, not from defect of strength, but from an increase of it. These truths, however, all follow so plainly from the definitions alone of love and the intellect, that there is no need to demonstrate them singly.

V

Necessary Evils

(i)

The emotions of hope and fear cannot exist without sorrow; for fear is sorrow, and hope cannot exist without fear. Therefore these emotions cannot be good of themselves, but only in so far as they are able to restrain the excesses of joy.

We may here add that these emotions indicate want of knowledge and impotence of mind, and, for the same reason, confidence, despair, gladness, and remorse are signs of weakness of mind. For although confidence and gladness are emotions of joy, they nevertheless suppose that sorrow has preceded them, namely, hope or fear. In proportion, therefore, as we endeavor to live according to the guidance of reason, shall we strive as much as possible to depend less on hope, to liberate ourselves from fear, to rule fortune, and to direct our actions by the sure counsels of reason.

Humility is sorrow, which springs from this, that a man contemplates his own weakness. But in so far as a man knows himself by true reason is he supposed to understand his essence, that is to say, his power. If, therefore, while contemplating himself, he perceives any impotence of his, this is not due to his understanding himself, but, as we have shown, to the fact that his power of actions is restrained. But if we suppose that he forms a conception of his own impotence because he understands something to be more powerful than himself, by the knowledge of which he limits his own power of action, in this case we simply conceive that he understands himself distinctly, and his power of action is increased. Humility or sorrow, therefore, which arises because a man contemplates his own impotence, does not spring from true contemplation or reason, and is not a virtue, but a passion.

Repentance is not a virtue, that is to say, it does not spring from reason; on the contrary, the man who repents of what he has done is doubly wretched or impotent. For, in the first place, we allow ourselves to be overcome by a depraved desire, and, in the second place, by sorrow.

Inasmuch as men seldom live as reason dictates, therefore these two emotions, humility and repentance, together with hope and fear, are productive of more profit than disadvantage, and therefore, since men must sin, it is better that they should sin in this way. For if men impotent in mind were all equally proud, were ashamed of nothing, and feared nothing, by what bonds could they be united or constrained? The multitude becomes a thing to be feared if it has nothing to fear. It is not to be wondered at, therefore, that the prophets, thinking rather of the good of the community than of a few, should have commended so greatly humility, repentance and reverence. Indeed, those who are subject to these emotions can be led much more easily than others, so that, at last, they come to live according to the guidance of reason, that is to say, become free men, and enjoy the life of the blessed.

(ii)

Pity is sorrow, and therefore is in itself evil. The good, however, which issues from pity, namely, that we endeavor to free from misery the man we pity, we desire to do from the dictate of reason alone; nor can we do anything except by the dictate of reason alone, which we are sure is good. Pity, therefore, in a man who lives according to the guidance of reason is in itself bad and unprofitable.

Hence it follows that a man who lives according to the dictates of reason endeavors as much as possible to prevent himself from being touched by pity.

The man who has properly understood that everything follows from the necessity of the divine nature, and comes to pass according to the eternal laws and rules of Nature, will in truth discover nothing which is worthy of hatred, laughter, or contempt, nor will he pity any one, but, so far as human virtue is able, he will endeavor to *do well*, as we say, and to *rejoice*. We must add also, that a man who is easily touched by the emotion of pity, and is moved by the misery or tears of another, often does something of which he afterward repents, both because from an emotion we do nothing which we certainly know to be good, and also because we are so easily deceived by false tears. But this I say expressly of the man who lives according to the guidance of reason. For he who is moved neither by reason nor pity to be of any service to others is properly called inhuman; for he seems to be unlike a man.

VI

Diseased Emotions

The primary foundation of virtue is the preservation of our being according to the guidance of reason. The man, therefore, who is ignorant of himself is ignorant of the foundation of all the virtues, and consequently is ignorant of all the virtues. Again, to act in conformity with virtue is nothing but acting according to the guidance of reason, and he who acts according to the guidance of reason must necessarily know that he acts according to the guidance of reason. He, therefore, who is ignorant of himself, and consequently (as we have just shown) altogether ignorant of all the virtues, cannot in any way act in conformity with virtue, that is to say, is altogether impotent in mind. Therefore the greatest pride or despondency indicates the greatest impotence of mind.

Hence follows, with the utmost clearness, that the proud and the desponding are above all others subject to emotions.

Despondency, nevertheless, can be corrected more easily than pride, since the former is an emotion of sorrow, while the latter is an emotion of joy, and is therefore stronger than the former.

Pride is joy arising from a man's having too high an opinion of himself. This opinion a proud man will endeavor, as much as he can, to cherish, and therefore, will love the presence of parasites or flatterers (the definitions of these people are omitted, because they are too well known), and will shun that of the noble-minded who think of him as is right.

It would take too much time to enumerate here all the evils of pride, for the proud are subject to all emotions, but to none are they less subject than to those of love and pity. It is necessary, however, to observe here that a man is also called proud if he thinks too little of other people, and so, in this sense, pride is to be defined as joy which arises from the false opinion that we are superior to other people, while despondency, the contrary to this pride, would be defined as sorrow arising from the false opinion that we are inferior to other people. This being understood, it is easy to see that the proud man is necessarily envious, and that he hates those above all others who are the most praised on account of their virtues. It follows, too, that his hatred of them is not easily overcome by love or kindness and that he is delighted by the presence of those only who humor his weakness, and from a fool make him a madman.

Although despondency is contrary to pride, the despondent man is closely akin to the proud man. For since the sorrow of the despondent man arises from his judging his own impotence by the power of virtue of others, his sorrow will be mitigated, that is to say, he will rejoice, if his imagination be occupied in contemplating the vices of others. Hence the proverb— It is a consolation to the wretched to have bad companions in their misfortunes. On the other hand, the more the despondent man believes himself to be below other people, the more will he sorrow; and this is the reason why none are more prone to envy than the despondent; and why they, above all others, try to observe men's actions with a view to finding fault with them rather than correcting them, so that at last they praise nothing but despondency and glory in it; but in such a manner, however, as always to seem despondent.

These things follow from this emotion as necessarily as it follows from the nature of a triangle that its three angles are equal to two right angles. It is true, indeed, that I have said that I call these and the like emotions evil, in so far as I attend to human profit alone; but the laws of Nature have regard to the common order of Nature of which man is a part—a remark I desired to make in passing, lest it should be thought that I talk about the vices and absurdities of men rather than attempt to demonstrate the nature and properties of things. As I said, I consider human emotions and their properties precisely as I consider other natural objects; and, indeed, the emotions of man, if they do not show his power, show at least the power and workmanship of Nature, no less than many other things which we admire and delight to contemplate.

VII

Reasonable Emotions

If we live according to the guidance of reason, we shall desire for others the good which we seek for ourselves. Therefore if we see one person do good to another, our endeavor to do good is assisted, that is to say, we shall rejoice, and our joy (by hypothesis) will be accompanied with the idea of the person who does good to the other, that is to say, we shall favor him. Favor is not opposed to reason, but agrees with it, and may arise from it.

Indignation, as it is defined by us, is necessarily evil; but it is to be observed that when the supreme authority, constrained by the desire of preserving peace, punishes a citizen who injures another, I do not say that it is indignant with the citizen, since it is not excited by hatred to destroy him, but punishes him from motives of piety.

Self-satisfaction is the joy which arises from a man's contemplating himself and his power of action. But man's true power of action or his virtue is reason itself, which he contemplates clearly and distinctly. Self-satisfaction therefore arises from reason. Again, man, when he contemplates himself, perceives nothing clearly and distinctly or adequately, excepting those things which follow from his power of action, that is to say, those things which follow from his power of understanding; and therefore from this contemplation alone the highest satisfaction which can exist arises.

Self-satisfaction is indeed the highest thing for which we can hope, for (as we have shown), no one endeavors to preserve his being for the sake of any end. Again, because this self-satisfaction is more and more nourished and strengthened by praise, and, on the contrary more and more disturbed by blame, therefore we are principally led by glory, and can scarcely endure life with disgrace.

Self-exaltation is not opposed to reason, but may spring from it.

What is called vainglory is self-satisfaction, nourished by nothing but the good opinion of the multitude, so that when that is withdrawn, the satisfaction, that is to say, the chief good which everyone loves, ceases. For this reason those who glory in the good opinion of the multitude anxiously and with daily care strive, labor, and struggle to preserve their fame. For the multitude is changeable and fickle, so that fame, if it be not preserved, soon passes away. As everyone, moreover, is desirous to catch the praises of the people, one person will readily destroy the fame of another; and consequently, as the object of contention is what is commonly thought to be the highest good, a great desire arises on the part of everyone to keep down his fellows by every possible means, and he who at last comes off conqueror boasts more because he has injured another person than because he has profited himself. This glory of self-satisfaction, therefore, is indeed vain, for it is really no glory.

What is worthy of notice with regard to shame may easily be gathered from what has been said about compassion and repentance. I will only add that pity, like shame, although it is not a virtue, is nevertheless good, in so far as it shows that a desire of living uprightly is present in the man who is possessed with shame, just as pain is called good in so far as it shows that the injured part has not yet putrefied. A man, therefore, who is ashamed of what he has done, although he is sorrowful, is nevertheless more perfect that the shameless man who has no desire of living uprightly.

These are the things which I undertook to establish with regard to the emotions of joy and sorrow. With reference to the desires, these are good or evil as they spring from good or evil emotions. All of them, however, in so far as they are begotten in us of emotions which are passions, are blind, as may easily be inferred from what has been said, nor would they be of any use if men could be easily persuaded to live according to the dictates of reason alone.

The Life of Virtue

I

All our efforts or desires follow from the necessity of our nature in such a manner that they can be understood either through it alone as their proximate cause, or in so far as we are a part of Nature, which part cannot be adequately conceived through itself and without the other individuals.

II

The desires which follow from our nature in such a manner that they can be understood through it alone, are those which are related to the mind, in so far as it is conceived to consist of adequate ideas. The remaining desires are not related to the mind, unless in so far as it conceives things inadequately, whose power and increase cannot be determined by human power, but by the power of objects which are without us. The first kind of desires, therefore, are properly called actions, but the latter passions; for the first always indicate our power, and the latter, on the contrary, indicate our impotence and imperfect knowledge.

III

Our actions, that is to say, those desires which are determined by man's power or reason, are always good; the others may be good as well as evil.

IV

It is therefore most profitable to us in life to make perfect the intellect or reason as far as possible, and in this one thing consists the highest happiness or blessedness of man; for blessedness is nothing but the peace of mind which springs from the intuitive knowledge of God, and to perfect the intellect is nothing but to understand God, together with the attributes and actions of God, which flow from the necessity of His nature. The final aim, therefore, of a man who is guided by reason, that is to say, the chief desire by which he strives to govern all his other desires, is that by which he is led adequately to conceive himself and all things which can be conceived by his intelligence.

V

There is no rational life, therefore, without intelligence and things are good only in so far as they assist man to enjoy that life of the mind which is determined by intelligence. Those things alone, on the other hand, we call evil which hinder man from perfecting his reason and enjoying a rational life.

VI

But because all those things of which man is the efficient cause are necessarily good, it follows that no evil can happen to man except from external causes, that is to say, except in so far as he is a part of the whole of Nature, whose laws human nature is compelled to obey—compelled also to accommodate himself to this whole of Nature in almost an infinite number of ways.

VII

It is impossible that a man should not be a part of Nature and follow her common order; but if he be placed amongst individuals who agree with his nature, his power of action will by that very fact be assisted and supported. But if, on the contrary, he be placed amongst individuals who do not in the least agree with his nature, he will scarcely be able without great change on his part to accommodate himself to them.

VIII

Anything that exists in Nature which we judge to be evil or able to hinder us from existing and enjoying a rational life, we are allowed to remove from us in that way which seems the safest; and whatever, on the other hand, we judge to be good or to be profitable for the preservation of our being or the enjoyment of a rational life, we are permitted to take for our use and use in any way we may think proper; and absolutely, everyone is allowed by the highest right of Nature to do that which he believes contributes to his own profit.

IX

Nothing, therefore, can agree better with the nature of any object than other individuals of the same kind, and so (see § VII) there is nothing more profitable to man for the preservation of his being and the enjoyment of a rational life than a man who is guided by reason. Again, since there is no single thing we know which is more excellent than a man who is guided by reason, it follows that there is nothing by which a person can better show how much skill and talent he possesses than by so educating men that at last they will live under the direct authority of reason.

X

In so far as men are carried away by envy or any emotion of hatred towards one another, so far are they contrary to one another, and consequently so much the more are they to be feared, as they have more power than other individuals of nature.

XI

Minds, nevertheless, are not conquered by arms, but by love and generosity.

XII

Above all things is it profitable to men to form communities and to unite themselves to one another by bonds which may make all of them as one man; and absolutely, it is profitable for them to do whatever may tend to strengthen their friendships.

XIII

But to accomplish this skill and watchfulness are required; for men are changeable (those being very few who live according to the laws of reason), and nevertheless generally envious and more inclined to vengeance than pity. To bear with each, therefore, according to his disposition and to refrain from imitating his emotions requires a singular power of mind. But those, on the contrary, who know how to revile men, to denounce vices rather than teach virtues, and not to strengthen men's minds but to weaken them, are injurious both to themselves and others, so that many of them through an excess of impatience and a false zeal for religion prefer living with brutes rather than amongst men; just as boys or youths, unable to endure with equanimity the rebukes of their parents, fly to the army, choosing the discomforts of war and the rule of a tyrant rather than the comforts of home and the admonitions of a father, suffering all kinds of burdens to be imposed upon them in order that they may revenge themselves upon their parents.

XIV

Although, therefore, men generally determine everything by their pleasure, many more advantages than disadvantages arise from their common union. It is better, therefore, to endure with equanimity the injuries inflicted by them, and to apply our minds to those things which subserve concord and the establishment of friendship.

XV

The things which beget concord are those which are related to justice, integrity, and honor; for besides that which is unjust and injurious, men take ill also anything which is esteemed base, or that any one should despise the received customs of the State. But in order to win love, those things are chiefly necessary which have reference to religion and piety.

XVI

Concord, moreover, is often produced by fear, but it is without good faith. It is to be observed, too, that fear arises from impotence of mind, and therefore is of no service to reason; nor is pity, although it seems to present an appearance of piety.

XVII

Men also are conquered by liberality, especially those who have not the means wherewith to procure what is necessary for the support of life. But to assist everyone who is needy far surpasses the strength or profit of a private person, for the wealth of a private person is altogether insufficient to supply such wants. Besides, the power of any one man is too limited for him to be able to unite everyone with himself in friendship. The care, therefore, of the poor is incumbent on the whole of society and concerns only the general profit.

XVIII

In the receipt of benefits and in returning thanks, care altogether different must be taken.

XIX

The love of a harlot, that is to say, the lust of sexual intercourse, which arises from mere external form, and absolutely all love which recognizes any other cause than the freedom of the mind, easily passes into hatred, unless, which is worse, it becomes a species of delirium, and thereby discord is cherished rather than concord.

XX

With regard to marriage, it is plain that it is in accordance with reason, if the desire of connection is engendered not merely by external form, but by a love of begetting children and wisely educating them; and if, in addition, the love both of the husband and wife has for its cause not external form merely, but chiefly liberty of mind.

XXI

Flattery, too, produces concord, but only by means of the disgraceful crime of slavery or perfidy; for there are none who are more taken by flattery than the proud, who wish to be first and are not so.

XXII

There is a false appearance of piety and religion in dejection; and although dejection is the opposite of pride, the humble dejected man is very near akin to the proud.

XXIII

Shame also contributes to concord, but only with regard to those matters which cannot be concealed. Shame, too, inasmuch as it is a kind of sorrow, does not belong to the service of reason.

XXIV

The remaining emotions of sorrow which have man for their object are directly opposed to justice, integrity, honor, piety, and religion; and although indignation may seem to present an appearance of equity, yet there is no law where it is allowed to everyone to judge the deeds of another, and to vindicate his own or another's right.

XXV

Affability, that is to say, the desire of pleasing men, which is determined by reason, is related to piety. But if affability arise from an emotion, it is ambition or desire, by which men, generally under a false pretense of piety, excite discords and seditions. For he who desires to assist other people, either by advice or by deed, in order that they may together enjoy the highest good, will strive, above all things, to win their love, and not to draw them into admiration, so that a doctrine may be named after him, nor absolutely to give any occasion for envy. In common conversation, too, he will avoid referring to the vices of men, and will take care only sparingly to speak of human impotence, while he will talk largely of human virtue or power, and of the way by which it may be made perfect, so that men being moved not by fear or aversion, but solely by the emotion of joy, may endeavor as much as they can to live under the rule of reason.

XXVI

Excepting man, we know no individual thing in Nature in whose mind we can take pleasure, nor any thing which we can unite with ourselves by friendship or any kind of intercourse, and therefore regard to our own profit does not demand that we should preserve anything which exists in Nature excepting men, but teaches us to preserve it or destroy it in accordance with its varied uses, or to adapt it to our own service in any way whatever.

XXVII

The profit which we derive from objects without us, over and above the experience and knowledge which we obtain because we observe them and change them from their existing forms into others, is chiefly the preservation of the body, and for this reason those objects are the most profitable to us which can feed and nourish the body, so that all its parts are able properly to perform their functions. For the more capable the body is of being affected in many ways, and affecting external bodies in many ways, the more capable of thinking is the mind. But there seem to be very few things in Nature of this kind, and it is consequently necessary for the requisite nourishment of the body to use many different kinds of food; for the human body is composed of a great number of parts of different nature, which need constant and varied food in order that the whole of the body may be equally adapted for all those things which can follow from its nature, and consequently that the mind also may be equally adapted to conceive many things.

XXVIII

The strength of one man would scarcely suffice to obtain these things if men did not mutually assist one another. As money has presented us with an abstract of everything, it has come to pass that its image above every other usually occupies the mind of the multitude, because they can imagine hardly any kind of joy without the accompanying idea of money as its cause.

XXIX

This, however, is a vice only in those who seek money not from poverty or necessity, but because they have learned the arts of gain, by which they keep up a grand appearance. As for the body itself, they feed it in accordance with custom, but sparingly, because they believe that they lose so much of their goods as they spend upon the preservation of their body. Those, however, who know the true use of money, and regulate the measure of wealth according to their needs, live contented with few things.

XXX

Since, therefore, those things are good which help the parts of the body to perform their functions, and since joy consists in this, that the power of man, in so far as he is made up of mind and body, is helped or increased, it follows that all things which bring joy are good. But inasmuch as things do not work to this end—that they may affect us with joy—nor is their power of action guided in accordance with our profit, and finally, since joy is generally related chiefly to some one part of the body, it follows that generally the emotions of joy (unless reason and watchfulness be present), and consequently the desires which are begotten from them, are excessive. It is to be added, that an emotion causes us to put that thing first which is sweet to us in the present, and that we are not able to judge the future with an equal emotion of the mind.

XXXI

Superstition, on the contrary, seems to affirm that what brings sorrow is good, and, on the contrary, that what brings joy is evil. But, as we have already said, no one, excepting an envious man, is delighted at my impotence or disadvantage, for the greater the joy with which we are affected, the greater the perfection to which we pass, and consequently the more do we participate in the divine nature; nor can joy ever be evil which is controlled by a true consideration for our own profit. On the other hand, the man who is led by fear, and does what is good that he may avoid what is evil, is not guided by reason.

XXXII

But human power is very limited, and is infinitely surpassed by the power of external causes, so that we do not possess an absolute power to adapt to our service the things which are without us. Nevertheless we shall bear with equanimity those things which happen to us contrary to what a consideration of our own profit demands, if we are conscious that we have performed our duty, that the power we have could not reach so far as to enable us to avoid those things, and that we are a part of the whole of Nature, whose order we follow. If we clearly and distinctly understand this, the part of us which is determined by intelligence, that is to say, the better part of us, will be entirely satisfied therewith, and in that satisfaction will endeavor to persevere; for, in so far as we understand, we cannot desire anything excepting what is necessary, nor, absolutely, can we be satisfied with anything but the truth. Therefore in so far as we understand these things properly will the efforts of the better part of us agree with the order of the whole of Nature.

FOOTNOTES:

[30] ... If it agreed better with a man's nature that he should hang himself, could any reasons be given for his not hanging himself? Can such a nature possibly exist? If so, I maintain (whether I do or do not grant free will), that

such an one, if he sees that he can live more conveniently on the gallows than sitting at his own table, would act most foolishly, if he did not hang himself. So any one who clearly saw that, by committing crimes, he would enjoy a really more perfect and better life and existence, than he could attain by the practice of virtue, would be foolish if he did not act on his convictions. For, with such a perverse human nature as his, crime would become virtue. *From a letter to Wm. Blyenbergh* (March 13, 1665).

[31] It is to be observed that here and in the following I understand by hatred, hatred towards men only.

CHAPTER XVI

OF THE FOUNDATIONS OF A STATE[132]

By the right and ordinance of Nature, I merely mean those natural laws wherewith we conceive every individual to be conditioned by Nature, so as to live and act in a given way. For instance, fishes are naturally conditioned for swimming, and the greater for devouring the less; therefore fishes enjoy the water, and the greater devour the less by sovereign natural right. For it is certain that Nature, taken in the abstract, has sovereign right to do anything she can; in other words, her right is co-extensive with her power. The power of Nature is the power of God, which has sovereign right over all things; and, inasmuch as the power of Nature is simply the aggregate of the powers of all her individual components, it follows that every individual has sovereign right to do all that he can, in other words, the rights of an individual extend to the utmost limits of his power as it has been conditioned.

Now it is the sovereign law and right of Nature that each individual should endeavor to preserve itself as it is, without regard to anything but itself; therefore this sovereign law and right belongs to every individual, namely, to exist and act according to its natural conditions. We do not here acknowledge any difference between mankind and other individual natural entities, nor between men endowed with reason and those to whom reason is unknown; nor between fools, madmen, and sane men. Whatsoever an individual does by the laws of its nature it has a sovereign right to do, inasmuch as it acts as it was conditioned by Nature, and cannot act otherwise. Wherefore among men, so long as they are considered as living under the sway of Nature, he who does not yet know reason, or who has not yet acquired the habit of virtue, acts solely according to the laws of his desire with as sovereign a right as he who orders his life entirely by the laws of reason.

That is, as the wise man has sovereign right to do all that reason dictates, or to live according to the laws of reason, so also the ignorant and foolish man has sovereign right to do all that desire dictates, or to live according to the laws of desire. This is identical with the teaching of Paul, who acknowledges that previous to the law—that is, so long as men are considered of as living under the sway of Nature, there is no sin.

The natural right of the individual man is thus determined, not by sound reason, but by desire and power. All are not naturally conditioned so as to act according to the laws and rules of reason; nay, on the contrary, all men are born ignorant, and before they can learn the right way of life and acquire the habit of virtue, the greater part of their life, even if they have been well brought up, has passed away. Nevertheless, they are in the meanwhile bound to live and preserve themselves as far as they can by the unaided impulses of desire. Nature has given them no other guide, and has denied them the present power of living according to sound reason; so that they are no more bound to live by the dictates of an enlightened mind than a cat is bound to live by the laws of the nature of a lion.

Whatsoever, therefore, an individual, considered as under the sway of Nature, thinks useful for himself, whether led by sound reason or impelled by the passions, that he has a sovereign right to seek and to take for himself as he best can, whether by force, cunning, entreaty, or any other means; consequently he may regard as an enemy anyone who hinders the accomplishment of his purpose.

It follows from what we have said that the right and ordinance of Nature, under which all men are born, and under which they mostly live, only prohibits such things as no one desires, and no one can attain: it does not forbid strife, nor hatred, nor anger, nor deceit, nor, indeed, any of the means suggested by desire.

This we need not wonder at, for Nature is not bounded by the laws of human reason, which aims only at man's true benefit and preservation. Her limits are infinitely wider, and have reference to the eternal order of Nature, wherein man is but a speck. It is by the necessity of this alone that all individuals are conditioned for living and acting in a particular way. If anything, therefore, in Nature seems to us ridiculous, absurd, or evil, it is because we only know in part, and are almost entirely ignorant of the order and interdependence of Nature as a whole, and also because we want everything to be arranged according to the dictates of our human reason; in reality that which reason considers evil is not evil in respect to the order and laws of Nature as a whole, but only in respect to the laws of our reason.

Nevertheless, no one can doubt that it is much better for us to live according to the laws and assured dictates of reason, for, as we said, they have men's true good for their object. Moreover, everyone wishes to live as far as possible securely beyond the reach of fear, and this would be quite impossible so long as everyone did everything he liked, and reason's claim was lowered to a par with those of hatred and anger. There is no one who is not ill at ease in the midst of enmity, hatred, anger and deceit, and who does not seek to avoid them as much as he can. When we reflect that men without mutual help, or the aid of reason, must needs live most miserably, ... we shall plainly see that men must necessarily come to an agreement to live together as securely and well as possible if they are to enjoy, as a whole, the rights which naturally belong to them as individuals, and their life should be no more conditioned by the force and desire of individuals, but by the power and will of the whole body. This end they will be unable to attain if desire be their only guide, for by the laws of desire each man is drawn in a different direction; they must, therefore, most firmly decree and establish that they will be guided in everything by reason, which nobody will dare openly to repudiate lest he should be taken for a madman, and will restrain any desire which is injurious to a man's fellows, that they will do to all as they would be done by, and that they will defend their neighbor's rights as their own.

How such a compact as this should be entered into, how ratified and established, we will now inquire.

Now it is a universal law of human nature that no one ever neglects anything which he judges to be good, except with the hope of gaining a greater good, or from the fear of a greater evil; nor does any one endure an evil except for the sake of avoiding a greater evil, or gaining a greater good. That is, everyone will, of two goods, choose that which he thinks the greatest; and, of two evils that which he thinks the least. I say advisedly that which he thinks the greatest or the least, for it does not necessarily follow that he judges right. This law is so deeply implanted in the human mind that it ought to be counted among eternal truths and axioms.

As a necessary consequence of the principle just enunciated, no one can honestly promise to forego the right which he has over all things,[33] and in general no one will abide by his promises, unless under the fear of a greater evil, or the hope of a greater good. An example will make the matter clearer. Suppose that a robber forces me to promise that I will give him my goods at his will and pleasure. It is plain (inasmuch as my natural right is, as I have shown, co-extensive with my power) that if I can free myself from this robber by stratagem, by assenting to his demands, I have the natural right to do so, and to pretend to accept his conditions. Or, again, suppose I have genuinely promised some one that for the space of twenty days I will not taste food or any nourishment; and suppose I afterwards find that my promise was foolish, and cannot be kept without very great injury to myself; as I am bound by natural law and right to choose the least of two evils, I have complete right to break any compact, and act as if my promise had never been uttered. I say that I should have perfect natural right to do so, whether I was actuated by true and evident reason, or whether I was actuated by mere opinion in thinking I had promised rashly; whether my reasons were true or false, I should be in fear of a greater evil, which, by the ordinance of Nature, I should strive to avoid by every means in my power.

We may, therefore, conclude that a compact is only made valid by its utility, without which it becomes null and void. It is therefore foolish to ask a man to keep his faith with us forever, unless we also endeavor that the violation of the compact we enter into shall involve for the violator more harm than good. This consideration should have very great weight in forming a state. However, if all men could be easily led by reason alone, and could recognize what is best and most useful for a state, there would be no one who would not forswear deceit, for everyone would keep most religiously to their compact in their desire for the chief good, namely, the preservation of the state, and would cherish good faith above all things as the shield and buckler of the commonwealth. However, it is far from being the case that all men can always be easily led by reason alone; everyone is drawn away by his pleasure, while avarice, ambition, envy, hatred, and the like so engross the mind that reason has no place therein. Hence, though men make promises with all the appearances of good faith, and agree that they will keep to their engagement, no one can absolutely rely on another man's promise unless there is something behind it. Everyone has by Nature a right to act deceitfully, and to break his compacts, unless he be restrained by the hope of some greater good, or the fear of some greater evil.

However, as we have shown that the natural right of the individual is only limited by his power, it is clear that by transferring, either willingly or under compulsion, this power into the hands of another, he in so doing necessarily cedes also a part of his right; and, further, that the sovereign right over all men belongs to him who has sovereign power, wherewith he can compel men by force, or restrain them by threats of the universally feared punishment of death. Such sovereign right he will retain only so long as he can maintain his power of enforcing his will; otherwise he will totter on his throne, and no one who is stronger than he will be bound unwillingly to obey him.

In this manner a society can be formed without any violation of natural right, and the covenant can always be strictly kept—that is, if each individual hands over the whole of his power to the body politic, the latter will then possess sovereign natural right over all things; that is, it will have sole and unquestioned dominion, and everyone will be bound to obey, under pain of the severest punishment. A body politic of this kind is called a Democracy, which may be defined as a society which wields all its power as a whole. The sovereign power is not restrained by any laws, but everyone is bound to obey it in all things; such is the state of things implied when men either tacitly or expressly handed over to it all their power of self-defense, or in other words, all their right. For if they had wished to retain any right for themselves, they ought to have taken precautions for its defense and preservation. As they have not done so, and indeed could not have done so without dividing and consequently ruining the state, they placed themselves absolutely at the mercy of the sovereign power; and, therefore, having acted (as we have shown) as reason and necessity demanded, they are obliged to fulfill the commands of the sovereign power, however absurd these may be, else they will be public enemies, and will act against reason, which urges the preservation of the state as a primary duty. For reason bids us choose the lesser of two evils.

Furthermore, this danger of submitting absolutely to the dominion and will of another, is one which may be incurred with a light heart: for we have shown that sovereigns only possess this right of imposing their will, so long as they have the full power to enforce it. If such power be lost their right to command is lost also, or lapses to those who have assumed it and can keep it. Thus it is very rare for sovereigns to impose thoroughly irrational commands, for they are bound to consult their own interests, and retain their power by consulting the public good and acting according to the dictates of reason, as Seneca says, "*violenta imperia nemo continuit diu.*" No one can long retain a tyrant's sway.

In a democracy, irrational commands are still less to be feared: for it is almost impossible that the majority of a people, especially if it be a large one, should agree in an irrational design: and, moreover, the basis and aim of a democracy is to avoid the desires as irrational, and to bring men as far as possible under the control of reason, so that they may live in peace and harmony. If this basis be removed the whole fabric falls to ruin.

Such being the ends in view for the sovereign power, the duty of subjects is, as I have said, to obey its commands, and to recognize no right save that which it sanctions.

It will, perhaps, be thought that we are turning subjects into slaves, for slaves obey commands and free men live as they like; but this idea is based on a misconception, for the true slave is he who is led away by his pleasures and can neither see what is good for him nor act accordingly: he alone is free who lives with free consent under the entire guidance of reason.

Action in obedience to orders does take away freedom in a certain sense, but it does not, therefore, make a man a slave; all depends on the object of the action. If the object of the action be the good of the state, and not the good of the agent, the latter is a slave and does himself no good; but in a state or kingdom where the weal of the whole people, and not that of the ruler, is the supreme law, obedience to the sovereign power does not make a man a slave, of no use to himself, but a subject. Therefore, that state is the freest whose laws are founded on sound reason, so that every member of it may, if he will, be free;[34] that is, live with full consent under the entire guidance of reason.

Children, though they are bound to obey all the commands of their parents, are yet not slaves; for the commands of parents look generally to the children's benefit.

We must, therefore, acknowledge a great difference between a slave, a son, and a subject; their positions may be thus defined. A slave is one who is bound to obey his master's orders, though they are given solely in the master's interest; a son is one who obeys his father's orders, given in his own interest; a subject obeys the orders of the sovereign power, given for the common interest, wherein he is included.

I think I have now shown sufficiently clearly the basis of a democracy. I have especially desired to do so, for I believe it to be of all forms of government the most natural, and the most consonant with individual liberty. In it no one transfers his natural right so absolutely that he has no further voice in affairs; he only hands it over to the majority of a society, whereof he is a unit. Thus all men remain, as they were in the state of Nature, equals.

This is the only form of government which I have treated of at length, for it is the one most akin to my purpose of showing the benefits of freedom in a state.

I may pass over the fundamental principles of other forms of government, for we may gather from what has been said whence their right arises without going into its origin. The possessor of sovereign power, whether he be one, or many, or the whole body politic, has the sovereign right of imposing any commands he pleases; and he who has either voluntarily, or under compulsion, transferred the right to defend him to another, has, in so doing, renounced his natural right and is therefore bound to obey, in all things, the commands of the sovereign power; and will be bound so to do so long as the king, or nobles, or the people preserve the sovereign power which formed the basis of the original transfer. I need add no more.

The bases and rights of dominion being thus displayed, we shall readily be able to define private civil right, wrong, justice, and injustice, with their relations to the state; and also to determine what constitutes an ally, or an enemy, or the crime of treason.

By private civil right we can only mean the liberty every man possesses to preserve his existence, a liberty limited by the edicts of the sovereign power, and preserved only by its authority. For when a man has transferred to another his right of living as he likes, which was only limited by his power, that is, has transferred his liberty and power of self-defense, he is bound to live as that other dictates, and to trust to him entirely for his defense. Wrong takes place when a citizen, or subject, is forced by another to undergo some loss or pain in contradiction to the authority of the law, or the edict of the sovereign power.

Wrong is conceivable only in an organized community; nor can it ever accrue to subjects from any act of the sovereign, who has the right to do what he likes. It can only arise, therefore, between private persons, who are bound by law and right not to injure one another. Justice consists in the habitual rendering to every man his lawful due; injustice consists in depriving a man, under the pretense of legality, of what the laws, rightly interpreted, would allow him. These last are also called equity and inequity, because those who administer the laws are bound to show no respect of persons, but to account all men equal, and to defend every man's right equally, neither envying the rich nor despising the poor.

The men of two states become allies, when for the sake of avoiding war, or for some other advantage, they covenant to do each other no hurt, but, on the contrary, to assist each other if necessity arises, each retaining his independence. Such a covenant is valid so long as its basis of danger or advantage is in force: no one enters into an engagement, or is bound to stand by his compacts unless there be a hope of some accruing good, or the fear of some evil: if this basis be removed the compact thereby becomes void: this has been abundantly shown by experience. For although different states make treaties not to harm one another, they always take every possible precaution against such treaties being broken by the stronger party, and do not rely on the compact, unless there is a sufficiently obvious object and advantage to both parties in observing it. Otherwise they would fear a breach of faith, nor would there be any wrong done thereby; for who in his proper senses, and aware of the right of the sovereign power, would trust in the promises of one who has the will and the power to do what he likes, and who aims solely at the safety and advantage of his dominion? Moreover, if we consult loyalty and religion, we shall see that no one in possession of power ought to abide by his promises to the injury of his dominion; for he cannot keep such promises without breaking the engagement he made with his subjects, by which both he and they are most solemnly bound.

An enemy is one who lives apart from the state, and does not recognize its authority either as a subject or as an ally. It is not hatred which makes a man an enemy, but the rights of the state. The rights of the state are the same in regard to him who does not recognize by any compact the state authority, as they are against him who has done the state an injury. It has the right to force him, as best it can, either to submit, or to contract an alliance.

Lastly, treason can only be committed by subjects, who by compact, either tacit or expressed, have transferred all their rights to the state. A subject is said to have committed this crime when he has attempted, for whatever reason, to seize the sovereign power, or to place it in different hands. I say, *has attempted*, for if punishment were not to overtake him till he had succeeded, it would often come too late, the sovereign rights would have been acquired or transferred already.

I also say, *has attempted, for whatever reasons, to seize the sovereign power*, and I recognize no difference whether such an attempt should be followed by public loss or public gain. Whatever be his reason for acting, the crime is treason, and he is rightly condemned. In war, everyone would admit the justice of his sentence. If a man does not keep to his post, but approaches the enemy without the knowledge of his commander, whatever may be his motive, so long as he acts on his own motion, even if he advances with the design of defeating the enemy, he is rightly put to death, because he has violated his oath, and infringed the rights of his commander. That all citizens are equally bound by these rights in time of peace, is not so generally recognized, but the reasons for obedience are in both cases identical. The state must be preserved and directed by the sole authority of the sovereign, and such authority and right have been accorded by universal consent to him alone. If, therefore, anyone else attempts, without his consent, to execute any public enterprise, even though the state might (as we said) reap benefit therefrom, such person has none the less infringed the sovereign's right, and would be rightly punished for treason.

In order that every scruple may be removed, we may now answer the inquiry, whether our former assertion that everyone who has not the practice of reason, may, in the state of Nature, live by sovereign natural right, according to the laws of his desires, is not in direct opposition to the law and right of God as revealed. For as all men absolutely (whether they be less endowed with reason or more) are equally bound by the Divine command to love their neighbor as themselves, it may be said that they cannot, without wrong, do injury to any one, or live according to their desires.

This objection, so far as the state of Nature is concerned, can be easily answered, for the state of Nature is, both in nature and in time, prior to religion. No one knows by nature that he owes any obedience to God,[35] nor can he attain thereto by any exercise of his reason, but solely by revelation confirmed by signs. Therefore, previous to revelation, no one is bound by a Divine law and right of which he is necessarily in ignorance. The state of Nature must by no means be confounded with a state of religion, but must be conceived as without either religion or law, and consequently without sin or wrong. This is how we have described it, and we are confirmed by the authority of Paul. It is not only in respect of ignorance that we conceive the state of Nature as prior to, and lacking the Divine revealed law and right; but in respect of freedom also, wherewith all men are born endowed....

It may be insisted that sovereigns are as much bound by the Divine law as subjects; whereas we have asserted that they retain their natural rights, and may do whatever they like.

In order to clear up the whole difficulty, which arises rather concerning the natural right than the natural state, I maintain that everyone is bound, in the state of Nature, to live according to Divine law, in the same way as he is bound to live according to the dictates of sound reason; namely, inasmuch as it is to his advantage, and necessary for his salvation; but, if he will not so live, he may do otherwise at his own risk. He is thus bound to live according to his own laws, not according to anyone else's, and to recognize no man as a judge, or as a superior in religion. Such, in my opinion, is the position of a sovereign, for he may take advice from his fellow men, but he is not bound to recognize any as a judge, nor any one besides himself as an arbitrator on any question of right, unless it be a prophet sent expressly by God and attesting his mission by indisputable signs. Even then he does not recognize a man, but God Himself as his judge.

If a sovereign refuses to obey God as revealed in His law, he does so at his own risk and loss, but without violating any civil or natural right. For the civil right is dependent on his own decree; and natural right is dependent on the laws of Nature, which latter are not adapted to religion, whose sole aim is the good of humanity, but to the order of Nature—that is, to God's eternal decree unknown to us.

This truth seems to be adumbrated in a somewhat obscurer form by those who maintain that men can sin against God's revelation, but not against the eternal decree by which He has ordained all things....

FOOTNOTES:

[32] From the *Tr. Th.-P.*, ch. xvi, same title.

[33] In the state of social life, where general right determines what is good or evil, stratagem is rightly distinguished as of two kinds, good and evil. But in the state of Nature, where every man is his own judge, possessing the absolute right to lay down laws for himself, to interpret them as he pleases, or to abrogate them if he thinks it convenient, it is not conceivable that stratagem should be evil.

[34] Whatever be the social state a man finds himself in, he may be free. For certainly a man is free, in so far as he is led by reason. Now reason (though Hobbes thinks otherwise) is always on the side of peace, which cannot be attained unless the general laws of the state be respected. Therefore the more a man is led by reason—in other words, the more he is free, the more constantly will he respect the laws of his country, and obey the commands of the sovereign power to which he is subject.

[35] When Paul says that men have in themselves no refuge, he speaks as a man: for in the ninth chapter of the same Epistle he expressly teaches that God has mercy on whom He will, and that men are without excuse, only because they are in God's power like clay in the hands of a potter, who out of the same lump makes vessels, some for honor and some for dishonor, not because they have been forewarned. As regards the Divine natural law whereof the chief commandment is, as we have said, to love God, I have called it a law in the same sense, as philosophers style laws those general rules of Nature, according to which everything happens. For the love of God is not a state of obedience: it is a virtue which necessarily exists in a man who knows God rightly. Obedience has regard to the will of a ruler, not to necessity and truth. Now as we are

ignorant of the nature of God's will, and on the other hand know that every-thing happens solely by God's power, we cannot, except through revelation, know whether God wishes in any way to be honored as a sovereign.

Again; we have shown that the Divine rights appear to us in the light of rights or commands, only so long as we are ignorant of their cause: as soon as their cause is known, they cease to be rights, and we embrace them no longer as rights but as eternal truths; in other words, obedience passes into love of God, which emanates from true knowledge as necessarily as light emanates from the sun. Reason then leads us to love God, but cannot lead us to obey Him; for we cannot embrace the commands of God as Divine, while we are in ignorance of their cause, neither can we rationally conceive God as a sovereign laying down laws as a sovereign.

CHAPTER XVII
OF SUPREME AUTHORITIES

I

Of the Right of Supreme Authorities[36]

Under every dominion the state is said to be Civil; but the entire body subject to a dominion is called a Commonwealth, and the general business of the dominion, subject to the direction of him that holds it, has the name of Affairs of State. Next we call men Citizens, as far as they enjoy by the civil law all the advantages of the commonwealth, and Subjects, as far as they are bound to obey its ordinances or laws. Lastly ... of the civil state there are three kinds— democracy, aristocracy and monarchy. Now, before I begin to treat of each kind separately, I will first deduce all the properties of the civil state in general. And of these, first of all comes to be considered the supreme right of the commonwealth, or the right of the supreme authorities.

It is clear that the right of the supreme authorities is nothing else than simple natural right, limited, indeed, by the power, not of every individual, but of the multitude, which is guided, as it were, by one mind—that is, as each individual in the state of Nature, so the body and mind of a dominion have as much right as they have power. And thus each single citizen or subject has the less right, the more the commonwealth exceeds him in power, and each citizen consequently does and has nothing but what he may by the general decree of the commonwealth defend.

If the commonwealth grant to any man the right, and therewith the authority (for else it is but a gift of words) to live after his own mind, by that very act it abandons its own right, and transfers the same to him, to whom it has given such authority. But if it has given this authority to two or more, I mean authority to live each after his own mind, by that very act it has divided the dominion, and if, lastly, it has given this same authority to every citizen, it has thereby destroyed itself, and there remains no more a commonwealth, but everything returns to the state of Nature; all of which is very manifest from what goes before. And thus it follows, that it can by no means be conceived, that every citizen should by the ordinance of the commonwealth live after his own mind, and accordingly this natural right of being one's own judge ceases in the civil state. I say expressly "by the ordinance of the commonwealth," for if we weigh the matter aright, the natural right of every man does not cease in the civil state. For man, alike in the natural and in the civil state, acts according to the laws of his own nature, and consults his own interest. Man, I say, in each state is led by fear or hope to do or leave undone this or that; but the main difference between the two states is this, that in the civil state all fear the same things, and all have the same ground of security, and manner of life; and this certainly does not do away with the individual's faculty of judgment. For he that is minded to obey all the commonwealth's orders, whether through fear of its power or through love of quiet, certainly consults after his own heart his own safety and interest.

Moreover, we cannot even conceive, that every citizen should be allowed to interpret the commonwealth's decrees or laws. For were every citizen allowed this, he would thereby be his own judge, because each would easily be able to give a color of right to his own deeds, which by the last section is absurd.

We see, then, that every citizen depends not on himself, but on the commonwealth, all whose commands he is bound to execute, and has no right to decide, what is equitable or iniquitous, just or unjust. But, on the contrary, as the body of the dominion should, so to speak, be guided by one mind, and consequently the will of the commonwealth must be taken to be the will of all; what the state decides to be just and good must be held to be so decided by every individual. And so, however iniquitous the subject may think the commonwealth's decisions, he is none the less bound to execute them.

But, it may be objected, is it not contrary to the dictate of reason to subject oneself wholly to the judgment of another, and, consequently, is not the civil state repugnant to reason? Whence it would follow that the civil state is irrational, and could only be created by men destitute of reason, not at all by such as are led by it. But since reason teaches nothing contrary to Nature, sound reason cannot therefore dictate that everyone should remain independent, so long as men are liable to passions, that is, reason pronounces against such independence. Besides, reason altogether teaches to seek peace, and peace cannot be maintained, unless the commonwealth's general laws be kept unbroken. And so, the more a man is guided by reason, that is, the more he is free, the more constantly he will keep the laws of the commonwealth, and execute the commands of the supreme authority, whose subject he is. Furthermore, the civil state is naturally ordained to remove general fear, and prevent general sufferings, and therefore pursue above everything the very end, after which everyone, who is led by reason, strives, but in the natural state strives vainly.

Wherefore, if a man, who is led by reason, has sometimes to do by the commonwealth's order what he knows to be repugnant to reason, that harm is far compensated by the good, which he derives from the existence of a civil state. For it is reason's own law, to choose the less of two evils; and accordingly we may conclude that no one is acting against the dictate of his own reason, so far as he does what by the law of the commonwealth is to be done. And this any one will more easily grant us, after we have explained how far the power and consequently the right of the commonwealth extends.

For, first of all, it must be considered that, as in the state of Nature the man who is led by reason is most powerful and most independent, so too that commonwealth will be most powerful and most independent which is founded and guided by reason. For the right of the commonwealth is determined by the power of the multitude, which is led, as it were, by one mind. But this unity of mind can in no wise be conceived, unless the commonwealth pursues chiefly the very end which sound reason teaches is to the interest of all men.

In the second place it comes to be considered that subjects are so far dependent, not on themselves but on the commonwealth, as they fear its power or threats, or as they love the civil state. Whence it follows, that such things, as no one can be induced to do by rewards or threats, do not fall within the rights of the commonwealth. For instance, by reason of his faculty of judgment, it is in no man's power to believe. For by what rewards or threats can a man be brought to believe that the whole is not greater than its part, or that God does not exist, or that that is an infinite being, which he sees to be finite, or, generally, anything contrary to his sense or thought? So, too, by what rewards or threats can a man be brought to love one whom he hates, or to hate one whom he loves? And to this head must likewise be referred such things as are so abhorrent to human nature, that it regards them as actually worse than any evil, as that a man should be witness against himself, or torture himself, or kill his parents, or not strive to avoid death, and the like, to which no one can be induced by rewards or threats. But if we still choose to say that the commonwealth has the right or authority to order such things, we can conceive of it in no other sense than that in which one might say that a man has the right to be mad or delirious. For what but a delirious fancy would such a right be, as could bind no one? And here I am speaking expressly of such things as cannot be subject to the right of a commonwealth and are abhorrent to human nature in general. For the fact that a fool or madman can by no rewards or threats be induced to execute orders, or that this or that person, because he is attached to this or that religion, judges the laws of a dominion worse than any possible evil, in no wise makes void the laws of the commonwealth, since by them most of the citizens are restrained. And so, as those who are without fear or hope are so far independent, they are, therefore, enemies of the dominion, and may lawfully be coerced by force.

Thirdly, and lastly, it comes to be considered that those things are not so much within the commonwealth's right, which cause indignation in the majority. For it is certain, that by the guidance of Nature men conspire together, either through common fear, or with the desire to avenge some common hurt; and as the right of the commonwealth is determined by the common power of the multitude, it is certain that the power and right of the commonwealth are so far diminished, as it gives occasion for many to conspire together. There are certainly some subjects of fear for a commonwealth, and as every separate citizen or in the state of Nature every man, so a commonwealth is the less independent, the greater reason it has to fear. So much for the right of supreme authorities over subjects. Now before I treat of the right of the said authorities as against others, we had better resolve a question commonly mooted about religion.

For it may be objected to us, Do not the civil state, and the obedience of subjects, such as we have shown is required in the civil state, do away with religion, whereby we are bound to worship God? But if we consider the matter, as it really is, we shall find nothing that can suggest a scruple. For the mind, so far as it makes use of reason, is dependent, not on the supreme authorities, but on itself. And so the true knowledge and the love of God cannot be subject to the dominion of any, nor yet can charity towards one's neighbor. And if we further reflect that the highest exercise of charity is that which aims at keeping peace and joining in unity, we shall not doubt that he does his duty, who helps everyone, so far as the commonwealth's laws, that is, so far as unity and quiet allow. As for external rites, it is certain, that they can do no good or harm at all in respect of the true knowledge of God, and the love which necessarily results from it; and so they ought not to be held of such importance, that it should be thought worth while on their account to disturb public peace and quiet. Moreover, it is certain that I am not a champion of religion by the law of Nature, that is, by the divine decree. For I have no authority, as once the disciples of Christ had, to cast out unclean spirits and work miracles; which authority is yet so necessary to the propagating of religion in places where it is forbidden, that without it one not only, as they say, wastes one's time[37] and trouble, but causes besides very many inconveniences, whereof all ages have seen most mournful examples. Everyone therefore, wherever he may be, can worship God with true religion, and mind his own business, which is the duty of a private man. But the care of propagating religion should be left to God, or the supreme authorities, upon whom alone falls the charge of affairs of state. But I return to my subject.

After explaining the right of supreme authorities over citizens and the duty of subjects, it remains to consider the right of such authorities against the world at large, which is now easily intelligible from what has been said. For since the right of the supreme authorities is nothing else but simple natural right, it follows that two dominions stand towards each other in the same relation as do two men in the state of Nature, with this exception, that a commonwealth can provide against being oppressed by another; which a man in the state of Nature cannot do, seeing that he is overcome daily by sleep, often by disease or mental infirmity, and in the end by old age, and is besides liable to other inconveniences, from which a commonwealth can secure itself.

A commonwealth, then, is so far independent, as it can plan and provide against oppression by another, and so far dependent on another commonwealth, as it fears that other's power, or is hindered by it from executing its own wishes, or, lastly, as it needs its help for its own preservation or increase. For we cannot at all doubt, that if two commonwealths are willing to offer each other mutual help, both together are more powerful, and therefore have more right, than either alone.

But this will be more clearly intelligible if we reflect that two commonwealths are naturally enemies. For men in the state of Nature are enemies. Those, then, who stand outside a commonwealth, and retain their natural rights, continue enemies. Accordingly, if one commonwealth wishes to make war on another and employ extreme measures to make that other dependent on itself, it may lawfully make the attempt, since it needs but the bare will of the commonwealth for war to be waged. But concerning peace it can decide nothing, save with the concurrence of another commonwealth's will. When it follows that laws of war regard every commonwealth by itself, but laws of peace regard not one, but at the least two commonwealths, which are therefore called "contracting parties."

This "contract" remains so long unmoved as the motive for entering into it, that is, fear of hurt or hope of gain, subsists. But take away from either commonwealth this hope or fear, and it is left independent, and the link, whereby the commonwealths were mutually bound, breaks of itself. And therefore every commonwealth has the right to break its contract, whenever it chooses, and cannot be said to act treacherously or perfidiously in breaking its word, as soon as the motive of hope or fear is removed. For every contracting party was on equal terms in this respect, that whichever could first free itself of fear should be independent, and make use of its independence after its own mind; and, besides, no one makes a contract respecting the future, but on the hypothesis of certain precedent circumstances. But when these circumstances change, the reason of policy applicable to the whole position changes with them; and therefore everyone of the contracting commonwealths retains the right of consulting its own interest, and consequently endeavors, as far as possible, to be free from fear and thereby independent, and to prevent another from coming out of the contract with greater power. If then a commonwealth complains that it has been deceived, it cannot properly blame the bad faith of another contracting commonwealth, but only its own folly in having entrusted its own welfare to another party, that was independent, and had for its highest law the welfare of its own dominion.

To commonwealths, which have contracted a treaty of peace, it belongs to decide the questions which may be mooted about the terms or rules of peace, whereby they have mutually bound themselves, inasmuch as laws of peace regard not one commonwealth, but the commonwealths which contract taken together. But if they cannot agree together about the conditions, they by that very fact return to a state of war.

The more commonwealths there are, that have contracted a joint treaty of peace, the less each of them by itself is an object of fear to the remainder, or the less it has the authority to make war. But it is so much the more bound to observe the conditions of peace; that is, the less independent, and the more bound to accommodate itself to the general will of the contracting parties.

But the good faith, inculcated by sound reason and religion, is not hereby made void; for neither reason nor Scripture teaches one to keep one's word in every case. For if I have promised a man, for instance, to keep safe a sum of money he has secretly deposited with me, I am not bound to keep my word, from the time that I know or believe the deposit to have been stolen, but I shall act more rightly in endeavoring to restore it to its owners. So likewise, if the supreme authority has promised another to do something, which subsequently occasion or reason shows or seems to show is contrary to the welfare of its subjects, it is surely bound to break its word. As then Scripture only teaches us to keep our word in general, and leaves to every individual's judgment the special cases of exception, it teaches nothing repugnant to what we have just proved.

But that I may not have so often to break the thread of my discourse, and to resolve hereafter similar objections, I would have it known that all this demonstration of mine proceeds from the necessity of human nature, considered in what light you will—I mean, from the universal effort of all men after self-preservation, an effort inherent in all men, whether learned or unlearned. And therefore, however one considers men are led, whether by passion or by reason, it will be the same thing; for the demonstration, as we have said, is of universal application.

II

Of the Functions of Supreme Authorities[38]

The right of the supreme authorities is limited by their power; the most important part of that right is, that they are, as it were, the mind of the dominion, whereby all ought to be guided; and accordingly, such authorities alone have the right of deciding what is good, evil, equitable or iniquitous, that is, what must be done or left undone by the subjects severally or collectively. And, accordingly, they have the sole right of laying down laws, and of interpreting the same, whenever their meaning is disputed, and of deciding whether a given case is in conformity with or violation of the laws; and, lastly, of waging war, and of drawing up and offering propositions for peace, or of accepting such when offered.

As all these functions, and also the means required to execute them, are matters which regard the whole body of the dominion, that is, are affairs of state, it follows that affairs of state depend on the direction of him only who holds supreme dominion. And hence it follows that it is the right of the supreme authority alone to judge the deeds of every individual, and demand of him an account of the same; to punish criminals, and decide questions of law between citizens, or appoint jurists acquainted with the existing laws, to administer these matters on its behalf; and, further, to use and order all means to war and peace, as to found and fortify cities, levy soldiers, assign military posts, and order what it would have done, and, with a view to peace, to send and give audience to ambassadors; and, finally, to levy the costs of all this.

Since, then, it is the right of the supreme authority alone to handle public matters, or choose officials to do so, it follows that that subject is a pretender to the dominion, who, without the supreme council's knowledge, enters upon any public matter, although he believe that his design will be to the best interest of the commonwealth.

But it is often asked, whether the supreme authority is bound by laws, and, consequently, whether it can do wrong. Now as the words "law" and "wrong-doing" often refer not merely to the laws of a commonwealth, but also to the general rules which concern all natural things, and especially to the general rules of reason, we cannot, without qualification, say that the commonwealth is bound by no laws, or can do no wrong. For were the commonwealth bound by no laws or rules, which removed, the commonwealth were no commonwealth, we should have to regard it not as a natural thing, but as a chimera. A commonwealth then does wrong, when it does, or suffers to be done, things which may be the cause of its own ruin; and we can say that it then does wrong, in the sense in which philosophers or doctors say that Nature does wrong; and in this sense we can say, that a commonwealth does wrong, when it acts against the dictate of reason. For a commonwealth is most independent when it acts according to the dictate of reason; so far, then, as it acts against reason, it fails itself, or does wrong. And we shall be able more easily to understand this if we reflect that when we say, that a man can do what he will with his own, this authority must be limited not only by the power of the agent, but by the capacity of the object. If, for instance, I say that I can rightfully do what I will with this table, I do not certainly mean that I have the right to make it eat grass. So, too, though we say, that men depend not on themselves, but on the commonwealth, we do not mean, that men lose their human nature and put on another; nor yet that the commonwealth has the right to make men wish for this or that, or (what is just as impossible) regard with honor things which excite ridicule or disgust. But it is implied that there are certain intervening circumstances which supposed, one likewise supposes the reverence and fear of the subjects towards the commonwealth, and which abstracted, one makes abstraction likewise of that fear and reverence, and therewith of the commonwealth itself. The commonwealth, then, to maintain its independence, is bound to preserve the causes of fear and reverence, otherwise it ceases to be a commonwealth. For the person or persons that hold dominion can no more combine with the keeping up of majesty the running with harlots drunk or naked about the streets, or the performances of a stage-player, or the open violation or contempt of laws passed by themselves, than they can combine existence with non-existence. But to proceed to slay and rob subjects, ravish maidens, and the like, turns fear into indignation and the civil state into a state of enmity.

We see, then, in what sense we may say, that a commonwealth is bound by laws and can do wrong. But if by "law" we understand civil law, and by "wrong" that which, by civil law, is forbidden to be done, that is, if these words be taken in their proper sense, we cannot at all say that a commonwealth is bound by laws or can do wrong. For the maxims and motives of fear and reverence which a commonwealth is bound to observe in its own interest, pertain not to civil jurisprudence, but to the law of Nature, since they cannot be vindicated by the civil law, but by the law of war. And a commonwealth is bound by them in no other sense than that in which in the state of Nature a man is bound to take heed that he preserve his independence and be not his own enemy, lest he should destroy himself; and in this taking heed lies not the subjection, but the liberty of human nature. But civil jurisprudence depends on the mere decree of the commonwealth, which is not bound to please any but itself, nor to hold anything to be good or bad, but what it judges to be such for itself. And, accordingly, it has not merely the right to avenge itself, or to lay down and interpret laws, but also to abolish the same, and to pardon any guilty person out of the fullness of its power.

Contracts or laws, whereby the multitude transfers its right to one council or man, should without doubt be broken, when it is expedient for the general welfare to do so. But to decide this point, whether, that is, it be expedient for the general welfare to break them or not, is within the right of no private person, but of him only who holds dominion; therefore of these laws he who holds dominion remains sole interpreter. Moreover, no private person can by right vindicate these laws, and so they do not really bind him who holds dominion. Notwithstanding, if they are of such a nature that they cannot be broken without at the same time weakening the commonwealth's strength, that is, without at the same time changing to indignation the common fear of most of the citizens, by this very fact the commonwealth is dissolved, and the contract comes to an end; and therefore such contract is vindicated not by the civil law, but by the law of war. And so he who holds dominion is not bound to observe the terms of the contract by any other cause than that, which bids a man in the state of Nature to beware of being his own enemy, lest he should destroy himself.

III

Of the Best State of a Dominion[39]

We have shown that man is then most independent when he is most led by reason, and, in consequence, that that commonwealth is most powerful and most independent which is founded and guided by reason. But, as the best plan of living, so as to assure to the utmost self-preservation, is that which is framed according to the dictate of reason, therefore it follows that that in every kind is best done, which a man or commonwealth does, so far as he or it is in the highest degree independent. For it is one thing to till a field by right, and another to till it in the best way. One thing, I say, to defend or preserve oneself, and to pass judgment by right, and another to defend or preserve oneself in the best way, and to pass the best judgment; and, consequently, it is one thing to have dominion and care of affairs of state by right, and another to exercise dominion and direct affairs of state in the best way. And so, as we have treated of the right of every commonwealth in general, it is time to treat of the best state of every dominion.

Now the quality of the state of any dominion is easily perceived from the end of the civil state, which end is nothing else but peace and security of life. And therefore that dominion is the best, where men pass their lives in unity, and the laws are kept unbroken. For it is certain, that seditions, wars, and contempt or breach of the laws are not so much to be imputed to the wickedness of the subjects, as to the bad state of a dominion. For men are not born fit for citizenship, but must be made so. Besides, men's natural passions are everywhere the same; and if wickedness more prevails, and more offenses are committed in one commonwealth than in another, it is certain that the former has not enough pursued the end of unity, nor framed its laws with sufficient forethought; and that, therefore, it has failed in making quite good its right as a commonwealth. For a civil state, which has not done away with the causes of seditions, where war is a perpetual object of fear, and where, lastly, the laws are often broken, differs but little from the mere state of Nature, in which everyone lives after his own mind at the great risk of his life.

But as the vices and inordinate license and contumacy of subjects must be imputed to the commonwealth, so, on the other hand, their virtue and constant obedience to the laws are to be ascribed in the main to the virtue and perfect right of the commonwealth. And so it is deservedly reckoned to Hannibal as an extraordinary virtue, that in his army there never arose a sedition.

Of a commonwealth, whose subjects are but hindered by terror from taking arms, it should rather be said, that it is free from war, than that it has peace. For peace is not mere absence of war, but is a virtue that springs from force of character: for obedience is the constant will to execute what, by the general decree of the commonwealth, ought to be done. Besides, that commonwealth whose peace depends on the sluggishness of its subjects, that are led about like sheep to learn but slavery, may more properly be called a desert than a commonwealth.

When, then, we call that dominion best, where men pass their lives in unity, I understand a human life, defined not by mere circulation of the blood, and other qualities common to all animals, but above all by reason, the true excellence and life of the mind.

But be it remarked that, by the dominion which I have said is established for this end, I intend that which has been established by a free multitude, not that which is acquired over a multitude by right of war. For a free multitude is guided more by hope than fear; a conquered one, more by fear than by hope: inasmuch as the former aims at making use of life, the latter but at escaping death. The former, I say, aims at living for its own ends, the latter is forced to belong to the conqueror; and so we say that this is enslaved, but that free. And, therefore, the end of a dominion, which one gets by right of war, is to be master, and have rather slaves than subjects. And although between the dominion created by a free multitude, and that gained by right of war, if we regard generally the right of each, we can make no essential distinction; yet their ends, as we have already shown, and further the means to the preservation of each are very different.

But what means a prince, whose sole motive is lust of mastery, should use to establish and maintain his dominion, the most ingenious Machiavelli has set forth at large,[40] but with what design one can hardly be sure. If, however, he had some good design, as one should believe of a learned man, it seems to have been to show, with how little foresight many attempt to remove a tyrant, though thereby the causes which make the prince a tyrant can in no wise be removed, but, on the contrary, are so much the more established, as the prince is given more cause to fear, which happens when the multitude has made an example of its prince, and glories in the parricide as in a thing well done. Moreover, he perhaps wished to show how cautious a free multitude should be of entrusting its welfare absolutely to one man, who, unless in his vanity he thinks he can please everybody, must be in daily fear of plots, and so is forced to look chiefly after his own interest, and, as for the multitude, rather to plot against it than consult its good. And I am the more led to this opinion concerning that most far-seeing man, because it is known that he was favorable to liberty, for the maintenance of which he has besides given the most wholesome advice.

FOOTNOTES:

[36] From *A Political Treatise*, ch. iii, same title.

[37] Literally, "oil and trouble"—a common proverbial expression in Latin.

[38] From *A Political Treatise*, ch. iv, same title.

[39] From *A Political Treatise*, ch. v, same title.

[40] In his book called "Il Principe," or "The Prince."

CHAPTER XVIII

FREEDOM OF THOUGHT AND SPEECH[411]

If men's minds were as easily controlled as their tongues, every king would sit safely on his throne, and government by compulsion would cease; for every subject would shape his life according to the intentions of his rulers, and would esteem a thing true or false, good or evil, just or unjust, in obedience to their dictates. However, ... no man's mind can possibly lie wholly at the disposition of another, for no one can willingly transfer his natural right of free reason and judgment, or be compelled so to do. For this reason government which attempts to control minds is accounted tyrannical, and it is considered an abuse of sovereignty and a usurpation of the rights of subjects to seek to prescribe what shall be accepted as true, or rejected as false, or what opinions should actuate men in their worship of God. All these questions fall within a man's natural right, which he cannot abdicate even with his own consent.

I admit that the judgment can be biased in many ways, and to an almost incredible degree, so that while exempt from direct external control it may be so dependent on another man's words, that it may fitly be said to be ruled by him; but although this influence is carried to great lengths, it has never gone so far as to invalidate the statement that every man's understanding is his own, and that brains are as diverse as palates.

Moses, not by fraud, but by Divine virtue, gained such a hold over the popular judgment that he was accounted superhuman, and believed to speak and act through the inspiration of the Deity; nevertheless, even he could not escape murmurs and evil interpretations. How much less then can other monarchs avoid them! Yet such unlimited power, if it exists at all, must belong to a monarch, and least of all to a democracy, where the whole or a great part of the people wield authority collectively. This is a fact which I think everyone can explain for himself.

However unlimited, therefore, the power of a sovereign may be, however implicitly it is trusted as the exponent of law and religion, it can never prevent men from forming judgments according to their intellect, or being influenced by any given emotion. It is true that it has the right to treat as enemies all men whose opinions do not, on all subjects, entirely coincide with its own; but we are not discussing its strict rights, but its proper course of action. I grant that it has the right to rule in the most violent manner, and to put citizens to death for very trivial causes, but no one supposes it can do this with the approval of sound judgment. Nay, inasmuch as such things cannot be done without extreme peril to itself, we may even deny that it has the absolute power to do them, or, consequently, the absolute right; for the rights of the sovereign are limited by his power.

Since, therefore, no one can abdicate his freedom of judgment and feeling; since every man is by indefeasible natural right the master of his own thoughts, it follows that men, thinking in diverse and contradictory fashions, cannot, without disastrous results, be compelled to speak only according to the dictates of the supreme power. Not even the most experienced, to say nothing of the multitude, know how to keep silence. Men's common failing is to confide their plans to others, though there be need for secrecy, so that a government would be most harsh which deprived the individual of his freedom of saying and teaching what he thought; and would be moderate if such freedom were granted. Still we cannot deny that authority may be as much injured by words as by actions. Hence, although the freedom we are discussing cannot be entirely denied to subjects, its unlimited concession would be most baneful; we must, therefore, now inquire, how far such freedom can and ought to be conceded without danger to the peace of the state, or the power of the rulers.

It follows, plainly, from the explanation given above, of the foundations of a state, that the ultimate aim of government is not to rule, or restrain by fear, nor to exact obedience, but, contrariwise, to free every man from fear that he may live in all possible security; in other words, to strengthen his natural right to exist and work without injury to himself or others.

No, the object of government is not to change men from rational beings into beasts or puppets, but to enable them to develop their minds and bodies in security, and to employ their reason unshackled; neither showing hatred, anger or deceit, nor watched with the eyes of jealousy and injustice. In fact, the true aim of government is liberty.

Now we have seen that in forming a state the power of making laws must either be vested in the body of the citizens, or in a portion of them, or in one man. For, although men's free judgments are very diverse, each one thinking that he alone knows everything, and although complete unanimity of feeling and speech is out of the question, it is impossible to preserve peace unless individuals abdicate their right of acting entirely on their own judgment. Therefore, the individual justly cedes the right of free action, though not of free reason and judgment; no one can act against the authorities without danger to the state, though his feelings and judgment may be at variance therewith; he may even speak against them, provided that he does so from rational conviction, not from fraud, anger or hatred, and provided that he does not attempt to introduce any change on his private authority.

For instance, supposing a man shows that a law is repugnant to sound reason, and should therefore be repealed; if he submits his opinion to the judgment of the authorities (who alone have the right of making and repealing laws), and meanwhile acts in nowise contrary to that law, he has deserved well of the state, and has behaved as a good citizen should; but if he accuses the authorities of injustice, and stirs up the people against them, or if he seditiously strives to abrogate the law without their consent, he is a mere agitator and rebel.

Thus we see how an individual may declare and teach what he believes, without injury to the authority of his rulers, or to the public peace; namely, by leaving in their hands the entire power of legislation as it affects action, and by doing nothing against their laws, though he be compelled often to act in contradiction to what he believes, and openly feels, to be best.

Such a course can be taken without detriment to justice and dutifulness, nay, it is the one which a just and dutiful man would adopt. We have shown that justice is dependent on the laws of the authorities, so that no one who contravenes their accepted decrees can be just, while the highest regard for duty, as we have pointed out, is exercised in maintaining public peace and tranquility. These could not be preserved if every man were to live as he pleased. Therefore it is no less than undutiful for a man to act contrary to his country's laws, for if the practice became universal the ruin of states would necessarily follow.

Hence, so long as a man acts in obedience to the laws of his rulers, he in nowise contravenes his reason, for in obedience to reason he transferred the right of controlling his actions from his own hands to theirs. This doctrine we can confirm from actual custom, for in a conference of great and small powers, schemes are seldom carried unanimously, yet all unite in carrying out what is decided on, whether they voted for or against. But I return to my proposition.

From the fundamental notions of a state, we have discovered how a man may exercise free judgment without detriment to the supreme power: from the same premises we can no less easily determine what opinions would be seditious. Evidently those which by their very nature nullify the compact by which the right of free action was ceded. For instance, a man who holds that the supreme power has no rights over him, or that promises ought not to be kept, or that everyone should live as he pleases, or other doctrines of this nature in direct opposition to the above-mentioned contract, is seditious, not so much from his actual opinions and judgment, as from the deeds which they involve; for he who maintains such theories abrogates the contract which tacitly, or openly, he made with his rulers. Other opinions which do not involve acts violating the contract, such as revenge, anger, and the like, are not seditious, unless it be in some corrupt state, where superstitious and ambitious persons, unable to endure men of learning, are so popular with the multitude that their word is more valued than the law.

However, I do not deny that there are some doctrines which, while they are apparently only concerned with abstract truths and falsehoods, are yet propounded and published with unworthy motives.... Reason should nevertheless remain unshackled. If we hold to the principle that a man's loyalty to the state should be judged, like his loyalty to God, from his actions only—namely, from his charity towards his neighbors; we cannot doubt that the best government will allow freedom of philosophical speculation no less than of religious belief. I confess that from such freedom inconveniences may sometimes arise, but what question was ever settled so wisely than no abuses could possibly spring therefrom? He who seeks to regulate everything by law is more likely to arouse vices than to reform them. It is best to grant what cannot be abolished, even though it be in itself harmful. How many evils spring from luxury, envy, avarice, drunkenness and the like, yet these are tolerated—vices as they are—because they cannot be prevented by legal enactments. How much more, then, should free thought be granted, seeing that it is in itself a virtue and that it cannot be crushed! Besides, the evil results can easily be checked, as I will show, by the secular authorities, not to mention that such freedom is absolutely necessary for progress in science and the liberal arts: for no man follows such pursuits to advantage unless his judgment be entirely free and unhampered.

But let it be granted that freedom may be crushed, and men be so bound down that they do not dare to utter a whisper, save at the bidding of their rulers; nevertheless this can never be carried to the pitch of making them think according to authority, so that the necessary consequences would be that men would daily be thinking one thing and saying another, to the corruption of good faith, that mainstay of government, and to the fostering of hateful flattery and perfidy, whence spring stratagems, and the corruption of every good art.

It is far from possible to impose uniformity of speech, for the more rulers strive to curtail freedom of speech the more obstinately are they resisted; not

indeed by the avaricious, the flatterers, and other numskulls, who think supreme salvation consists in filling their stomachs and gloating over their mon-
ey-bags, but by those whom good education, sound morality, and virtue have
rendered more free. Men, as generally constituted, are most prone to resent the
branding as criminal of opinions which they believe to be true, and the pro-
scription as wicked of that which inspires them with piety towards God and
man; hence they are ready to forswear the laws and conspire against the authorities, thinking it not shameful but honorable to stir up seditions and per-
petuate any sort of crime with this end in view. Such being the constitution of
human nature, we see that laws directed against opinions affect the generous
minded rather than the wicked, and are adapted less for coercing criminals than
for irritating the upright; so that they cannot be maintained without great peril
to the state.

Moreover, such laws are almost always useless, for those who hold that the
opinions proscribed are sound, cannot possibly obey the law; whereas those
who already reject them as false, accept the law as a kind of privilege, and
make such boast of it, that authority is powerless to repeal it, even if such a
course be subsequently desired.

... And, lastly, how many schisms have arisen in the Church from the attempt
of the authorities to decide by law the intricacies of theological controversy! If
men were not allured by the hope of getting the law and the authorities on their
side, of triumphing over their adversaries in the sight of an applauding multitude, and of acquiring honorable distinctions, they would not strive so mali-
ciously, nor would such fury sway their minds. This is taught not only by reason but by daily examples, for laws of this kind prescribing what every man
shall believe and forbidding any one to speak or write to the contrary, have
often been passed as sops or concessions to the anger of those who cannot
tolerate men of enlightenment, and who, by such harsh and crooked enactments, can easily turn the devotion of the masses into fury and direct it against
whom they will.

How much better would it be to restrain popular anger and fury, instead of
passing useless laws, which can only be broken by those who love virtue and
the liberal arts, thus paring down the state till it is too small to harbor men of
talent. What greater misfortune for a state can be conceived than that honorable men should be sent like criminals into exile, because they hold diverse
opinions which they cannot disguise? What, I say, can be more hurtful than
that men who have committed no crime or wickedness should, simply because
they are enlightened, be treated as enemies and put to death, and that the scaf-

fold, the terror of evil-doers, should become the arena where the highest examples of tolerance and virtue are displayed to the people with all the marks of
ignominy that authority can devise?

He that knows himself to be upright does not fear the death of a criminal, and
shrinks from no punishment. His mind is not wrung with remorse for any disgraceful deed. He holds that death in a good cause is no punishment, but an
honor, and that death for freedom is glory.

What purpose, then, is served by the death of such men, what example is proclaimed? The cause for which they die is unknown to the idle and the foolish,
hateful to the turbulent, loved by the upright. The only lesson we can draw
from such scenes is to flatter the persecutor, or else to imitate the victim.

If formal assent is not to be esteemed above conviction, and if governments are
to retain a firm hold of authority and not be compelled to yield to agitators, it is
imperative that freedom of judgment should be granted, so that men may live
together in harmony, however diverse, or even openly contradictory their opinions may be. We cannot doubt that such is the best system of government and
open to the fewest objections, since it is the one most in harmony with human
nature. In a democracy (the most natural form of government) everyone submits to the control of authority over his actions, but not over his judgment and
reason; that is, seeing that all cannot think alike, the voice of the majority has
the force of law, subject to repeal if circumstances bring about a change of
opinion. In proportion as the power of free judgment is withheld we depart
from the natural condition of mankind, and consequently the government becomes more tyrannical.

In order to prove that from such freedom no inconvenience arises which cannot easily be checked by the exercise of the sovereign power, and that men's
actions can easily be kept in bounds, though their opinions be at open variance,
it will be well to cite an example. Such an one is not very far to seek. The city
of Amsterdam reaps the fruit of this freedom in its own great prosperity and in
the admiration of all other people. For in this most flourishing state, and most
splendid city, men of every nation and religion live together in the greatest
harmony, and ask no questions before trusting their goods to a fellow-citizen,
save whether he be rich or poor, and whether he generally acts honestly, or the
reverse. His religion and sect is considered of no importance: for it has no effect before the judges in gaining or losing a cause, and there is no sect so despised that its followers, provided that they harm no one, pay every man his

due, and live uprightly, are deprived of the protection of the magisterial authority.

On the other hand, when the religious controversy between Remonstrants and Counter-Remonstrants began to be taken up by politicians and the States, it grew into a schism, and abundantly showed that laws dealing with religion and seeking to settle its controversies are much more calculated to irritate than to reform, and that they give rise to extreme license. Further, it was seen that schisms do not originate in a love of truth, which is a source of courtesy and gentleness, but rather in an inordinate desire for supremacy. From all these considerations it is clearer than the sun at noonday, that the true schismatics are those who condemn other men's writings, and seditiously stir up the quarrelsome masses against their authors, rather than those authors themselves, who generally write only for the learned, and appeal solely to reason. In fact, the real disturbers of the peace are those who, in a free state, seek to curtail the liberty of judgment which they are unable to tyrannize over.

I have thus shown:—I. That it is impossible to deprive men of the liberty of saying what they think. II. That such liberty can be conceded to every man without injury to the rights and authority of the sovereign power, and that every man may retain it without injury to such rights, provided that he does not presume upon it to the extent of introducing any new rights into the state, or acting in any way contrary to the existing laws. III. That every man may enjoy this liberty without detriment to the public peace, and that no inconveniences arise therefrom which cannot easily be checked. IV. That every man may enjoy it without injury to his allegiance. V. That laws dealing with speculative problems are entirely useless. VI. Lastly, that not only may such liberty be granted without prejudice to the public peace, to loyalty, and to the rights of rulers, but that it is even necessary for their preservation. For when people try to take it away, and bring to trial, not only the acts which alone are capable of offending, but also the opinions of mankind, they only succeed in surrounding their victims with an appearance of martyrdom, and raise feelings of pity and revenge rather than of terror. Uprightness and good faith are thus corrupted, flatterers and traitors are encouraged, and sectarians triumph, inasmuch as concessions have been made to their animosity, and they have gained the state sanction for the doctrines of which they are the interpreters. Hence they arrogate to themselves the state authority and rights, and do not scruple to assert that they have been directly chosen by God, and that their laws are Divine, whereas the laws of the state are human, and should therefore yield obedience to the laws of God—in other words, to their own laws. Everyone must see that this is not a state of affairs conducive to public welfare. Wherefore, the safest way for a state is to lay down the rule that religion is comprised solely in the exercise of charity and justice, and that the rights of rulers in sacred, no less than in secular matters, should merely have to do with actions, but that every man should think what he likes and say what he thinks.

FOOTNOTES:

[41] From the *Tr. Th.-P.*, ch. xx, same title.

CHAPTER XIX

OF HUMAN FREEDOM

Introductory

I pass at length to the other part of ethics which concerns the method or way which leads to liberty. In [the following], therefore, I shall treat of the power of reason, showing how much reason itself can control the emotions, and then what is freedom of mind or blessedness. Thence we shall see how much stronger the wise man is than the ignorant. In what manner and what way the intellect should be rendered perfect, and with what art the body is to be cared for in order that it may properly perform its functions, I have nothing to do with here; for the former belongs to logic, the latter to medicine. I shall occupy myself here, as I have said, solely with the power of the mind or of reason, first of all showing the extent and nature of the authority which it has over the emotions in restraining them and governing them; for that we have not absolute authority over them we have already demonstrated. The Stoics indeed thought that the emotions depend absolutely on our will, and that we are absolutely masters over them; but they were driven, by the contradiction of experience, though not by their own principles, to confess that not a little practice and study are required in order to restrain and govern the emotions. This one of them attempted to illustrate, if I remember rightly, by the example of two dogs, one of a domestic and the other of a hunting breed; for he was able by habit to make the house dog hunt, and the hunting dog, on the contrary, to desist from running after hares.

To the Stoical opinion Descartes much inclines. He affirms that the soul or mind is united specially to a certain part of the brain called the pineal gland, which the mind by the mere exercise of the will is able to move in different ways, and by whose help the mind perceives all the movements which are excited in the body and external objects. This gland, he affirms, is suspended in the middle of the brain in such a manner that it can be moved by the least motion of the animal spirits. Again, he affirms that any variation in the manner in which the animal spirits impinge upon this gland is followed by a variation in the manner in which it is suspended in the middle of the brain, and moreover that the number of different impressions on the gland is the same as that of the different external objects which propel the animal spirits toward it. Hence it comes to pass that if the gland, by the will of the soul moving it in different directions, be afterwards suspended in this or that way in which it had once been suspended by the spirits agitated in this or that way, then the gland itself will propel and determine the animal spirits themselves in the same way as that in which they had before been repelled by a similar suspension of the gland. Moreover, he affirmed that each volition of the mind is united in Nature to a certain motion of the gland. For example, if a person wishes to behold a remote object, this volition will cause the pupil of the eye to dilate, but if he thinks merely of the dilation of the pupil, to have that volition will profit him nothing, because Nature has not connected a motion of the gland which serves to impel the animal spirits towards the optic nerve in a way suitable for dilation or contraction of the pupil with the volition or dilation or contraction, but only with the volition of beholding objects afar off or close at hand. Finally, he maintained that although each motion of this gland appears to be connected by Nature from the commencement of our life with an individual thought, these motions can nevertheless be connected by habit with other thoughts, a proposition which he attempts to demonstrate in his "Passions of the Soul" (art. 50, pt. 1).

From this he concludes that there is no mind so feeble that it cannot, when properly directed, acquire absolute power over its passions; for passions, as defined by him, are "perceptions, or sensations, or emotions of the soul which are related to it specially, and which (N.B.) are produced, preserved, and strengthened by some motion of the spirits." (See the "Passions of Soul," art. 27, pt. 1.) But since it is possible to join to a certain volition any motion of the gland, and consequently of the spirits, and since the determination of the will depends solely on our power, we shall be able to acquire absolute mastery over our passions provided only we determine our will by fixed and firm decisions by which we desire to direct our actions and bind with these decisions the movements of the passions we wish to have.

So far as I can gather from his own words, this is the opinion of that distinguished man, and I could scarcely have believed it possible for one so great to have put it forward if it had been less subtle. I can hardly wonder enough that a philosopher who firmly resolved to make no deduction except from self-evident principles, and to affirm nothing but what he clearly and distinctly perceived, and who blamed all the Schoolmen because they desired to explain obscure matters by occult qualities, should accept a hypothesis more occult than any occult quality.

What does he understand, I ask, by the union of the mind and body? What clear and distinct conception has he of thought intimately connected with a certain small portion of matter? I wish that he had explained this union by its proximate cause. But he conceived the mind to be so distinct from the body that he was able to assign no single cause of this union, nor of the mind itself, but was obliged to have recourse to the cause of the whole universe, that is to say, to God. Again, I should like to know how many degrees of motion the mind can give to that pineal gland, and with how great a power the mind can hold it suspended. For I do not understand whether this gland is acted on by the mind more slowly or more quickly than by the animal spirits, and whether the movements of the passions, which we have so closely bound with firm decisions, might not be separated from them again by bodily causes, from which it would follow that although the mind had firmly determined to meet danger, and had joined to this decision the motion of boldness, the sight of the danger might cause the gland to be suspended in such a manner that the mind could think of nothing but flight. Indeed, since there is no relation between the will and motion, so there is no comparison between the power or strength of the body and that of the mind, and consequently the strength of the body can never be determined by the strength of the mind. It is to be remembered also that this gland is not found to be so situated in the middle of the brain that it can be driven about so easily and in so many ways, and that all the nerves are not extended to the cavities of the brain.

Lastly, I omit all that Descartes asserts concerning the will and the freedom of the will, since I have shown over and over again that it is false. Therefore, inasmuch as the power of the mind, as I have shown above, is determined by intelligence alone, we shall determine by the knowledge of the mind alone the remedies against the emotions—remedies which everyone, I believe, has experienced, although there may not have been any accurate observation or distinct perception of them, and from this knowledge of the mind alone shall we deduce everything which relates to its blessedness.

Axioms

I. If two contrary actions be excited in the same subject, a change must necessarily take place in both, or in one alone, until they cease to be contrary.

II. The power of an emotion is limited by the power of its cause, in so far as the essence of the emotion is manifested or limited by the essence of the cause itself.

The Strength of the Emotions

The emotion towards an object which we imagine to be free is greater than towards one which is necessary, and consequently still greater than towards one which we imagine as possible or contingent. But to imagine an object as free can be nothing else than to imagine it simply, while we know not the causes by which it was determined to action. An emotion, therefore, towards an object which we simply imagine is, other things being equal, greater than towards one which we imagine as necessary, possible, or contingent, and consequently greatest of all.

The mind understands all things to be necessary and determined by an infinite chain of causes to existence and action, and therefore so far enables itself to suffer less from the emotions which arise from these things, and to be less affected towards them.

The more this knowledge that things are necessary is applied to individual things which we imagine more distinctly and more vividly, the greater is this power of the mind over the emotions—a fact to which experience also testifies. For we see that sorrow for the loss of anything good is diminished if the person who has lost it considers that it could not by any possibility have been preserved. So also we see that nobody pities an infant because it does not know how to speak, walk, or reason, and lives so many years not conscious, as it were, of itself. But if a number of human beings were born adult, and only a few here and there were born infants, everyone would pity the infants, because we should then consider infancy not as a thing natural and necessary, but as a defect or fault of Nature. Many other facts of a similar kind we might observe.

We do not contemplate an object as absent by reason of the emotion by which we imagine it, but by reason of the fact that the body is affected with another modification, which excludes the existence of that object. The emotion, therefore, which is related to an object which we contemplate as absent, is not of such a nature as to overcome the other actions and power of man, but, on the contrary, is of such a nature that it can in some way be restrained by those modifications which exclude the existence of its external cause. But the emotion which arises from reason is necessarily related to the common properties of things, which we always contemplate as present for nothing can exist which excludes their present existence, and which we always imagine in the same way. This emotion, therefore, always remains the same, and consequently the emotions which are contrary to it, and which are not maintained by their external cause, must more and more accommodate themselves to it until they are no longer contrary to it. So far, therefore, the emotion which springs from reason is the stronger.

A number of simultaneous causes can do more than if they were fewer, and therefore the greater the number of the simultaneous causes by which an emotion is excited, the greater it is.

An emotion is bad or injurious only in so far as it hinders the mind from thinking and therefore that emotion by which the mind is determined to the contemplation of a number of objects at the same time is less injurious than another emotion equally great which holds the mind in the contemplation of one object alone or of a few objects, so that it cannot think of others. Again, since the essence of the mind, that is to say, its power, consists in thought alone, the mind suffers less through an emotion by which it is determined to the contemplation of a number of objects at the same time than through an emotion equally great which holds it occupied in the contemplation of one object alone or of a few objects. Finally, this emotion, in so far as it is related to a number of external causes, is therefore less towards each.

The Power of the Intellect Over the Emotions

I

General Principles

The order and connection of ideas is the same as the order and connection of things, and *vice versa*, the order and connection of things is the same as the order and connection of ideas. Therefore, as the order and connection of ideas in the mind is according to the order and connection of the modifications of the body it follows *vice versa*, that the order and connection of the modifications of the body is according to the order and connection in the mind of the thoughts and ideas of things.

If we detach an emotion of the mind from the thought of an external cause and connect it with other thoughts, then the love or hatred towards the external cause and the fluctuations of the mind which arise from these emotions will be destroyed.

An emotion which is a passion is a confused idea. If, therefore, we form a clear and distinct idea of this emotion, the idea will not be distinguished—except by reason—from this emotion, in so far as the emotion is related to the mind alone, and therefore the emotion will cease to be a passion.

261

In proportion, then, as we know an emotion better is it more within our control, and the less does the mind suffer from it.

Those things which are common to all cannot be otherwise than adequately conceived and therefore there is no modification of the body of which we cannot form some clear and distinct conception.

Hence it follows that there is no emotion of which we cannot form some clear and distinct conception. For an emotion is an idea of a modification of the body, and this idea therefore must involve some clear and distinct conception.

Since nothing exists from which some effect does not follow, and since we understand clearly and distinctly everything which follows from an idea which is adequate in us, it is a necessary consequence that everyone has the power, partly at least, if not absolutely, of understanding clearly and distinctly himself and his emotions, and consequently of bringing it to pass that he suffers less from them. We have therefore mainly to strive to acquire a clear and distinct knowledge as far as possible of each emotion, so that the mind may be led to pass from the emotion to think those things which it perceives clearly and distinctly, and with which it is entirely satisfied, and to strive also that the emotion may be separated from the thought of an external cause and connected with true thoughts. Thus not only love, hatred, etc., will be destroyed, but also the appetites or desires to which the emotion gives rise cannot be excessive. For it is above everything to be observed that the appetite by which a man is said to act is one and the same appetite as that by which he is said to suffer. For example, we have shown that human nature is so constituted that everyone desires that other people should live according to his way of thinking, a desire which in a man who is not guided by reason is a passion which is called ambition, and is not very different from pride; while, on the other hand, in a man who lives according to the dictates of reason it is an action or virtue which is called piety. In the same manner, all the appetites or desires are passions only in so far as they arise from inadequate ideas, and are classed among the virtues whenever they are excited or begotten by adequate ideas; for all the desires by which we are determined to any action may arise either from adequate or inadequate ideas. To return, therefore, to the point from which we set out: there is no remedy within our power which can be conceived more excellent for the emotions than that which consists in true knowledge of them, since the mind possesses no other power than that of thinking and forming adequate ideas, as we have shown above.

II

The Natural Basis of Rational Control

The greater the number of objects to which an image or emotion is related, the greater is the number of causes by which it can be excited and cherished. All these causes the mind contemplates simultaneously by means of the emotion (by hypothesis), and therefore the more constant is the emotion, or the more frequently does it present itself, and the more does it occupy the mind.

Things which we clearly and distinctly understand are either the common properties of things or what are deduced from them, and consequently are more frequently excited in us; and therefore it is easier for us to contemplate other things together with these which we clearly and distinctly understand than with any others, and consequently it is easier to connect things with these which we clearly and distinctly understand than with any others.

The greater the number of other things with which any image is connected, the more frequently does it present itself. For the greater the number of other things with which an image is connected, the greater is the number of causes by which it may be excited.

There is no modification of the body of which the mind cannot form some clear and distinct conception and therefore it can cause all the modifications of the body to be related to the idea of God.

III

The Function of the Intellectual Order

The emotions which are contrary to our nature, that is to say, which are evil, are evil so far as they hinder the mind from understanding. So long, therefore, as we are not agitated by emotions which are contrary to our nature, so long the power of the mind by which it endeavors to understand things is not hindered, and therefore so long does it possess the power of forming clear and distinct ideas, and of deducing them the one from the other. So long, consequently, do we possess the power of arranging and connecting the modifications of the body according to the order of the intellect.

Through this power of properly arranging and connecting the modifications of the body we can prevent ourselves from being easily affected by evil emotions.

For a greater power is required to restrain emotions which are arranged and connected according to the order of the intellect than is required to restrain those which are uncertain and unsettled. The best thing, therefore, we can do, so long as we lack a perfect knowledge of our emotions, is to conceive a right rule of life, or sure maxims (*dogmata*) of life—to commit these latter to memory, and constantly to apply them to the particular cases which frequently meet us in life, so that our imagination may be widely affected by them, and they may always be ready to hand. For example, amongst the maxims of life we have placed this, that hatred is to be conquered by love or generosity, and is not to be met with hatred in return. But in order that we may always have this prescript of reason in readiness whenever it will be of service, we must think over and often meditate upon the common injuries inflicted by men, and consider how and in what way they may best be repelled by generosity; for thus we shall connect the image of injury with the imagination of this maxim, and it will be at hand whenever an injury is offered to us. If we also continually have regard to our own true profit, and the good which follows from mutual friendship and common fellowship, and remember that the highest peace of mind arises from a right rule of life, and also that man, like other things, acts according to the necessity of Nature, then the injury or the hatred which usually arises from that necessity will occupy but the least part of the imagination, and will be easily overcome: or supposing that the anger which generally arises from the greatest injuries is not so easily overcome, it will nevertheless be overcome, although not without fluctuation of mind, in a far shorter space of time than would have been necessary if we had not possessed those maxims on which we had thus meditated beforehand.

Concerning strength of mind, we must reflect in the same way for the purpose of getting rid of fear, that is to say, we must often enumerate and imagine the common dangers of life, and think upon the manner in which they can best be avoided and overcome by presence of mind and courage. It is to be observed, however, that in the ordering of our thoughts and images we must always look to those qualities which in each thing are good, so that we may be determined to action always by an emotion of joy.

For example, if a man sees that he pursues glory too eagerly, let him think on its proper use, for what end it is to be followed, and by what means it can be obtained; but let him not think upon its abuse and vanity, and on the inconstancy of men, and things of this sort, about which no one thinks unless through disease of mind. For with such thoughts do those who are ambitious greatly torment themselves when they despair of obtaining the honors for which they are striving; and while they vomit forth rage, wish to be thought wise. Indeed it is certain that those covet glory the most who are loudest in declaiming against its abuse and the vanity of the world. Nor is this a peculiarity of the ambitious, but is common to all to whom fortune is adverse and who are impotent in mind; for we see that a poor and avaricious man is never weary of speaking about the abuse of money and the vices of the rich, thereby achieving nothing save to torment himself and show to others that he is unable to bear with equanimity not only his own poverty but also the wealth of others. So also a man who has not been well deceived by his mistress thinks of nothing but the fickleness of women, their faithlessness, and their other oft-proclaimed failing—all of which he forgets as soon as he is taken into favor by his mistress again. He, therefore, who desires to govern his emotions and appetites from a love of liberty alone will strive as much as he can to know virtues and their causes, and to fill his mind with that joy which springs from a true knowledge of them. Least of all will he desire to contemplate the vices of men and disparage men, or to delight in a false show of liberty. He who will diligently observe these things (and they are not difficult), and will continue to practice them, will assuredly in a short space of time be able for the most part to direct his actions in accordance with the command of reason.

IV

Summary

I have, in what has preceded, included all the remedies for the emotions, that is to say, everything which the mind, considered in itself alone, can do against them. It appears therefrom that the power of the mind over the emotions consists—

1. In the knowledge itself of the emotions.

2. In the separation by the mind of the emotions from the thought of an external cause, which we imagine confusedly.

3. In duration, in which the emotions which are related to objects we understand surpass those related to objects conceived in a mutilated or confused manner.

4. In the multitude of causes by which the emotions which are related to the common properties of things or to God are nourished.

5. In the order in which the mind can arrange its emotions and connect them one with the other.

But that this power of the mind over the emotions may be better understood, it is to be carefully observed that we call the emotions great when we compare the emotion of one man with that of another, and see that one man is agitated more than another by the same emotion, or when we compare the emotions of one and the same man with one another, and discover that he is affected or moved more by one emotion than by another.

For the power of any emotion is limited by the power of the external cause as compared with our own power. But the power of the mind is limited solely by knowledge, whilst impotence or passion is estimated solely by privation of knowledge, or, in other words, by that through which ideas are called inadequate; and it therefore follows that that mind suffers the most whose largest part consists of inadequate ideas, so that it is distinguished rather by what it suffers than by what it does, while, on the contrary, that mind acts the most whose largest part consists of adequate ideas, so that although it may possess as many inadequate ideas as the first, it is nevertheless distinguished rather by those which belong to human virtue than by those which are a sign of human impotence. Again, it is to be observed that our sorrows and misfortunes mainly proceed from too much love towards an object which is subject to many changes, and which we can never possess. For no one is troubled or anxious about any object he does not love, neither do wrongs, suspicions, hatreds, etc., arise except from love towards objects of which no one can be truly the possessor.

From all this we easily conceive what is the power which clear and distinct knowledge, and especially that third kind of knowledge whose foundation is the knowledge itself of God, possesses over the emotions; the power, namely, by which it is able, in so far as they are passions, if not actually to destroy them, at least to make them constitute the smallest part of the mind. Moreover, it begets a love towards an immutable and eternal object of which we are really partakers; a love which therefore cannot be vitiated by the defects which are in common love, but which can always become greater and greater, occupy the largest part of the mind, and thoroughly affect it.

I have now concluded all that I had to say relating to this present life. For any one who will attend to what has been urged will easily be able to see the truth of what I said—that in these few words all the remedies for the emotions are comprehended. It is time, therefore, that I should now pass to the consideration of those matters which appertain to the duration of the mind without relation to the body.

CHAPTER XX

OF HUMAN BLESSEDNESS AND THE ETERNITY OF THE MIND

Human Blessedness: The Intellectual Love of God

I

The third kind of knowledge proceeds from an adequate idea of certain attributes of God to an adequate knowledge of the essence of things; and the more we understand things in this manner, the more we understand God; and therefore the highest virtue of the mind, that is to say, the power or nature of the mind, or the highest effort, is to understand things by the third kind of knowledge.

The better the mind is adapted to understand things by the third kind of knowledge, the more it desires to understand them by this kind of knowledge.

The highest virtue of the mind is to know God, or to understand things by the third kind of knowledge. This virtue is greater the more the mind knows things by this kind of knowledge, and therefore he who knows things by this kind of knowledge passes to the highest human perfection, and consequently is affected with the highest joy, which is accompanied with the idea of himself and his own virtue; and therefore from this kind of knowledge arises the highest possible peace of mind.

The effort or the desire to know things by the third kind of knowledge cannot arise from the first kind, but may arise from the second kind of knowledge. This proposition is self-evident. For everything that we clearly and distinctly understand, we understand either through itself or through something which is conceived through itself; or, in other words, ideas which are clear and distinct in us, or which are related to the third kind of knowledge, cannot follow from mutilated and confused ideas, which are related to the first kind of knowledge, but from adequate ideas, that is to say, from the second and third kinds of knowledge.

II

Eternity is the very essence of God, in so far as that essence involves necessary existence. To conceive things therefore under the form of eternity, is to conceive them in so far as they are conceived through the essence of God as actually existing things, or in so far as through the essence of God they involve existence. Therefore our mind, in so far as it conceives itself and its body under the form of eternity, necessarily has a knowledge of God, and knows that it is in God and is conceived through Him.

We delight in whatever we understand by the third kind of knowledge, and our delight is accompanied with the idea of God as its cause.

From the third kind of knowledge necessarily springs the intellectual love of God. For from this kind of knowledge arises joy attended with the idea of God as its cause, that is to say, the love of God, not in so far as we imagine Him as present, but in so far as we understand that He is eternal; and that is what I call the intellectual love of God.

He who clearly and distinctly understands himself and his emotions rejoices, and his joy is attended with the idea of God, therefore he loves God, and (by the same reasoning) loves Him better the better he understands himself and his emotions.

This intellectual love necessarily follows from the nature of the mind, in so far as it is considered, through the nature of God, as an eternal truth. If there were anything, therefore, contrary to this love, it would be contrary to the truth, and consequently whatever might be able to negate this love would be able to make the true false, which, as is self-evident, is absurd. There exists, therefore, nothing in Nature contrary to this intellectual love, or which can negate it.

III

This love to God above everything else ought to occupy the mind, for this love is connected with all the modifications of the body, by all of which it is cherished.

The idea of God which is in us is adequate and perfect, and therefore in so far as we contemplate God do we act and consequently no sorrow can exist with the accompanying idea of God; that is to say, no one can hate God.

Love to God cannot be turned into hatred. But some may object, that if we understand God to be the cause of all things, we do for that very reason consider Him to be the cause of sorrow. But I reply, that in so far as we understand the causes of sorrow, it ceases to be a passion, that is to say, it ceases to be sorrow; and therefore in so far as we understand God to be the cause of sorrow do we rejoice.

This love to God is the highest good which we can seek according to the dictate of reason; is common to all men; and we desire that all may enjoy it. It cannot, therefore, be sullied by the emotion of envy, nor by that of jealousy, but, on the contrary, it must be the more strengthened the more people we imagine to rejoice in it.

It is possible to show in the same manner that there is no emotion directly contrary to this love and able to destroy it, and so we may conclude that this love to God is the most constant of all the emotions, and that, in so far as it is related to the body, it cannot be destroyed unless with the body itself. What its nature is, in so far as it is related to the mind alone, we shall see hereafter.

IV

All ideas, in so far as they are related to God, are true; that is to say, are adequate, and therefore, (by the general definition of the Emotions), God is free from passions. Again, God can neither pass to a greater nor to a less perfection, and therefore He cannot be affected with any emotion of joy or sorrow.

He who loves God cannot strive that God should love him in return. If a man were to strive after this, he would desire that God, whom he loves, should not be God, and consequently he would desire to be sad, which is absurd.

V

God is absolutely infinite, that is to say, the nature of God delights in infinite perfection accompanied with the idea of Himself, that is to say, with the idea of Himself as cause, and this is what we have called intellectual love. God loves Himself with an infinite intellectual love.

The intellectual love of the mind towards God is the very love with which He loves Himself, not in so far as He is infinite, but in so far as He can be manifested through the essence of the human mind, considered under the form of eternity; that is to say, the intellectual love of the mind towards God is part of the infinite love with which God loves Himself.

Hence it follows that God, in so far as He loves Himself, loves men, and consequently that the love of God towards men and the intellectual love of the mind towards God are one and the same thing.

Hence it follows that God, in so far as He loves Himself, loves men, and consequently that the love of the mind towards God are one and the same thing.

Hence we clearly understand that our salvation, or blessedness, or liberty consists in a constant and eternal love towards God, or in the love of God towards men. This love or blessedness is called Glory in the sacred writings, and not without reason. For whether it be related to God or to the mind, it may properly be called repose of mind, which is, in truth, not distinguished from glory. For in so far as it is related to God, it is joy (granting that it is allowable to use this word), accompanied with the idea of Himself, and it is the same thing when it is related to the mind.

Again, since the essence of our mind consists in knowledge alone, whose beginning and foundation is God, it is clear to us in what manner and by what method our mind, with regard both to essence and existence, follows from the divine nature, and continually depends upon God. I thought it worthwhile for me to notice this here, in order that I might show, by this example, what that knowledge of individual objects which I have called intuitive or of the third kind is able to do, and how much more potent it is than the universal knowledge, which I have called knowledge of the second kind. For although I have shown generally that all things, and consequently also the human mind, depend upon God both with regard to existence and essence, yet that demonstration, although legitimate, and placed beyond the possibility of a doubt, does not, nevertheless, so affect our mind as a proof from the essence itself of any individual object which we say depends upon God. The more we understand individual objects, the more we understand God.

The Eternity of the Mind

I

The mind does not express the actual existence of its body, nor does it conceive as actual the modifications of the body, except while the body exists, and consequently it conceives no body as actually existing except while its own body exists. It can therefore imagine nothing, nor can it recollect anything that is past, except while the body exists.

An imagination is an idea by which the mind contemplates any object as present. This idea nevertheless indicates the present constitution of the human body rather than the nature of the external object. An emotion, therefore (by the general definition of the Emotions), is an imagination in so far as it indicates the present constitution of the body, and therefore the mind, only so long as the body exists, is subject to emotions which are related to passions.

Hence it follows that no love except intellectual love is eternal.

If we look at the common opinion of men, we shall see that they are indeed conscious of the eternity of their minds, but they confound it with duration, and attribute it to imagination or memory, which they believe remain after death.

God is not only the cause of the existence of this or that human body, but also of its essence, which therefore must necessarily be conceived through the essence of God itself and by a certain eternal necessity. This conception, moreover, must necessarily exist in God. In God there necessarily exists an idea which expresses the essence of this or that human body under the form of eternity.

In God there necessarily exists a conception or idea which expresses the essence of the human body. This conception or idea is therefore necessarily something which pertains to the essence of the human mind. But we ascribe to the human mind no duration which can be limited by time, unless in so far as it expresses the actual existence of the body, which is manifested through duration, and which can be limited by time, that is to say, we cannot ascribe duration to the mind except while the body exists.

But, nevertheless, since this something is that which is conceived by a certain eternal necessity through the essence itself of God, this something which pertains to the essence of the mind will necessarily be eternal.

This idea which expresses the essence of the body under the form of eternity is, as we have said, a certain mode of thought which pertains to the essence of the mind, and is necessarily eternal. It is impossible, nevertheless, that we should recollect that we existed before the body, because there are no traces of any such existence in the body, and also because eternity cannot be defined by time, or have any relationship to it. Nevertheless we feel and know by experience that we are eternal. For the mind is no less sensible of those things which

272

it conceives through intelligence than of those which it remembers, for demonstrations are the eyes of the mind by which it sees and observes things.

Although, therefore, we do not recollect that we existed before the body, we feel that our mind, in so far as it involves the essence of the body under the form of eternity, is eternal, and that this existence of the mind cannot be limited by time nor manifested through duration. Only in so far, therefore, as it involves the actual existence of the body can the mind be said to possess duration, and its existence be limited by a fixed time, and so far only has it the power of determining the existence of things in time, and of conceiving them under the form of duration.

II

In so far as the mind conceives the present existence of its body does it conceive duration which can be determined in time, and so far only has it the power of conceiving things in relation to time. But eternity cannot be manifested through duration, therefore the mind so far has not the power of conceiving things under the form of eternity: but because it is the nature of reason to conceive things under the form of eternity, and because it also pertains to the nature of the mind to conceive the essence of the body under the form of eternity, and excepting these two things nothing else pertains to the nature of the mind, therefore this power of conceiving things under the form of eternity does not pertain to the mind except in so far as it conceives the essence of the body under the form of eternity.

Things are conceived by us as actual in two ways; either in so far as we conceive them to exist with relation to a fixed time and place, or in so far as we conceive them to be contained in God, and to follow from the necessity of the divine nature. But those things which are conceived in this second way as true or real we conceive under the form of eternity, and their ideas involve the eternal and infinite essence of God.

The mind conceives nothing under the form of eternity, unless in so far as it conceives the essence of its body under the form of eternity, that is to say, unless in so far as it is eternal. Therefore in so far as the mind is eternal it has a knowledge of God, which is necessarily adequate, and therefore in so far as it is eternal it is fitted to know all those things which can follow from this knowledge of God, that is to say, it is fitted to know things by the third kind of knowledge of which, in so far as the mind is eternal, it is the adequate or formal cause.

As each person therefore becomes stronger in this kind of knowledge, the more is he conscious of himself and of God; that is to say, the more perfect and the happier he is, a truth which will still more clearly appear from what follows. Here, however, it is to be observed, that although we are now certain that the mind is eternal in so far as it conceives things under the form of eternity, yet, in order that what we wish to prove may be more easily explained and better understood, we shall consider the mind, as we have hitherto done, as if it had just begun to be, and had just begun to understand things under the form of eternity. This we can do without any risk of error, provided only we are careful to conclude nothing except from clear premises.

The third kind of knowledge is eternal, and therefore the love which springs from it is necessarily eternal.

Although this love to God has no beginning, it nevertheless has all the perfections of love, just as if it had originated. Nor is there here any difference, excepting that the mind has eternally possessed these same perfections which we imagined as now accruing to it, and has possessed them with the accompanying idea of God as the eternal cause. And if joy consist in the passage to a greater perfection, blessedness must indeed consist in this, that the mind is endowed with perfection itself.

III

The essence of the mind consists in knowledge. The more things, therefore, the mind knows by the second and third kinds of knowledge, the greater is that part which abides and consequently the greater is that part which is not touched by emotions which are contrary to our nature, that is to say, which are evil. The more things, therefore, the mind understands by the second and third kinds of knowledge, the greater is that part which remains unharmed, and the less consequently does it suffer from the emotions.

We are thus enabled to understand that death is by so much the less injurious to us as the clear and distinct knowledge of the mind is greater, and consequently as the mind loves God more. Again, since from the third kind of knowledge there arises the highest possible peace, it follows that it is possible for the human mind to be of such a nature that that part of it which we have shown perishes with its body, in comparison with the part of it which remains, is of no consequence. But more fully upon this subject presently.

He who possesses a body fitted for doing many things is least of all agitated by those emotions which are evil, that is to say, by emotions which are contrary to our nature, and therefore he possesses the power of arranging and connecting the modifications of the body according to the order of the intellect, and consequently of causing all the modifications of the body to be related to the idea of God; in consequence of which he is affected with a love to God, which must occupy or form the greatest part of his mind, and therefore he possesses a mind of which the greatest part is eternal.

Inasmuch as human bodies are fit for many things, we cannot doubt the possibility of their possessing such a nature that they may be related to minds which have a large knowledge of themselves and of God, and whose greatest or principal part is eternal, so that they scarcely fear death. To understand this more clearly, it is to be here considered that we live in constant change, and that according as we change for the better or the worse we are called happy or unhappy. For he who passes from infancy or childhood to death is called unhappy, and, on the other hand, we consider ourselves happy if we can pass through the whole period of life with a sound mind in a sound body. Moreover, he who, like an infant or child, possesses a body fit for very few things, and, almost altogether dependent on external causes, has a mind which, considered in itself alone, is almost entirely unconscious of itself, of God, and of objects. On the other hand, he who possesses a body fit for many things possesses a mind which, considered in itself alone, is largely conscious of itself, of God, and of objects. In this life, therefore, it is our chief endeavor to change the body of infancy, so far as its nature permits and is conducive thereto, into another body which is fitted for many things, and which is related to a mind conscious as much as possible of itself, of God, and of objects; so that everything which is related to its memory or imagination, in comparison with the intellect is scarcely of any moment, as I have already said.

The more perfect a thing is, the more reality it possesses, and consequently the more it acts and the less it suffers. Inversely also it may be demonstrated in the same way that the more a thing acts the more perfect it is. Hence it follows that that part of the mind which abides, whether great or small, is more perfect than the other part. For the part of the mind which is eternal is the intellect, through which alone we are said to act, but that part which, as we have shown, perishes, is the imagination itself, through which alone we are said to suffer. Therefore that part which abides, whether great or small, is more perfect than the latter.

These are the things I proposed to prove concerning the mind, in so far as it is considered without relation to the existence of the body, and from these, and other propositions, it is evident that our mind, in so far as it understands, is an eternal mode of thought, which is determined by another eternal mode of thought, and this again by another, and so on *ad infinitum*, so that all taken together form the eternal and infinite intellect of God.

Conclusion

The primary and sole foundation of virtue or of the proper conduct of life is to seek our own profit. But in order to determine what reason prescribes as profitable, we had no regard to the eternity of the mind. Therefore, although we were at that time ignorant that the mind is eternal, we considered as of primary importance those things which we have shown are related to strength of mind and generosity; and therefore, even if we were now ignorant of the eternity of the mind, we should consider those commands of reason as of primary importance.

The creed of the multitude seems to be different from this; for most persons seem to believe that they are free in so far as it is allowed them to obey their lusts, and that they give up a portion of their rights, in so far as they are bound to live according to the commands of divine law. Piety, therefore, and religion,[42] and absolutely all those things that are related to greatness of soul, they believe to be burdens which they hope to be able to lay aside after death; hoping also to receive some reward for their bondage, that is to say, for *their* piety and religion. It is not merely this hope, however, but also and chiefly fear of dreadful punishments after death, by which they are induced to live according to the commands of divine law, that is to say, as far as their feebleness and impotent mind will permit; and if this hope and fear were not present to them, but if they, on the contrary, believed that minds perish with the body, and that there is no prolongation of life for miserable creatures exhausted with the burden of their piety, they would return to ways of their own liking. They would prefer to let everything be controlled by their own passions, and to obey fortune rather than themselves.

This seems to me as absurd as if a man, because he does not believe that he will be able to feed his body with good food to all eternity, should desire to satiate himself with poisonous and deadly drugs; or as if, because he sees that the mind is not eternal or immortal, he should therefore prefer to be mad and to live without reason—absurdities so great that they scarcely deserve to be repeated.

Blessedness consists in love towards God, which arises from the third kind of knowledge, and this love, therefore, must be related to the mind in so far as it acts. Blessedness, therefore, is virtue itself. Again, the more the mind delights in this divine love or blessedness, the more it understands, that is to say, the greater is the power it has over its emotions and the less it suffers from emotions which are evil. Therefore, it is because the mind delights in this divine love or blessedness that it possesses the power of restraining the lusts; and because the power of man to restrain the emotions is in the intellect alone, no one, therefore, delights in blessedness because he has restrained his emotions, but, on the contrary, the power of restraining his lusts springs from blessedness itself.

I have finished everything I wished to explain concerning the power of the mind over the emotions and concerning its liberty. From what has been said we see what is the strength of the wise man, and how much he surpasses the ignorant who is driven forward by lust alone. For the ignorant man is not only agitated by external causes in many ways, and never enjoys true peace of soul, but lives also ignorant, as it were, both of God and of things, and as soon as he ceases to suffer ceases also to be. On the other hand, the wise man, in so far as he is considered as such, is scarcely ever moved in his mind, but, being conscious by a certain eternal necessity of himself, of God, and of things, never ceases to be, and always enjoys true peace of soul.

If the way which, as I have shown, leads hither seem very difficult, it can nevertheless be found. It must indeed be difficult since it is so seldom discovered; for if salvation lay ready to hand and could be discovered without great labor, how could it be possible that it should be neglected almost by everybody? But all noble things are as difficult as they are rare.

FOOTNOTES:

[42] Everything which we desire and do, of which we are the cause in so far as we possess an idea of God, or in so far as we know God, I refer to *Religion*. The desire of doing well which is born in us, because we live according to the guidance of reason, I call *Piety*.

APPENDIX

Spinoza's *Ethics*, demonstrated in geometrical order, consists of five parts; from these parts the following selections have been taken:

Part I.   *Of God*

    Definitions, Axioms, and the Appendix.

    Propositions: 11; 15-18; 26; 27; 29; 33.

Part II.   *Of the Nature and Origin of the Mind*

    Preface, Definitions, and Axioms.

    Propositions: 1; 4-7; 11-13; 15-18; 24-26; 28-32; 35; 36; 38-49.

Part III.   *Of the Origin and Nature of the Emotions*

    Preface, Definitions, and Postulates; Definitions of the Emotions.

    Propositions: 1; 2; 4; 6; 9; 11; 14; 16; 18; 25; 27-32; 40; 41; 43-46; 48-51; 56; 57.

Part IV.   *Of Human Bondage or Of the Strength of the Emotions*

    Preface, Definitions, Axioms, and the Appendix.

    Propositions: 3-9; 11-27; 38; 39; 41-47; 50-54; 56-58.

Part V.   *Of the Power of the Intellect or Of Human Liberty*

    Preface and Axioms.

    Propositions: 1-28; 30-42.

THE END

Made in the USA
Las Vegas, NV
03 August 2023

75576942R00173